# ISO 9001:2008 Explained

## Third Edition

ASQ Quality Press
Milwaukee, Wisconsin

NEW AGE

# ISO 9001:2008 Explained

## Third Edition

Charles A. Cianfrani
Joseph J. Tsiakals
John E. (Jack) West

PUBLISHING FOR ONE WORLD

NEW AGE INTERNATIONAL (P) LIMITED, PUBLISHERS
New Delhi • Bangalore • Chennai • Cochin • Guwahati • Hyderabad
Jalandhar • Kolkata • Lucknow • Mumbai • Ranchi
Visit us at www.newagepublishers.com

First Indian Sub-Continent Edition : 2010
by New Age International (P) Ltd., Publishers

This special low-priced edition is for sale in India, Bangladesh, Bhutan, Myanmar (Burma), Sri Lanka, Nepal, Pakistan, Southeast Asia and the Middle East.

Originally Published by *American Society for Quality, USA*



**BRANCHES**

- **Bangalore** 37/10, 8th Cross (Near Hanuman Temple), Azad Nagar, Chamarajpet Bangalore-560 018. Tel.: (080) 26756823, Telefax: 26756820 E-mail:bangalore@newagepublishers.com
- **Chennai** 26, Damodaran Street, T. Nagar, Chennai-600 017 Tel.: (044) 24353401, Telefax: 24351463 E-mail: chennai@newagepublishers.com
- **Cochin** CC-39/1016, Carrier Station Road, Ernakulam South Cochin-682 016. Tel.: (0484) 2377004, Telefax: 4051303 E-mail: cochin@newagepublishers.com
- **Guwahati** Hemsen Complex, Mohd. Shah Road, Paltan Bazar, Near Starline Hotel, Guwahati-781 008. Tel.: (0361) 2513881, Telefax: 2543669 E-mail: guwahati@newagepublishers.com
- **Hyderabad** 105, 1st Floor, Madhiray Kaveri Tower, 3-2-19, Azam Jahi Road Nimboliadda, Hyderabad-500 027. Tel.: (040) 24652456 Telefax: 24652457, E-mail: hyderabad@newagepublishers.com
- **Kolkata** RDB Chambers (Formerly Lotus Cinema) 106A, 1st Floor S.N. Banerjee Road, Kolkata-700 014. Tel.: (033) 22273773 Telefax: 22275247, E-mail: kolkata@newagepublishers.com
- **Lucknow** 16-A, Jopling Road, Lucknow-226 001. Tel.: (0522) 2209578 4045297, Telefax: 2204098, E-mail: lucknow@newagepublishers.com
- **Mumbai** 142C, Victor House, Ground Floor, N.M. Joshi Marg, Lower Parel Mumbai- 400 013. Tel.: (022) 24927869, Telefax: 24915415 E-mail: mumbai@newagepublishers.com
- **New Delhi** 22, Golden House, Daryaganj, New Delhi-110 002 Tel.: (011) 23262368, 23262370, Telefax: 43551305 E-mail: sales@newagepublishers.com

---

Printed in India at Glorious Printers, Delhi.
C-13-02-6744

ISBN : 978-81-224-3101-8
Original Edition Price: $ 105.00
Indian Edition Price: ₹ 395.00

**PUBLISHING FOR ONE WORLD**

**NEW AGE INTERNATIONAL (P) LIMITED, PUBLISHERS**
7/30 A, Daryaganj, New Delhi-110002
Visit us at **www.newagepublishers.com**

# Contents

# Tables and Figures

# Preface

The ISO 9000 series of quality management system standards was initially issued in 1987 and reissued with minor revisions in 1994. A major revision was issued in 2000 to update the standards and to make the documents more user friendly. ISO 9001:2008 is the fourth edition of ISO 9001. The purpose of ISO 9001:2008 is to clarify, not to change, the requirements. So, systems conforming to the requirements and intent of ISO 9001:2000 should conform to the new document with little or no change. The major features of ISO 9001:2000 have been retained and include emphasis on the following:

- Consistently providing product that meets customer and applicable statutory and regulatory requirements
- The customer, including understanding needs, meeting requirements, and monitoring information related to customer satisfaction
- Use of a process approach and a structure for the standard which is built around a process model that considers all work in terms of suppliers, inputs, processing activities, process interactions, outputs, and customers
- Managing a system of effective processes rather than on documenting the system in procedures
- The role of top management
- Setting measurable objectives and on measuring product and process performance
- Analysis and use of data to define opportunities for improvement
- Continual improvement of processes and of quality management system effectiveness

- Use of commonly understood wording that can be easily understood by people in all product sectors—not just hardware
- Provision via the Applications Clause to adapt ISO 9001:2008 to all sizes and kinds of organizations and to all sectors of the marketplace

This book addresses the needs of the following:

- Organizations seeking a general understanding of the contents of ISO 9001:2008
- Organizations that desire to have the best material available for staff reference and learning
- Organizations desiring guidance to ensure that their ISO 9001:2000 quality management system also meets the new version
- Organizations considering the use of ISO 9001:2008 as a foundation for the development of a comprehensive quality management system
- Educators who require a textbook to accompany a training class or course on ISO 9001:2008
- Auditors who desire to increase their level of auditing competence

This book explains the meaning and intent of the requirements of ISO 9001:2008 and discusses the requirements as they relate to each product category. Where appropriate, it elaborates on why the requirements are important. It includes a list of typical audit-type questions that an organization may consider using to appraise compliance with the requirements.

## NEW IN THIS THIRD EDITION

The book now includes some recommendations for implementation. Some implementation guidance was provided in earlier editions. They had focused on achieving understanding of the requirements, not on their implementation. Each clause now has a section on tips for implementation. Where tips were included in previous editions, they have been moved to this section. New tips have also been added. ISO 9001:2008 itself provides requirements for what activities and processes are needed; it does not tell the user how these requirements are to be carried out. So, the authors have included some recommendations for implementation actions that have proved successful. It should be recognized that these implementation tips may go beyond the requirements of ISO 9001:2008. It is provided because much of what is needed for successful quality management systems involves how the requirements are implemented, not the requirements themselves.

There are also new chapters on Implementation, Auditing the Process-Based Quality Management System, and use of ISO 9001 and Sector Applications.

Symbols designate the following:

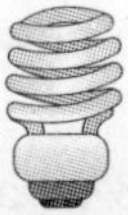
Provides tips implementation

Gives definitions of key terms used in ISO 9001:2008 as they are defined in ISO 9000:2005

Lists typical assessment questions an organization may ask to appraise conformity with the requirements of ISO 9001:2008

Describes considerations for documentation

This book contains the text of ISO 9001:2008 as contained in the U.S. adoption of this standard. It also provides the ISO 9000:2005 definitions of key words as contained in the proposed U.S. adoption of this standard.

ISO 9001:2000 introduced users to a simple process model for structuring and implementing a contemporary quality management system. That model has proven to be quite robust and useful for organizations implementing the standard. ISO 9001:2008 uses that same model. This book facilitates an understanding of what the standard says and what it means, and how to apply it in any organization to achieve internal operating effectiveness, and improved performance as viewed by customers.

# CHAPTER

# 1

# Introduction

## 0 Introduction

### 0.1 General

The adoption of a quality management system should be a strategic decision of an organization. The design and implementation of an organization's quality management system is influenced by

— its organizational environment, changes in that environment, and the risks associated with that environment,

— its varying needs,

— its particular objectives,

— the products it provides,

— the processes it employs,

— its size and organizational structure.

It is not the intent of this International Standard to imply uniformity in the structure of quality management systems or uniformity of documentation.

The quality management system requirements specified in this International Standard are complementary to requirements for products. Information marked "NOTE" is for guidance in understanding or clarifying the associated requirement.

This International Standard can be used by internal and external parties, including certification bodies, to assess the organization's ability to meet customer, statutory and regulatory requirements applicable to the product, and the organization's own requirements.

The quality management principles stated in ISO 9000 and ISO 9004 have been taken into consideration during the development of this International Standard.

*Source:* ANSI/ISO/ASQ Q9001-2008

Clause 0.1 of ISO 9001:2008 is identical to clause 0.1 of ISO 9001:2000. The introductory material in clause 0 and its subclauses is called "informative" in ISO language, meaning that it does not form part of the requirements of ISO 9001:2008. It exists to provide context, general understanding, and background.

This subclause discusses the intent of ISO 9001:2008, the flexibility of the standard, and why organizations should use it. This can be summarized as follows:

- As with its predecessor, ISO 9001:2000, ISO 9001:2008 contains the *requirements* for quality management systems.
- *Any organization* can use the standard to *demonstrate* its *ability to consistently meet* customers', regulators', and the organization's own internal requirements.
- *Any organization* can also enhance customer satisfaction by improving its ability to consistently meet requirements.
- The standard can also be used to *assess* the organization's ability to meet customer requirements by the use of either internal or external parties (for example, a certification audit by a third-party auditor, by a customer, or by internal auditors).
- ISO 9001:2008 is very *flexible and does not imply uniformity* of quality management systems; as such, it does not imply a requirement for any specific structure or format of quality management system documentation.

## THE EIGHT QUALITY MANAGEMENT PRINCIPLES

Subclause 0.1 recognizes that ISO 9001:2008 has been developed with the eight quality management principles given in ISO 9000:2005 as a basis. While they help form the foundation of ISO 9001, these principles do not appear in ISO 9001 and are not part of the requirements. The principles as they appear in ISO 9000:2005 are as follows:

> To lead and operate an organization successfully, it is necessary to direct and control it in a systematic and transparent manner. Success can result from implementing and maintaining a management system that is designed to continually improve performance while addressing the needs of all interested parties. Managing an

organization encompasses quality management amongst other management disciplines. Eight quality management principles have been identified that can be used by top management in order to lead the organization towards improved performance.

a) Customer focus

Organizations depend on their customers and therefore should understand current and future customer needs, should meet customer requirements and strive to exceed customer expectations.

b) Leadership

Leaders establish unity of purpose and direction of the organization. They should create and maintain the internal environment in which people can become fully involved in achieving the organization's objectives.

c) Involvement of people

People at all levels are the essence of an organization and their full involvement enables their abilities to be used for the organization's benefit.

d) Process approach

A desired result is achieved more efficiently when activities and related resources are managed as a process.

e) System approach to management

Identifying, understanding and managing interrelated processes as a system contributes to the organization's effectiveness and efficiency in achieving its objectives.

f) Continual improvement

Continual improvement of the organization's overall performance should be a permanent objective of the organization.

g) Factual approach to decision making

Effective decisions are based on the analysis of data and information.

h) Mutually beneficial supplier relationships

An organization and its suppliers are interdependent and a mutually beneficial relationship enhances the ability of both to create value.

These eight quality management principles form the basis for the quality management system standards within the ISO 9000 family.

*Source:* ANSI/ISO/ASQ Q9000-2005

## 0.2 Process approach

This International Standard promotes the adoption of a process approach when developing, implementing and improving the effectiveness of a quality management system, to enhance customer satisfaction by meeting customer requirements.

For an organization to function effectively, it has to determine and manage numerous linked activities. An activity or set of activities using resources, and managed in order to enable the transformation of inputs into outputs, can be considered a process. Often the output from one process directly forms the input to the next.

The application of a system of processes within an organization, together with the identification and interactions of these processes, and their management to produce the desired outcome, can be referred to as the "process approach".

An advantage of the process approach is the ongoing control that it provides over the linkage between the individual processes within the system of processes, as well as over their combination and interaction.

When used within a quality management system, such an approach emphasizes the importance of

a) understanding and meeting requirements,

b) the need to consider processes in terms of added value,

c) obtaining results of process performance and effectiveness, and

d) continual improvement of processes based on objective measurement.

The model of a process-based quality management system shown in Figure 1 illustrates the process linkages presented in Clauses 4 to 8. This illustration shows that customers play a significant role in defining requirements as inputs. Monitoring of customer satisfaction requires the evaluation of information relating to customer perception as to whether the organization has met the customer requirements. The model shown in Figure 1 covers all the requirements of this International Standard, but does not show processes at a detailed level.

NOTE In addition, the methodology known as "Plan-Do-Check-Act" (PDCA) can be applied to all processes. PDCA can be briefly described as follows.

> Plan: establish the objectives and processes necessary to deliver results in accordance with customer requirements and the organization's policies.
>
> Do: implement the processes.
>
> Check: monitor and measure processes and product against policies, objectives and requirements for the product and report the results.
>
> Act: take actions to continually improve process performance.

*Source:* ANSI/ISO/ASQ Q9001-2008

Clause 0.2, *Process approach,* is almost identical to clause 0.2 of ISO 9001:2000, with only minimal editing for clarity. This clause explains why organizations need to base their quality management systems on the process approach and the system approach to management. Clause 4.1 of ISO 9001:2008 requires the organization to identify and manage quality management system processes and their interactions. Clause 0.2 gives brief guidance on this subject. Figure 1 describes graphically one possible model of how the process approach applies to the quality management system. The text of clause 0.2 explains the model. Key concepts to remember from the clause include the following:

- Organizations will be more effective if they manage a system of interlinked processes. Identification and management of these processes can make the overall quality

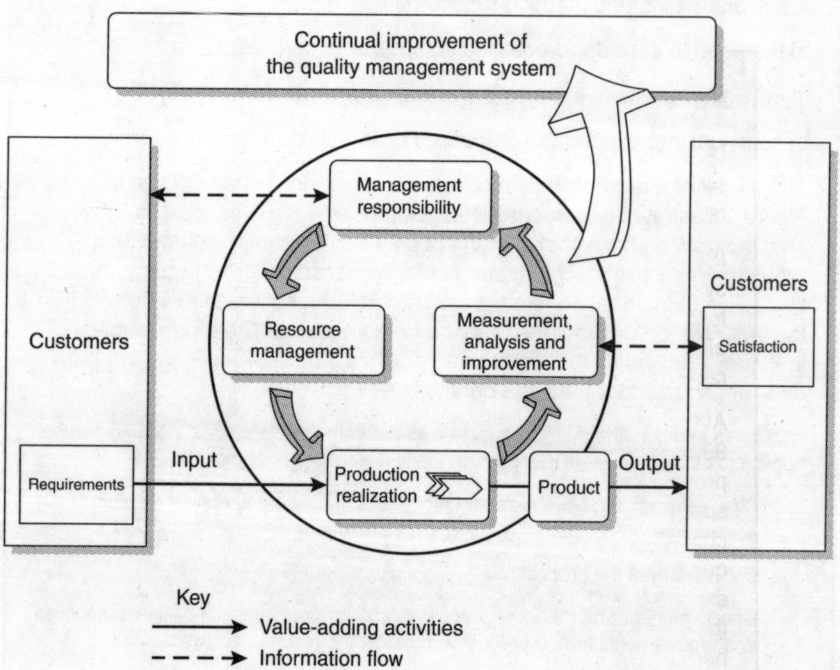


**Figure 1** Model of a process-based quality management system

*Source:* ANSI/ISO/ASQ Q9001-2008

management system more effective in meeting customer requirements.

- The process approach itself is a very different way to understand the quality system than the understanding that is provided by the element approach (sometimes called the life-cycle model) used as the basis for ISO 9001:1994.
- The process approach has been adopted as a means to facilitate improvement.
- Figure 1 is not intended to reflect all of the processes in a quality management system. It is provided to enhance understanding and is not a part of the requirements.
- Figure 1 represents one model that can be used to describe how the process approach may be applied to quality management systems. There is no implication that Figure 1 is the ideal model or that it is the only model that can be used.

**0.3 Relationship with ISO 9004**

ISO 9001 and ISO 9004 are quality management system standards which have been designed to complement each other, but can also be used independently.

ISO 9001 specifies requirements for a quality management system that can be used for internal application by organizations, for certification, or for contractual purposes. It focuses on the effectiveness of the quality management system in meeting customer requirements.

At the time of publication of this International Standard, ISO 9004 is under revision. The revised edition of ISO 9004 will provide guidance to management for achieving sustained success for any organization in a complex, demanding, and ever changing, environment. ISO 9004 provides a wider focus on quality management than ISO 9001; it addresses the needs and expectations of all interested parties and their satisfaction, by the systematic and continual improvement of the organization's performance. However, it is not intended for certification, regulatory or contractual use.

*Source:* ANSI/ISO/ASQ Q9001-2008

This clause is the same as clause 0.3 of ISO 9001:2000, except that the note regarding revision to ISO 9004 has been added.

Clause 0.3 describes the relationship between the ISO 9001:2008 requirements document and ISO 9004, which provides guidelines for a quality management system that is focused on performance improvement (ISO 9004:2000) and broader application to long-term survival (drafts of a new revision to ISO 9004). ISO 9001:2008 can be compared to ISO 9004 as follows:

- The standards have very different scopes. ISO 9004 is not intended for certification or contractual use, while ISO 9001:2008 is specifically designed to be suitable for both of these uses. ISO 9004 is not intended to provide guidance for implementing ISO 9001:2008. ISO 9004 also is not intended to be used as a basis for auditing the quality management system but does contain an assessment process based on maturity model concepts.
- ISO 9004 provides guidance that can be used to improve the overall performance of the organization.

It is expected that the revised ISO 9004 will be issued in 2009. The purpose statement for that revision is: "To help organizations who are users of ISO 9001 obtain sustained benefit from the implementation of a more broad-based and in-depth quality management system." The objectives for the revised ISO 9004 as stated by the committee responsible for the revision are as follows:

- "Facilitate improvement in users' quality management systems
- Provide guidance to an organization for the creation of a quality management system that:
    - creates value for its customers, via the products it provides
    - creates value for other interested parties,
    - balances interested-party viewpoints.
- Provide guidance for managers on leading their organization towards sustainable success.
- Forward compatibility to allow organizations to build on existing quality management systems."

> **0.4 Compatibility with other management systems**
>
> During the development of this International Standard, due consideration was given to the provisions of ISO 14001:2004 to enhance the compatibility of the two standards for the benefit of the user community. Annex A shows the correspondence between ISO 9001:2008 and ISO 14001:2004.
>
> This International Standard does not include requirements specific to other management systems, such as those particular to environmental management, occupational health and safety management, financial management or risk management. However, this International Standard enables an organization to align or integrate its own quality management system with related management system requirements. It is possible for an organization to adapt its existing management system(s) in order to establish a quality management system that complies with the requirements of this International Standard.

*Source:* ANSI/ISO/ASQ Q9001-2008

Clause 0.4, *Compatibility with other management systems,* states that the standard has been developed with the specific intent to be compatible with the ISO 14001:2004 *Environmental management systems—Specification with guidance for use.* The first paragraph of this clause has been updated to recognize the publication of ISO 14000:2004 and to use current ISO language. In the opinion of most experts, there has always been good compatibility between ISO 14001 and ISO 9001. The drafters of the two families worked together during the development of ISO 9001:2000 and ISO 14001:2004 to ensure that this compatibility was maintained. In fact, experts from ISO TC 207, the technical committee responsible for ISO 14001, were participants in the working group that drafted ISO 9001:2000. Maintaining and enhancing compatibility was also a significant consideration during development of ISO 9001:2008.

Considerations related to compatibility include the following:

- ISO 9001:2008 is structured to enhance its usability with ISO 14001:2004.

- ISO 9001:2008 and ISO 14001:2004 can be used together without unnecessary duplication or conflicting requirements.
- Common requirements can form a basis for integrated management systems.
- Quality management system processes need not be established separately from an existing management system.

> ## 1 Scope
>
> ### 1.1 General
>
> This International Standard specifies requirements for a quality management system where an organization
>
> a) needs to demonstrate its ability to consistently provide product that meets customer and applicable statutory and regulatory requirements, and
>
> b) aims to enhance customer satisfaction through the effective application of the system, including processes for continual improvement of the system and the assurance of conformity to customer and applicable statutory and regulatory requirements.
>
> NOTE 1 In this International Standard, the term "product" only applies to
>
> — product intended for, or required by, a customer,
>
> — any intended output resulting from the product realization processes.
>
> NOTE 2 Statutory and regulatory requirements can be expressed as legal requirements.

*Source:* ANSI/ISO/ASQ Q9001-2008

This clause is identical to clause 1.1 of ISO 9001:2000 except:

- In paragraphs a) and b) "regulatory requirements" has been changed to "statutory and regulatory requirements" to reflect original intent to cover written regulations and laws. The addition of the word "statutory" is intended to ensure that users understand that written laws (statutes) must be considered in quality management system implementation.

  - Statute—a law passed by a legislative body such as a congress or parliament
  - Regulation—an authoritative rule (generally issued by an executive authority of a government) having the force of law

- The second dashed paragraph of note 1 and all of note 2 has been added to clarify the original intent of ISO 9001:2000.

Earlier it was indicated that clause 0 and its subclauses are "informative" and do not form part of the requirements of ISO 9001:2008. The scope is a normative part of the standard, but the ISO Directives also specify that the topics in clause 1 also must not contain requirements. Part 2 of the ISO Directives, fifth edition (2004), clause 6.2, states that the scope of a standard ". . . shall be succinct so that it can be used as a summary for bibliographic purposes. This element shall be worded as a series of statements of fact." Clause 1 of ISO 9001:2008 therefore does not use the word "shall," the keyword in ISO standards that makes a statement a requirement. As summarized in the following list, the scope contains material that describes how the standard is used.

- The intent is that ISO 9001:2008 be directly usable by all types and sizes of organizations regardless of product category.
- The scope makes it clear that a quality management system conforming to ISO 9001:2008 is aimed at achieving customer satisfaction by consistently meeting customer and applicable statutory and regulatory requirements. Thus product and services delivered by the system need to consistently meet the needs of customers. ***The outputs of the system matter to both customers and to other stakeholders as well.***

ISO 9001:2008 is comprehensive in that it applies to all quality management system processes from the identification of requirements to the delivery and addressing of customer satisfaction.

## 1.2 Application

All requirements of this International Standard are generic and are intended to be applicable to all organizations, regardless of type, size and product provided.

Where any requirement(s) of this International Standard cannot be applied due to the nature of an organization and its product, this can be considered for exclusion.

Where exclusions are made, claims of conformity to this International Standard are not acceptable unless these exclusions are limited to requirements within Clause 7, and such exclusions do not affect the organization's ability, or responsibility, to provide product that meets customer and applicable statutory and regulatory requirements.

*Source:* ANSI/ISO/ASQ Q9001-2008

This clause of ISO 9001:2008 is identical to clause 1.2 of ISO 9001:2000 except the last paragraph. "Regulatory" has been changed to "statutory and regulatory" to reflect more accurately the original intent.

Key points of the application clause include the following:

- An organization can exclude requirements within clause 7 that are not required in order to meet customer requirements or are not required by the nature of the product or service provided.
- An organization cannot exclude requirements that affect the ability to produce and provide conforming product or service.

Organizations had excluded activities covered by the 1994 editions when those activities were not performed and had no effect on conformity with customer requirements. Organizations typically use the quality manual to designate the requirements that are excluded. The application clause recognizes this reality.

Many organizations that perform product design activities had used ANSI/ISO/ASQC Q9002-1994, which excludes design. With ISO 9001:2000 and ISO 9001:2008, this is not acceptable. Organizations that perform design work and wish to achieve compliance with ISO 9001:2008 must address design requirements in their quality management systems based on ISO 9001:2008.

The exclusions must be defined in the quality manual, but they do not absolve the organization of its responsibility to meet customer requirements.

Organizations need to exercise great care in excluding activities from their systems. The clause clearly states that an organization may not claim compliance with ISO 9001:2008 if quality management system exclusions exceed what is permitted in clause 1.2.

A second important aspect of the application clause is the relationship of ISO 9001:2008 to legal (statutory and regulatory) requirements. Applicable statutes and regulations absolutely take precedence. This issue is critical to many users of the standard. Therefore, ISO 9001:2008 has been carefully developed to address statutory and regulatory needs. Today, ISO 9001:2000 is indicated in certain regulations as one approach for meeting the regulatory requirements for the design and production of various products. The intent of the application clause is to facilitate the continued use of ISO 9001:2008 by organizations that must address applicable statutes and regulatory requirements.

When scope is reduced, regulatory requirements are still applicable. If scope is reduced further than permitted by the standard, the system is not ISO 9001:2008 compliant.

## 2 Normative references

The following referenced documents are indispensable for the application of this document. For dated references, only the edition cited applies. For undated references, the latest edition of the referenced document (including any amendments) applies.

ISO 9000:2005, *Quality management systems—Fundamentals and vocabulary*

*Source:* ANSI/ISO/ASQ Q9001-2008

> **3 Terms and definitions**
>
> For the purposes of this document, the terms and definitions given in ISO 9000 apply.
>
> Throughout the text of this International Standard, wherever the term "product" occurs, it can also mean "service".

*Source:* ANSI/ISO/ASQ Q9001-2008

Clause 2, *normative reference,* has been updated to use wording specified in the latest edition of the ISO Directives. Note the statement that the reference is "indispensable for the application of ISO 9001:2008." This is a part of the language mandated by ISO Directives. It means ISO committees should list as normative references only those documents that are "indispensable." The only normative reference in ISO 9001:2008 is ISO 9000:2005, which contains the terms and definitions used in the ISO 9000 family. The only normative content of ISO 9000:2005 is the actual definitions. This is because the text of ISO 9000:2005 clause 2 is written in descriptive language without words like "should" or "shall." This has led some users to ignore the fundamentals of quality management given in ISO 9000:2005 clause 2. This is a mistake. Users leading quality management system implementation should clearly understand the fundamentals as well as the terminology. The fundamentals of ISO 9000:2005 clause 2 provide a framework of understanding that is very useful during implementation of ISO 9001:2008.

The second and third paragraphs of clause 3 of ISO 9001:2000 have been deleted. It was considered that the explanation of supply chain terminology and reference to ISO 9001:1994 are no longer needed.

Key points from clauses 2 and 3 include the following:

- ISO 9000:2005 contains definitions that are normative and form part of the requirements.
- ISO 9000:2005 is an indispensable reference for users of ISO 9001:2008.
- Wherever the term "product" is used, it can also mean "service."

# CHAPTER

# 2

# Quality Management System and General Documentation

## 4 Quality management system

### 4.1 General requirements

The organization shall establish, document, implement and maintain a quality management system and continually improve its effectiveness in accordance with the requirements of this International Standard.

The organization shall

a) determine the processes needed for the quality management system and their application throughout the organization (see 1.2),

b) determine the sequence and interaction of these processes,

c) determine criteria and methods needed to ensure that both the operation and control of these processes are effective,

d) ensure the availability of resources and information necessary to support the operation and monitoring of these processes,

e) monitor, measure where applicable, and analyse these processes, and

f) implement actions necessary to achieve planned results and continual improvement of these processes.

These processes shall be managed by the organization in accordance with the requirements of this International Standard.

Where an organization chooses to outsource any process that affects product conformity to requirements, the organization shall ensure control over such processes. The type and extent of control to be applied to these outsourced processes shall be defined within the quality management system.

NOTE 1 Processes needed for the quality management system referred to above include processes for management activities, provision of resources, product realization, measurement, analysis and improvement.

NOTE 2 An "outsourced process" is a process that the organization needs for its quality management system and which the organization chooses to have performed by an external party.

NOTE 3 Ensuring control over outsourced processes does not absolve the organization of the responsibility of conformity to all customer, statutory and regulatory requirements. The type and extent of control to be applied to the outsourced process can be influenced by factors such as

a) the potential impact of the outsourced process on the organization's capability to provide product that conforms to requirements,

b) the degree to which the control for the process is shared,

c) the capability of achieving the necessary control through the application of 7.4.

*Source:* ANSI/ISO/ASQ Q9001-2008

The requirements of clause 4.1 have not changed. The text of 4.1e has been edited by the addition of "(where applicable)" to clarify that process measurement may not be possible or practical in every case. The last paragraph and note 1 have been edited for clarity. Notes 2 and 3 have been added to clarify the intent related to outsourcing.

The basic requirement for a quality management system is that the organization must identify and manage the family of processes needed to ensure conformity of the quality management system to the standard and of product to requirements. This basic requirement has not changed from ISO 9001:2000. ***The quality management system ensures compliance with the quality policy, ensures that quality objectives are met, and it ensures that products consistently meet customer and applicable regulatory requirements.*** For a discussion of this concept see Chapter 1 on the scope of ISO 9001:2008. Organizations should not lose sight of this basic concept. It is easy to get so absorbed in documenting a system that the basic concept is lost. While documentation is important, the primary emphasis should be on developing and implementing effective quality management system processes.

It is critical to understand the difference between managing a system and documenting a system. Clause 4.1 does not directly address documentation. Rather, clause 4.1 requires that processes be developed and implemented to make up the overall system. It also requires that processes be managed and continually improved. Improvement activities must include monitoring, measurement, and analysis of the processes. This is at the heart of the process approach.

Examples of activities that organizations will need to consider include:

- Identification of processes and their interrelationships, sequences, and interactions
- Establishment of criteria and means to effectively operate, monitor, measure, analyze, and control the processes
- Improvement of quality management system effectiveness including improvement of these processes
- Control of quality management system processes that are outsourced to another organization that affect product conformity

Understanding and using this process approach is critical to compliance with ISO 9001:2008.

## IMPLEMENTATION TIPS AND TYPICAL QUESTIONS TO ASK FOR CONFORMITY

The first steps to take in developing the quality management system are given in Chapter 3 and involve establishing management commitment, developing the quality policy, determining quality objectives, and aligning the policy and objectives with the overall mission of the organization. It is also important to explore and understand basic customer needs and requirements. This understanding is key input to the development of the processes of the quality management system. Most organizations already have at least some of the processes that are needed for a complete system. The next step is to identify these existing processes and determine what other processes must be developed for the quality management system to be effective and conform to ISO 9001:2008. Each process should be mapped or flowcharted. Then the organization must determine how all of the processes relate to each other. Understanding these relationships is important because problems often occur at process interactions. Map or chart existing processes as they are. Then map or chart any new processes that are required and improve those that already exist to keep the process maps up to date. Process development should include understanding the inputs and outputs of each process, determination of what measurements are to be used and how those measures relate to the measurable quality objectives. Controls also need to be established so that each process operates under controlled conditions. See also Chapters 5 and 9.

Questions to consider asking to assess conformity to this clause include:

- Have the processes needed for quality management been identified?
- Have sequence and interaction of these processes been determined?

- Have criteria and control methods been determined for control of the processes in the quality management system?
- Is information available to support the operation and monitoring of the processes?
- Are processes measured, monitored, and analyzed with appropriate actions taken to achieve planned results and continual improvement?
- Is the quality management system established, documented, implemented, maintained, and continually improved?
- Has provision been made to ensure control of quality management system processes that are outsourced?

## DEFINITIONS

*Management system* (3.2.2)—**system** (3.2.1) to establish policy and objectives and to achieve those objectives

NOTE A management system of an **organization** (3.3.1) can include different management systems, such as a **quality management system** (3.2.3), a financial management system or an environmental management system.

*Organization* (3.3.1)—group of people and facilities with an arrangement of responsibilities, authorities and relationships

EXAMPLE Company, corporation, firm, enterprise, institution, charity, sole trader, association, or parts or combination thereof.

NOTE 1 The arrangement is generally orderly.

NOTE 2 An organization can be public or private.

NOTE 3 This definition is valid for the purposes of quality management system (3.2.3) standards. The term "organization" is defined differently in ISO/IEC Guide 2.

*Process* (3.4.1)—set of interrelated or interacting activities which transforms inputs into outputs

NOTE 1 Inputs to a process are generally outputs of other processes.

NOTE 2 Processes in an **organization** (3.3.1) are generally planned and carried out under controlled conditions to add value.

NOTE 3 A process where the **conformity** (3.6.1) of the resulting **product** (3.4.2) cannot be readily or economically verified is frequently referred to as a "special process".

*Quality* (3.1.1)—degree to which a set of inherent **characteristics** (3.5.1) fulfils **requirements** (3.1.2)

NOTE 1 The term "quality" can be used with adjectives such as poor, good or excellent.

NOTE 2 "Inherent", as opposed to "assigned", means existing in something, especially as a permanent characteristic.

*Quality management system* (3.2.3)—**management system** (3.2.2) to direct and control an **organization** (3.3.1) with regard to **quality** (3.1.1)

*Requirement* (3.1.2)—need or expectation that is stated, generally implied or obligatory

NOTE 1 "Generally implied" means that it is custom or common practice for the **organization** (3.3.1), its **customers** (3.3.5) and other **interested parties** (3.3.7), that the need or expectation under consideration is implied.

NOTE 2 A qualifier can be used to denote a specific type of requirement, e.g. product requirement, quality management requirement, customer requirement.

NOTE 3 A specified requirement is one that is stated, for example in a **document** (3.7.2).

NOTE 4 Requirements can be generated by different **interested parties** (3.3.7).

NOTE 5 This definition differs from that provided in 3.12.1 of ISO/IEC Directives, Part 2:2004.

> **3.12.1**
> **requirement**
> expression in the content of a document conveying criteria to be fulfilled if compliance with the document is to be claimed and from which no deviation is permitted

*Source:* ANSI/ISO/ASQ Q9000-2005

> ## 4.2 Documentation requirements
>
> ### 4.2.1 General
>
> The quality management system documentation shall include
>
> a) documented statements of a quality policy and quality objectives,
>
> b) a quality manual,
>
> c) documented procedures and records required by this International Standard, and
>
> d) documents, including records, determined by the organization to be necessary to ensure the effective planning, operation and control of its processes.
>
> NOTE 1 Where the term "documented procedure" appears within this International Standard, this means that the procedure is established, documented, implemented and maintained. A single document may address the requirements for one or more procedures. A requirement for a documented procedure may be covered by more than one document.
>
> NOTE 2 The extent of the quality management system documentation can differ from one organization to another due to
>
> a) the size of organization and type of activities,
>
> b) the complexity of processes and their interactions, and
>
> c) the competence of personnel.
>
> NOTE 3 The documentation can be in any form or type of medium.

*Source:* ANSI/ISO/ASQ Q9001-2008

The requirements of clause 4.2 and 4.2.1 have not changed. Clause 4.2.d) has been edited for clarity by replacing the word "needed" with "determined" and the requirements related to records have been moved from 4.2.1e) into sub clauses c) and d). Clause e has been deleted. Note 1 has been expanded to improve clarity.

Documentation forms a basis for understanding the system, communicating its processes and requirements within the organization, describing it to other organizations, and determining the effectiveness of implementation. The organization is required to establish, document, maintain, and improve the quality management system. It is top management's responsibility to facilitate the establishment of the system. Top management must also ensure that the system is actually implemented; it is obviously insufficient to have a documented system that is not implemented. The documented system must reflect activities that are actually performed to ensure conformity.

On the other hand, the perceived requirement for an excessive number of documented procedures was one of the most criticized aspects of ISO 9001:1987 and ISO 9001:1994. ISO 9001:2000 made a significant step toward changing that perception by greatly simplifying documentation required. The documentation requirements of ISO 9001:2008 retain the simplicity of ISO 9001:2000. *The emphasis is on managing a system of processes to achieve specific quality objectives and achieve customer requirements rather than on documenting procedures.* It is the process management described earlier that is emphasized. Organizations have always had the freedom to determine the extent of documentation that is appropriate. ISO 9001:2008 continues to provide great flexibility to select documentation methods and structures that are appropriate for the organization's needs.

The system must also be maintained. Nothing is static; changes occur constantly in most organizations. This means the system must be used on an ongoing basis and must be kept current.

The extent of the quality management system documentation for an organization depends on the organization's situation. As a minimum, the documentation must include an appropriate combination of the following documents:

- Documents describing the quality policy required by clause 5.3 and giving the quality objectives required by clause 5.4.1.
- The quality manual must describe the interaction of the processes in the quality management system. The organization is required to have a quality manual, and the manual must meet certain requirements. The details of these requirements are given in clause 4.2.2 and will be discussed later in this chapter. The manual must either contain or reference the documented procedures related to the system's processes.

- There must be documented procedures that describe the system. These documents must either be included as a part of or be referenced in the quality manual.

As with ISO 9001:2000, ISO 9001:2008 specifically requires "documented procedures" in only six places, but remember that the organization must also have documentation of the system's processes and their interactions. Once the processes of the quality management system have been defined and their interactions established, the key processes should be described in documented procedures. Along with the quality manual, these documented procedures provide a mechanism for communication of the processes to the organization. A well-prepared quality manual along with easily understood documented procedures will help to ensure that all employees understand the quality management system. Many organizations will choose to maintain their quality manual and other quality system documentation in electronic format, so the distinction between one comprehensive quality manual that includes all quality system documentation and a quality manual that references additional documentation becomes academic.

It may come as a surprise to many that ISO 9001:2008 has few specific requirements for documented procedures. Table 2.1 describes the requirements. While specific requirements are few, it is important to remember that clause 4.2.1d requires the organization to identify and prepare any documents necessary for the effective planning, operation, and control of its processes. *Organizations typically need additional documentation to fully describe the quality management system beyond the six explicitly required documented procedures.*

- Other system documentation is required as necessary to document the sequences and activities required for the operation of the system. In addition to the quality manual and the documented procedures that describe the overall processes of the quality management system, organizations are specifically required to prepare other documentation needed for control of processes. The type and extent of these documents must be determined by the organization.

Table 2.1 ISO 9001:2008 requirements for documented procedures.

| ANSI/ISO/ASQ Q9001-2008 Clause | Documented Procedure Required |
|---|---|
| 4.2.3 | Control of documents |
| 4.2.4 | Control of records |
| 8.3 | Control of nonconforming product |
| 8.5.2 | Corrective action |
| 8.5.3 | Preventive action |
| 8.2.2 | Internal quality audits |

*Source:* ANSI/ISO/ASQ Q9001-2008

This documentation is typically in the form of written procedures or work instructions. Table 2.2 lists the clauses in ISO 9001:2008 where such documentation is discussed or required.

For example, in clause 5.3 there is no requirement to create a documented procedure for describing the process of creating a quality policy. However, the organization must have a quality policy, and this quality policy is a document that needs to be controlled. This means that processes must ensure that the most current version of the quality policy has been issued and that obsolete versions have been removed or appropriately marked as such. It would be confusing to have obsolete versions of an organization's quality policy still present within the organization.

Organizations have many options for documenting their systems. Note, for example, that the quality manual need not be a separate document. Systems can be developed in which the manual contains documented procedures. In fact, for a small organization it may be appropriate to include most or all of the system documentation in a single manual. Depending on the size and complexity of the organization, it may also be appropriate that the documents describing the sequences and interactions of processes be combined with the documented procedures that describe

**Table 2.2** Requirements for documentation other than specifically required documented procedures and records.

| ANSI/ISO/ASQ Q9001-2008 Clause | Documented Procedure Required |
|---|---|
| 4.1 | "The organization shall establish, document, . . . a quality management system. . . ." |
| 4.2.1 | ". . . quality management system documentation shall include:<br>a) . . . quality policy and quality objectives . . .<br>b) . . . quality manual . . .<br>c) . . . documented procedures and records . . .<br>d) . . . documents including records, determined by the organization to be necessary to ensure the effective planning, operation and control of its processes. . . ." |
| 7.1 | ". . . In planning product realization, the organization shall determine the following<br>". . . b) need to establish processes, documents, and. . . ." |
| 7.3.3 | Design output ". . . shall be in a form suitable for verification" |
| 7.5.1 | b) "the availability of work instructions, as necessary" |

*Source:* ANSI/ISO/ASQ Q9001-2008

the system. Certainly other combinations are possible. Remember that the extent of required documentation depends on the following:

- Size and type of organization
- Complexity and interaction of the organization's processes
- Competency of the organization's people

Organizations may use any form or media for any of the documents in the quality management system. This means that the quality manual, the documented procedures, and the other documents of the system may be published in any way the organization chooses; there are no restrictions. However, the organization must remember in selecting its documentation media that the document control provisions of clause 4.2.3 must be met.

## IMPLEMENTATION TIPS AND TYPICAL QUESTIONS TO ASK FOR CONFORMITY

Keep the priorities correct. Development of the processes of the system and properly assigning resources is of much greater benefit to the organization than writing procedures. Focus on the process maps, flowcharts, measures, controls, activities, and resources. Think carefully about what processes need documented procedures using the criteria given above. Over time you may need to add procedures where the situations change (e.g., more temporary workers may require procedures not previously needed). It is also common to see organizations add procedures in response to problems. Resist this temptation and seek real, root causes to your problems. As the system matures, don't be afraid to eliminate unneeded documents. It is also advisable to use electronic documentation. Even very small organizations have gotten real benefit from simple electronic systems with hyperlinked documents. And most important, keep the documentation as simple as you can. Simple documentation generally improves performance and conformity. Don't over complicate that which can be simplified. And don't over simplify the documentation of that which is truly complicated.

Questions to consider asking to assess conformity to this clause include:

- Have documented procedures been prepared where specifically required by ISO 9001:2008 (see Table 2.1)?
- Is the extent of quality management system documentation dependent on the size and type of the organization?
- Is the extent of quality management system documentation dependent on the complexity and interaction of processes in the organization?
- Is the extent of quality management system documentation dependent on the competence of personnel in the organization?

## DEFINITIONS

*Document* (3.7.2)—**information** (3.7.1) and its supporting medium

EXAMPLE **Record** (3.7.6), **specification** (3.7.3), procedure document, drawing, report, standard.

NOTE 1 The medium can be paper, magnetic, electronic or optical computer disc, photograph or master sample, or a combination thereof.

NOTE 2 A set of documents, for example specifications and records, is frequently called "documentation".

NOTE 3 Some **requirements** (3.1.2) (e.g. the requirement to be readable) relate to all types of documents, however there can be different requirements for specifications (e.g. the requirement to be revision controlled) and records (e.g. the requirement to be retrievable).

*Procedure* (3.4.5)—specified way to carry out an activity or a **process** (3.4.1)

NOTE 1 Procedures can be documented or not.

NOTE 2 When a procedure is documented, the term "written procedure" or "documented procedure" is frequently used. The **document** (3.7.2) that contains a procedure can be called a "procedure document".

*Source:* ANSI/ISO/ASQ Q9000-2005

**4.2.2 Quality manual**

The organization shall establish and maintain a quality manual that includes

a) the scope of the quality management system, including details of and justification for any exclusions (see 1.2),

b) the documented procedures established for the quality management system, or reference to them, and

c) a description of the interaction between the processes of the quality management system.

*Source:* ANSI/ISO/ASQ Q9001-2008

The requirements and text of this clause are identical to ISO 9001:2000. The quality manual is the document that describes the overall quality management system, its processes, and the interrelationship among those processes. It can either contain or reference more detailed documented procedures. The manual should be useful to facilitate understanding of the quality management system, and the organization should not feel constrained to a specific format for the manual's content.

The format and content should be developed in a way that describes how the organization's quality management system really works.

ISO 9001:2008 requires the manual to have a description of the "interaction between" the processes that make up the system. This is a key concept for the quality manual. There is also a requirement in clause 4.2.2a) that the quality manual include the scope of the quality management system, including the details of and justification for any exclusions the organization has taken under clause 1.2, Application.

## IMPLEMENTATION TIPS AND TYPICAL QUESTIONS TO ASK FOR CONFORMITY

The best quality manuals are very simple. They focus on the very things that are required in ISO 9001:2008. They give the scope of coverage of the quality management system, briefly discuss any exclusions or special conditions affecting the system, and focus on providing understanding of the process interactions. Some good quality manuals include this basic material as the first section in a larger document, which also contains the procedures. Great manuals always provide easy-to-understand, simple descriptions of process interactions. The best way to do this is with a brief text description and one or more simplified maps of the basic system processes showing the important interactions. Even in a small organization it may be impractical to show all interactions. Instead of worrying about showing them all, focus on how the major interactions work and spend your analytical time on fixing problems at these important process interfaces. Organizations should also consider turning the quality manual into an overall management system manual using the same concepts but showing additional processes, such as those related to financial controls, safety, and environmental management. Remember, the manual describes your system. It is not just a list of clauses from the standard followed by your commitment to comply. If such information is required by customers, include it, but it is not sufficient; you must describe your system's process interfaces.

Questions to consider when assessing conformity to this clause include:

- Does the organization have a quality manual that describes the interaction of the processes in the quality management system?
- Does the quality manual either include or reference the documented procedures describing the processes of the quality management system?
- Does the quality manual include the scope of the quality management system, including details of and justification for any exclusions taken under clause 1.2?
- Is the quality manual a controlled document?

## DEFINITIONS

*Quality* (3.1.1)—degree to which a set of inherent **characteristics** (3.5.1) fulfils **requirements** (3.1.2)

NOTE 1 The term "quality" can be used with adjectives such as poor, good or excellent.

NOTE 2 "Inherent", as opposed to "assigned", means existing in something, especially as a permanent characteristic.

*Quality management* (3.2.8)—coordinated activities to direct and control an **organization** (3.3.1) with regard to **quality** (3.1.1)

NOTE Direction and control with regard to quality generally includes establishment of the **quality policy** (3.2.4) and **quality objectives** (3.2.5), **quality planning** (3.2.9), **quality control** (3.2.10), **quality assurance** (3.2.11) and **quality improvement** (3.2.12).

*Quality manual* (3.7.4)—**document** (3.7.2) specifying the **quality management system** (3.2.3) of an **organization** (3.3.1)

NOTE Quality manuals can vary in detail and format to suit the size and complexity of an individual organization.

*Source:* ANSI/ISO/ASQ Q9000-2005

### 4.2.3 Control of documents

Documents required by the quality management system shall be controlled. Records are a special type of document and shall be controlled according to the requirements given in 4.2.4.

A documented procedure shall be established to define the controls needed

a) to approve documents for adequacy prior to issue,

b) to review and update as necessary and re-approve documents,

c) to ensure that changes and the current revision status of documents are identified,

d) to ensure that relevant versions of applicable documents are available at points of use,

e) to ensure that documents remain legible and readily identifiable,

f) to ensure that documents of external origin determined by the organization to be necessary for the planning and operation of the quality management system are identified and their distribution controlled, and

g) to prevent the unintended use of obsolete documents, and to apply suitable identification to them if they are retained for any purpose.

*Source:* ANSI/ISO/ASQ Q9001-2008

### 4.2.4 Control of records

Records established to provide evidence of conformity to requirements and of the effective operation of the quality management system shall be controlled.

The organization shall establish a documented procedure to define the controls needed for the identification, storage, protection, retrieval, retention and disposition of records.

Records shall remain legible, readily identifiable and retrievable.

*Source:* ANSI/ISO/ASQ Q9001-2008

The requirements and text of clause 4.2.3 are almost identical to those of ISO 9001:2000. Clause 4.2.3f) has been expanded to clarify documents of external origin. The requirements of clause 4.2.4 also have not changed, but that clasue has been edited for clarity.

Documents that are part of the quality management system must be controlled to ensure that correct requirements are available. Controls for documents must include a number of specific activities.

Approval prior to issue for use is required to ensure that documents are adequate. Written document control procedures should specify how this approval is accomplished. Many organizations find it worthwhile to include a process for internal review of the documents by all affected units of the organizations as part of the pre-issue review process.

Review, updating, and reapproval are required as necessary. Some organizations create systems to ensure that documents are reviewed for continued suitability on a periodic, scheduled basis. There is no stated requirement that the review be periodic or scheduled, just that it occur as necessary. If the documentation system is vibrant and its documents are used daily, it may prove sufficient to conduct the reviews only when there is a known need to make a change. Each organization should define a document review, revision, and reapproval process that suits its own business needs.

Controls are required to ensure that the correct revisions of documents are identified and available at the points of use, including controls (such as identification) to prevent unintended use of obsolete documents. Many organizations have migrated to computer-based processes for tracking the current issue of documents. Also, means are required to ensure that documents remain legible, retrievable, and readily identifiable.

And controls must extend to documents of external origin, such as industry and customer specifications and standards.

A record is a special type of document and has its own control requirements. Records are documents that provide evidence that an activity has been accomplished or that an event has happened. Records are also used to provide information on the condition (such as conformity or nonconformity) of a product. While the other types of documents in the quality management system may indicate what is to be done (the current and future action), records provide evidence of what has occurred (past action).

As with documented procedures, there is emphasis on the organization's defining the required records rather than specifying them in the standards. Table 2.3 gives a listing of the specified record requirements as well as the requirements for the organization to identify its own record needs.

**Table 2.3** Record-related requirements.

| ANSI/ISO/ASQ Q9001-2008 Clause | Record-Related Requirements |
|---|---|
| 4.2.1 | The quality management system documentation shall include<br>"c) . . . records required by this international standard<br>"d) . . . documents, including records determined by the organization to be necessary to ensure the effective planning, operation and control of its processes." |
| 4.2.3 | ". . . Records are a special type of document and shall be controlled . . . 4.2.4." |
| 4.2.4 | "Records established to provide evidence of conformity to requirements and of the effective operation of the quality management system; shall be controlled." |
| 5.5.2[2] | The management representative reports to top management on the performance of the quality management system. |
| 5.6.1 | "Records for management review shall be maintained. (see 4.2.4)" |
| 6.2.2 | Records of education, training, skills, and experience. |
| 7.1.d[1] | The "records needed to provide evidence that the realization processes and resulting product meet requirements." |
| 7.2.2 | Records of review of product requirements |
| 7.3.2 | Records of inputs to product requirements in design and development |

**Table 2.3** Continued.

| ANSI/ISO/ASQ Q9001-2008 Clause | Record-Related Requirements |
|---|---|
| 7.3.4 | Records of design and development review and follow-up actions |
| 7.3.5 | Records of the design and development verification and subsequent follow-up actions |
| 7.3.6 | Records of the design and development validation and subsequent follow-up actions |
| 7.3.7 | Design and development changes ". . . identified and records maintained . . . Records of result of review of changes and any necessary actions. . . ." |
| 7.4.1 | Records of supplier evaluation results and follow-up actions |
| 7.5.2d[1] | Requirements for records related to process validation |
| 7.5.3 | Record of unique product identification (where traceability is a requirement) |
| 7.5.4 | Records of any customer property that is lost, damaged, or otherwise found unsuitable |
| 7.6.a | The basis used for calibration |
| 7.6 | Record validity of previous measurement results when equipment is found outside of requirements. |
| 7.6 | Results of calibration and verification |
| 7.6.c[2] | "Have identification in order to determine its calibration status; . . ." |
| 8.2.2 | Records of audits and their results |
| 8.2.2[2] | Follow-up audit actions including verification of actions taken and reporting of verification results |
| 8.2.4[2] | Evidence of conformity with the acceptance criteria shall be maintained; |
| 8.2.4 | Records shall indicate the authority responsible for release of product. |

*Continued*

**Table 2.3** Continued.

| ANSI/ISO/ASQ Q9001-2008 Clause | Record-Related Requirements |
|---|---|
| 8.3 | Record of nature of nonconformity, action taken, and any concessions |
| 8.5.2e | Records of results of corrective actions taken |
| 8.5.3d | Records of results of preventive actions taken |

[1]Requirement for a process or procedure to define quality records to be controlled.

[2]Requirement for "reporting" or reporting of results; may or may not involve quality records. No reference to clause 4.2.4 of ISO 9001:2008.

*Source:* ANSI/ISO/ASQ Q9001-2008

Organizations must identify the records to be retained along with the length of time each type of record must be retained. Many organizations do not have lengthy retention times and need only provide for the normal filing of records. In such cases, the documented procedure can be very simple, with a matrix giving the information required. Other organizations have very long retention times for some records and need to consider long-term indexing and retrieval from off-site archives. For all cases, controls should be appropriate to the circumstances and the retention times needed.

Organizations also need to identify the storage conditions and protection required for the records that they maintain. It is particularly important to consider how the organization would be affected if the records became lost or were destroyed. Organizations should look at each type of record and determine appropriate protection based on importance to the continued operation of the quality management system. For many noncritical records, storage in normal file cabinets may be appropriate. Critical records should be protected from potential fire and other damage. Provisions need to be made for backup of records stored on magnetic media and for appropriate protection of the backup copies. In the event of a fire, it will do little good to have computer backup files stored on a shelf next to the computer. Although it is not a specified requirement, many organizations create and maintain a disaster recovery plan to address such situations.

## IMPLEMENTATION TIPS AND TYPICAL QUESTIONS TO ASK FOR CONFORMITY

Keep the document and record control processes as simple as possible. One of the reasons for recommending that documentation for items other than records be electronic is that today's technology can greatly simplify controls. For example, it is easy to restrict document changes to only authorized personnel, or to permit printing of only copies clearly marked as having specific limited life. To the extent practical, it is also best to computerize record keeping. The world of computers gives us virtually unlimited choice of control mechanisms for both records and other documents.

Questions to consider asking to assess conformity to this clause include:

- Has a documented procedure been established for document control?
- Are documents approved for adequacy prior to use?
- Are documents reviewed and updated as necessary?
- Are document changes reapproved to ensure adequacy prior to use?
- Is current document revision status maintained?
- Are relevant versions of applicable documents available at points of use?
- Is there a process to ensure that documents remain legible, readily identifiable, and retrievable?
- Are documents of external origin identified and their distribution controlled?
- Are obsolete documents retained for any purpose suitably identified to prevent unintended use?

Questions related to control of records:

- Is there a documented procedure for the control of records?
- Have the organization's records been identified?
- Have retention times and disposition requirements been determined for all records?

- Are records disposed of as required by the organization's documented procedures?
- Have storage and retrieval requirements been determined and implemented for records?
- Have protection requirements been determined and implemented for records?

## DEFINITIONS

*Document* (3.7.2)—**information** (3.7.1) and its supporting medium

EXAMPLE **Record** (3.7.6), **specification** (3.7.3), procedure document, drawing, report, standard.

NOTE 1 The medium can be paper, magnetic, electronic or optical computer disc, photograph or master sample, or a combination thereof.

NOTE 2 A set of documents, for example specifications and records, is frequently called "documentation".

NOTE 3 Some **requirements** (3.1.2) (e.g. the requirement to be readable) relate to all types of documents, however there can be different requirements for specifications (e.g. the requirement to be revision controlled) and records (e.g. the requirement to be retrievable).

*Procedure* (3.4.5)—specified way to carry out an activity or a **process** (3.4.1)

NOTE 1 Procedures can be documented or not.

NOTE 2 When a procedure is documented, the term "written procedure" or "documented procedure" is frequently used. The **document** (3.7.2) that contains a procedure can be called a "procedure document".

*Quality* (3.1.1)—degree to which a set of inherent **characteristics** (3.5.1) fulfils **requirements** (3.1.2)

NOTE 1 The term "quality" can be used with adjectives such as poor, good or excellent.

NOTE 2 "Inherent", as opposed to "assigned", means existing in something, especially as a permanent characteristic.

*Quality management system* (3.2.3)—**management system** (3.2.2) to direct and control an **organization** (3.3.1) with regard to **quality** (3.1.1)

*Record* (3.7.6)—**document** (3.7.2) stating results achieved or providing evidence of activities performed

NOTE 1 Records can be used, for example, to document **traceability** (3.5.4) and to provide evidence of **verification** (3.8.4), **preventive action** (3.6.4) and **corrective action** (3.6.5).

NOTE 2 Generally records need not be under revision control.

*Review* (3.8.7)—activity undertaken to determine the suitability, adequacy and **effectiveness** (3.2.14) of the subject matter to achieve established objectives

NOTE Review can also include the determination of **efficiency** (3.2.15).

EXAMPLE Management review, design and development review, review of customer requirements and nonconformity review.

*Source:* ANSI/ISO/ASQ Q9000-2005

## CONSIDERATIONS FOR DOCUMENTATION

There must be a documented procedure to describe how document control is accomplished, and it must address the requirements of clauses 4.2.3a) through 4.2.3g). There also must be a documented procedure for the control of quality records covering the items listed in clause 4.2.4. Since control considerations for records are different from those for other documents, a separate documented procedure is required for the control of records.

NOTE 2 A qualifier can be applied to indicate the nature of what is being designed and developed (e.g. product design and development or process design and development).

*Process* (3.4.1)—set of interrelated or interacting activities which transforms inputs into outputs.

NOTE 1 Inputs to a process are generally outputs of other processes.

NOTE 2 Processes in an organization (3.3.1) are generally planned and carried out under controlled conditions to add value.

NOTE 3 A process where the conformity (3.6.1) of the resulting product (3.4.2) cannot be readily or economically verified is frequently referred to as a "special process".

*Project* (3.4.3)—unique process (3.4.1), consisting of a set of coordinated and controlled activities with start and finish dates, undertaken to achieve an objective conforming to specific requirements (3.1.2), including the constraints of time, cost and resources.

NOTE 1 An individual project can form part of a larger project structure.

NOTE 2 In some projects the objectives are refined and the product characteristics defined progressively as the project proceeds.

NOTE 3 The outcome of a project may be one or several units of product (3.4.2).

NOTE 4 Adapted from ISO 10006:2003.

*Characteristic* (3.5.1)—distinguishing feature.

NOTE 1 A characteristic can be inherent or assigned.

NOTE 2 A characteristic can be qualitative or quantitative.

NOTE 3 There are various classes of characteristic, such as the following:

— physical (e.g. mechanical, electrical, chemical or biological characteristics);
— sensory (e.g. related to smell, touch, taste, sight, hearing);
— behavioral (e.g. courtesy, honesty, veracity);
— temporal (e.g. punctuality, reliability, availability);
— ergonomic (e.g. physiological characteristic, or related to human safety);
— functional (e.g. maximum speed of an aircraft).

*System* (3.2.1)—set of interrelated or interacting elements.

Source: ANSI/ISO/ASQ Q9000-2005

## CONSIDERATIONS FOR DOCUMENTATION

Considerations should include a documented procedure that states the expectations for formal project plans, including the minimum level of detail for each project. The planning and

# CHAPTER 3

# Management Responsibility

## 5 Management responsibility

### 5.1 Management commitment

Top management shall provide evidence of its commitment to the development and implementation of the quality management system and continually improve its effectiveness by

a) communicating to the organization the importance of meeting customer as well as statutory and regulatory requirements,

b) establishing the quality policy,

c) ensuring that quality objectives are established,

d) conducting management reviews, and

e) ensuring the availability of resources.

### 5.2 Customer focus

Top management shall ensure that customer requirements are determined and are met with the aim of enhancing customer satisfaction (see 7.2.1 and 8.2.1).

*Source:* ANSI/ISO/ASQ Q9001-2008

The requirements and text are the same as that found in ISO 9001:2000. Top management commitment is required not only to develop the quality management system but also to continually improve its effectiveness.

Top management is required to demonstrate commitment by conducting specific activities. It is not sufficient for top managers merely to proclaim their commitment. There are specific responsibilities that must be fulfilled. Some of these responsibilities were required of top managers by the 1994 version of ISO 9001; others may well have been delegated. As with the 1994 version, top management must provide resources and must perform management reviews. They must also be actively involved in ensuring that the quality policy and objectives are established. Active participation of senior leaders in the development and deployment of both the quality policy and related objectives is a must for attaining compliance. Top management is also required to communicate the organization's policy and goals as required by earlier versions.

ISO 9001:2000 and ISO 9001:2008 include two additional requirements in this clause. Top management is required to communicate to the organization the importance of meeting customer requirements and regulatory and statutory requirements. In addition a process is required not only to create awareness of the organization's quality policy and quality objectives but also to maintain this awareness. Leaders demonstrate this commitment by both words and actions.

Top management is required to ensure that customer requirements are determined, understood, and met. Top managers are not expected to accomplish all of this on their own, but they must be able to demonstrate that they have processes to ensure that these requirements are met.

## IMPLEMENTATION TIPS AND TYPICAL QUESTIONS TO ASK FOR CONFORMITY

Developing a true sense of commitment on the part of top managers starts with a clear understanding of the organization's mission and vision of the future. If these are clear to top managers, it should be easy to develop a clear relationship between that mission and vision and product quality. To develop this alignment:

- A clear understanding of the general needs, expectations, and requirements of customers and other stakeholders is important.
- Determine the potential benefits of a formal quality management system: improved sales, lower costs, more customers.
- Describe for top managers *why* they need to do the important activities required by ISO 9001:2008.

Top managers need to understand enough about market and customer requirements to believe a quality management system is necessary to achieve the organization's mission and to reach the organization's future vision. These are aspects of top managers' commitments that are critical to success, such as:

- Be the recognized leaders of the quality management system—they need to feel and act the system.
- Create an environment in which the quality management system can be effective—make it the way they manage the organization.
- Demand conformance to requirements while encouraging innovation and positive change.
- Focus on improving processes, not blaming people.
- Supply required resources to operate and continually improve the quality management system and consistently meet requirements.
- Review quality management system effectiveness continually with the attitude that it always can be improved.
- Expect outstanding performance while looking at failures as learning experiences.
- Lead efforts to continually improve the quality management system, customer satisfaction, and performance.
- Maintain and articulate the business reasons for the formal quality management system.

While meeting the ISO 9001:2008 requirements is important, the real long term success of the quality management system is dependant more on top management attitude. If top managers adopt the quality management system as their key mechanism for operational control, the system will flourish. Otherwise it is likely to wither over time. The ISO 9001:2008 requirements for top managers' action all fit nicely in the aspects listed above.

Questions to consider asking to assess conformity to this clause include:

- Has top management established a quality policy?
- Has top management developed quality objectives?

- Do top managers regularly perform management reviews and assess opportunities for improvement?
- Does top management provide and regularly review the adequacy of resources?
- Is top management involved in the process to determine customer requirements and to ensure that they are met?
- Is there a process to ensure that employees understand the importance of meeting customer, regulatory, and statutory requirements?
- Is there evidence of top management commitment to continually improve QMS effectiveness?

## DEFINITIONS

*Customer* (3.3.5)—**organization** (3.3.1) or person that receives a **product** (3.4.2)

EXAMPLE Consumer, client, end-user, retailer, beneficiary and purchaser.

NOTE A customer can be internal or external to the organization.

*Management system* (3.2.2)—**system** (3.2.1) to establish policy and objectives and to achieve those objectives

NOTE A management system of an **organization** (3.3.1) can include different management systems, such as a **quality management system** (3.2.3), a financial management system or an environmental management system.

*Organization* (3.3.1)—group of people and facilities with an arrangement of responsibilities, authorities and relationships

EXAMPLE Company, corporation, firm, enterprise, institution, charity, sole trader, association, or parts or combination thereof.

NOTE 1 The arrangement is generally orderly.

NOTE 2 An organization can be public or private.

NOTE 3 This definition is valid for the purposes of **quality management system** (3.2.3) standards. The term "organization" is defined differently in ISO/IEC Guide 2.

*Quality* (3.1.1)—degree to which a set of inherent **characteristics** (3.5.1) fulfils **requirements** (3.1.2)

NOTE 1 The term "quality" can be used with adjectives such as poor, good or excellent.

NOTE 2 "Inherent", as opposed to "assigned", means existing in something, especially as a permanent characteristic.

*Quality management system* (3.2.3)—**management system** (3.2.2) to direct and control an **organization** (3.3.1) with regard to **quality** (3.1.1)

*Top management* (3.2.7)—person or group of people who directs and controls an **organization** (3.3.1) at the highest level

*Source:* ANSI/ISO/ASQ Q9000-2005

## CONSIDERATIONS FOR DOCUMENTATION

Although not specifically required to do so, organizations should consider documenting their processes to communicate customer, regulatory, and legal requirements. This clause does not require any specific quality records.

### 5.3 Quality policy

Top management shall ensure that the quality policy

a) is appropriate to the purpose of the organization,

b) includes a commitment to comply with requirements and continually improve the effectiveness of the quality management system,

c) provides a framework for establishing and reviewing quality objectives,

d) is communicated and understood within the organization, and

e) is reviewed for continuing suitability.

*Source:* ANSI/ISO/ASQ Q9001-2008

Clause 5.3 is identical to clause 5.3 of ISO 9001:2000. Clause 5.1 requires that top management establish the quality policy. Clause 5.3 elaborates on the substance of the policy. The clause has three requirements for the content of the policy itself and two requirements that deal with how it is to be communicated and reviewed.

The policy must first be appropriate to the needs of the organization and its customers. This means that the organization should not adopt a policy that it cannot carry out. The organization must have both the capability and the dedication required to implement the policy. It will do no good to create a policy with lofty goals if it is impossible for the organization to meet those goals. On the other hand, the policy must also meet the needs of the organization's customers, which is a basic concept of ISO 9001. In developing the policy, it is important to think through the elements of policy needed to meet customer needs. The needs can then be defined in terms of the key processes or activities of the organization.

Clause 5.3b) specifies two basic requirements that the policy must meet. It must include commitment to meeting requirements and commitment to improving the effectiveness of the quality management system. Although meeting requirements was a fundamental of ISO 9001:1994, specific reference to improvement of the quality management system was new with ISO 9001:2000. Meeting requirements and improvement are foundations of the system, and there must be a commitment to both of these concepts.

There is a new emphasis on the concept of continual improvement. Improvement is not new; the 1994 version of ISO 9001 had requirements to use corrective and preventive actions as a means for improvement, and these concepts are retained. With ISO 9001:2008, the organization must plan its activities for improvement, and the measurable objectives of the organization must be set with improvement in mind. Measurement, collection, and analysis of data are required for identifying areas for improvement. This process of improving the effectiveness of meeting the requirements of the quality management system must be done on a continual basis through methods such as periodic management reviews.

The quality policy must create the framework for setting and reviewing objectives, and the framework should be appropriate to the needs of the organization. It must also provide for the establishment of objectives at the various levels and functions of the organization. The standard requires this to be done at "relevant functions and levels." Organizations must define what this means for them. In making this determination, they must consider their own needs and those of their customers. The relevance of having an objective at any particular level or function is left to the organization to determine.

Once the policy is established, the organization must deploy it. This means it must be communicated to all involved in ways that are understandable. Understanding of the policy implies that everyone in the organization knows his or her role in carrying out the policy. This is much more than being able to quote what the policy says; everyone should clearly understand their roles in ensuring that the policy is implemented.

The policy must also be reviewed to ensure its continuing suitability. This review should be conducted at a time and in a manner that best suits the organization's needs. If goals and objectives are tightly tied to the policy, then the review can become an ongoing activity. In some organizations it might be more appropriate for the policy to be reviewed periodically as part of a strategic planning process or as part of management review. In any event, the policy should not be considered a static one but rather one that evolves as the organization, its customers, and its products change.

The objectives need not be included in the policy itself, but the policy must provide some basis for establishing and reviewing them.

ISO 9001:1994 required that policy be relevant to the expectations and needs of customers. ISO 9001:2000 and ISO 9001:2008 go further by mandating commitment to meeting requirements. The requirements include those of the organization itself, any applicable regulatory requirements, and customer-specified requirements. Requirements also include those derived from customer expectations and needs that customers may not have directly stated or specified.

Some organizations have dynamic quality policies that actually include the objectives and numerical goals for overall organizational performance. Because the goals change from time to time, this type of policy must be updated often. This provides a clear opportunity to validate the objectives and commitment components of the policy.

Other organizations find the inclusion of objectives in the policy to be cumbersome. It is important for each organization to find a method of developing, deploying, and reviewing the quality policy that fits its needs.

The notes to the definition of quality policy in ISO 9000:2005 provide some insight into policy development.

These notes are informative, and thus they are not among the requirements.

Managers who want successful quality management systems should align the quality policy with the strategies and needs of their businesses. Organizations should consider the eight quality management principles stated in ISO 9000:2005 as a guide to policy development. These principles were input for developing the ISO 9000 series of standards, but they are not requirements of ISO 9001:2008, and they should never be used as a basis for compliance audits to ISO 9001:2008.

## IMPLEMENTATION TIPS AND TYPICAL QUESTIONS TO ASK FOR CONFORMITY

The most important aspect of quality policy development is alignment of the policy with overall business mission, vision, and objectives. If the quality policy is not so aligned, it is unlikely the policy will be carried out. On the other hand, if there is good alignment, achievement of the quality policy can become a key driver for improved overall organizational performance. If the organization's mission is to develop and sell products or services that ignore customer and market needs, there is little chance a policy to "meet customer requirements" will be carried out. In such a case, achieving real conformance to ISO 9001:2008 would not be possible. It is also critical for the policy to include only commitments you can keep. A commitment to address "customer aspirations and wants" would not be practical in some industries where "minimum conformity" to requirements is the norm. So be careful. Of course the three major things that need to be included are given in ISO 9001:2008. They need to be stated in your policy in a manner that makes sense in your industry, industry segment, and organization. The three things required to be included in the policy are:

- Commitment to meet requirements
- Commitment to continually improve the quality management system
- A framework for establishing and reviewing quality objectives

Keep the policy statement as simple as possible. The best policies are clear and simple enough that each employee can state it in his or her own words and get it right.

Questions to consider asking to assess conformity to this clause include:

- Has a quality policy been developed?
- Does the quality policy include commitment to meeting requirements and commitment to continual improvement?
- Does the quality policy provide a framework for establishing and reviewing the quality objectives?
- Are quality objectives quantified?
- Has top management determined that the quality policy meets the needs of the organization and its customers?
- Is the policy communicated to and understood by all in the organization?
- Are the members of the organization clear as to their role in carrying out the policy?
- Is the quality policy included in the document control process?
- Is the quality policy reviewed for continuing suitability?

## DEFINITIONS

*Quality policy* (3.2.4)—overall intentions and direction of an **organization** (3.3.1) related to **quality** (3.1.1) as formally expressed by **top management** (3.2.7)

NOTE 1 Generally the quality policy is consistent with the overall policy of the organization and provides a framework for the setting of **quality objectives** (3.2.5).

NOTE 2 Quality management principles presented in this International Standard can form a basis for the establishment of a quality policy. (See 0.2.)

*Requirement* (3.1.2)—need or expectation that is stated, generally implied or obligatory

NOTE 1 "Generally implied" means that it is custom or common practice for the **organization** (3.3.1), its **customers** (3.3.5) and other **interested parties** (3.3.7), that the need or expectation under consideration is implied.

NOTE 2 A qualifier can be used to denote a specific type of requirement, e.g. product requirement, quality management requirement, customer requirement.

NOTE 3 A specified requirement is one that is stated, for example in a **document** (3.7.2).

NOTE 4 Requirements can be generated by different **interested parties** (3.3.7).

NOTE 5 This definition differs from that provided in 3.12.1 of ISO/IEC Directives, Part 2:2004.

**3.12.1**
**requirement**
expression in the content of a document conveying criteria to be fulfilled if compliance with the document is to be claimed and from which no deviation is permitted

*Source:* ANSI/ISO/ASQ Q9000-2005

## 5.4 Planning

### 5.4.1 Quality objectives

Top management shall ensure that quality objectives, including those needed to meet requirements for product [see 7.1 a)], are established at relevant functions and levels within the organization. The quality objectives shall be measurable and consistent with the quality policy.

### 5.4.2 Quality management system planning

Top management shall ensure that

a) the planning of the quality management system is carried out in order to meet the requirements given in 4.1, as well as the quality objectives, and

b) the integrity of the quality management system is maintained when changes to the quality management system are planned and implemented.

*Source:* ANSI/ISO/ASQ Q9001-2008

The requirements and text are identical to that found in ISO 9001:2000. The quantification of objectives implied in ISO 9001:1994 became a specific requirement with the introduction of ISO 9001:2000. Clause 5.4.1 requires that objectives be measurable. In many organizations, quality objectives are quantitative targets or goals. Where more abstract statements are used as quality objectives, organizations may need to review them to ensure they are measurable. Thus, objectives may be stated in any form suitable to the circumstances but eventually must be quantified so that performance can be measured. Many organizations find that quantifiable objectives are a useful tool in achieving conformity and continual improvement. The term objective is to be interpreted broadly to be similar to a goal, target, or aim.

The organization is required to include the objectives needed to meet the requirements for products.

There is also a requirement that the objectives be consistent with continual improvement of the effectiveness of the quality management system. Where output does not meet customer requirements, targeting quality management system improvements can lead to improved effectiveness in achieving an acceptable level of performance. Where output meets customer needs, the objectives may relate to maintaining or improving the system so that the customer requirements can be met more rapidly or with fewer in-process defects.

Clause 5.4.2 also requires management of change so that the integrity of the quality management system is maintained when the system is changed. Changes to the system can result from modifications to organizational structure, the introduction of new technology, turnover of personnel, or significant increases or decreases in volume. Change can also be driven by a need to improve the system's efficiency by eliminating activities perceived as non–value-adding. The organization needs a basic process to deal with quality management system changes as they occur. The process should provide for addressing quality management system changes in a controlled manner. The details of the controls needed for implementing any specific change will require specific decisions at the time, but the basic process should be worked out as part of quality system planning. This process must include the identification of changes that could affect the quality management system as an input to management reviews.

## IMPLEMENTATION TIPS AND TYPICAL QUESTIONS TO ASK FOR CONFORMITY

ISO 9001:2008 provides users with a great deal of flexibility and generally avoids prescribing how requirements are to be implemented. As with much of ISO 9001:2008 implementation, your potential for success is related more to *how* you implement the requirements. Some of the notions needed for success are not found in ISO 9001:2008. The following concepts are important to setting good objectives:

- Objectives need to be measurable because it is the things the organization measures that get focused attention. ***What gets measured gets done.***
- Alignment of quality objectives with quality policy and with overall business objectives. Ideally achieving the quality objectives is a necessary step to meeting the overall objectives of the organization.
- Flow down objectives to ensure all lower level objectives support achievement of top level objectives.
- Set objectives cross functionally so they are mutually supportive.
- Ensure top level and lower level objectives are mutually supportive and achievable.
- Simple and few is better than complex and more. There is a degree of art in this, but finding the set of key drivers that really matter is necessary. If this is not done well, the organization can find itself measuring a lot of things that do not really matter.

To set such objectives, there must be an understanding of the processes that are important to meet requirements. Key process outputs need to be identified. Focus on those that are important to the customer and to meeting statutory and regulatory requirements. Determine and understand the processes that create those outputs. This basic process information can be used as the first step in determining the important objectives.

To determine lower-level objectives, relevant processes can be broken down so that the key objectives are defined at each organizational level and function. As the objectives flow through the levels and functions of the organization, they may take on different terms. For example, a waste reduction objective may be stated in dollars at one level but in tons at another. It is also common for a number of lower-level objectives to be needed to support a higher-level objective.

Once objectives have been set, the organization is required to identify and plan the resources needed to achieve them. See Chapter 4 for a discussion of resource determination. It may be useful to determine the activities and associated resources required to meet objectives. This includes resources needed to identify and plan the quality management system processes and their interactions. Basic product-realization processes should be identified and understood in sufficient detail to plan the quality management system. Planning of product-realization processes is a separate concept and is covered in clause 7.1.

Top management needs to play a prominent role in planning the quality management system. Inputs to this planning include the organization's overall objectives, quality objectives, organizational strategies, current results, as well as current business risks and opportunities. Often, it is only top managers who fully understand these things, so their full engagement is necessary. To be determined during quality management system planning are such things as the organization's abilities (skills, knowledge), financial and other resources (capital, people, metrics, methods, and tools). Planning needs to address how the organization will prevent nonconformities, how processes will be controlled, and how continual improvement will be carried out.

Planning is required to include considerations for meeting all of the requirements of clause 4.1, including the actions needed for continually improving the processes of the quality management system. This includes identification of the measurement, analysis, and review processes needed for achieving the enhanced effectiveness of the quality management system. It means these activities become linked as an improvement process to meet the requirements of clauses 8.1 and 8.5.1.

Resource needs are required to be determined in accordance with clause 6.1, addressed in Chapter 4. This determination is best made by considering the processes necessary to operate and improve the quality management system. The quality management system should be effective in helping the organization to meet its objectives. For this reason, as the objectives are reviewed and changed over time, the quality management system must also evolve; it must be improved.

The requirement for controlling change and maintaining the integrity of the quality management system as the system changes was added with ISO 9001:2000. Because we live in an era of constant change, this is a very important concept to understand. It is not intended that the requirements prevent change; rather, organizations must conduct change activities in a controlled manner that does not negatively affect the quality management system. Change management is crucial to the success of today's organizations. Organizations' external environments are constantly changing, and great agility is required to remain competitive. It is important to plan for change rather than to just wait for it to happen. The objective is to make changes smoothly and in a controlled manner.

For *hardware, software, and processed materials,* the most important objectives may relate directly to the organization's hardware, software, or processed materials, but there may be other aspects of the customers' needs (such as delivery timing, customer service, or price) that are equally important and should not be ignored in determining objectives.

For *service,* organizations should consider in the planning process the differences in setting objectives for the parts of the organization that provide service in direct contact with the customer. Objectives that relate to levels of service performance can sometimes be established between the organization and the customer. Defining the key processes that actually create the service for the customer can help in the determination of the objectives.

Questions to consider asking to assess conformity to this clause include:

- Have quality objectives been established at each relevant function and level in the organization?
- Do quality objectives include those needed to meet requirements for the organization's products or services?
- Has the organization identified the activities and processes required to meet objectives? Quality management system

processes? Product or service-realization processes? Verification processes? Exclusions under clause 1.2?

- Does quality planning include continual improvement of the processes of the quality management system?
- Does quality planning take into account the needs of the organization as changes occur?

## DEFINITIONS

*Process* (3.4.1)—set of interrelated or interacting activities which transforms inputs into outputs

NOTE 1 Inputs to a process are generally outputs of other processes.

NOTE 2 Processes in an **organization** (3.3.1) are generally planned and carried out under controlled conditions to add value.

NOTE 3 A process where the **conformity** (3.6.1) of the resulting **product** (3.4.2) cannot be readily or economically verified is frequently referred to as a "special process".

*Quality objective* (3.2.5)—something sought, or aimed for, related to **quality** (3.1.1)

NOTE 1 Quality objectives are generally based on the organization's **quality policy** (3.2.4).

NOTE 2 Quality objectives are generally specified for relevant functions and levels in the **organization** (3.3.1).

*Quality planning* (3.2.9)—part of **quality management** (3.2.8) focused on setting **quality objectives** (3.2.5) and specifying necessary operational **processes** (3.4.1) and related resources to fulfil the quality objectives

NOTE Establishing **quality plans** (3.7.5) can be part of quality planning.

*Source:* ANSI/ISO/ASQ Q9000-2005

## CONSIDERATIONS FOR DOCUMENTATION

ISO 9001:2008 does not require specific documented procedures for this clause. The requirements of clause 4.2.1, *General documentation requirements,* state that the organization must determine the documentation to "ensure the effective planning, operation and control of its processes." The quality manual or other documents can be used to discuss how the planning activities take place and how planning is periodically updated. This clause does not require any specific quality records.

## 5.5 Responsibility, authority and communication

### 5.5.1 Responsibility and authority

Top management shall ensure that responsibilities and authorities are defined and communicated within the organization.

### 5.5.2 Management representative

Top management shall appoint a member of the organization's management who, irrespective of other responsibilities, shall have responsibility and authority that includes

a) ensuring that processes needed for the quality management system are established, implemented and maintained,

b) reporting to top management on the performance of the quality management system and any need for improvement, and

c) ensuring the promotion of awareness of customer requirements throughout the organization.

NOTE The responsibility of a management representative can include liaison with external parties on matters relating to the quality management system.

### 5.5.3 Internal communication

Top management shall ensure that appropriate communication processes are established within the organization and that communication takes place regarding the effectiveness of the quality management system.

*Source:* ANSI/ISO/ASQ Q9001-2008

The requirements and text are the same as that found in ISO 9001:2000 except for the edit in the first paragraph of clause 5.5.2. That text is changed from ". . . appoint a member of management . . ." to read: ". . . appoint a member of the organization's management. . . ."

The various roles of personnel in the organization must be defined so that their responsibility, authority, and interactions are clear. These roles must be communicated clearly to all in the organization who have a need to know them. This type of clarity is important for all key personnel involved with the quality management system. This was fundamental in ISO 9001:1994. ISO 9001:2000 went further by requiring that these responsibilities and authorities be defined and communicated.

There is also a specific requirement that top management appoint a management representative. Management representatives are required to fulfill specific duties, including the following:

- Ensure that the quality management system is implemented and maintained in accordance with ISO 9001:2008. The representatives act as a link with top management and ensure that the system's status and improvement needs are communicated to top management. Normally it is the management representative who acts as the primary interface person with outside parties in relation to the quality management system. This often includes interaction with, for example, customer representatives or third-party auditing organizations.
- Ensure that there is awareness of customer requirements throughout the organization. This means that a process is required for communicating customer requirements. The management representative has flexibility in determining how to address this requirement.

Although adequate communication has always been a key to successful quality management system implementation, the requirement for internal communications was new with ISO 9001:2000. There must be adequate communications about the effectiveness of the system. These communications can take place in any manner that best suits the needs of the organization.

## IMPLEMENTATION TIPS AND TYPICAL QUESTIONS TO ASK FOR CONFORMITY

Organization charts are often used to document and communicate the responsibility and authority of personnel.

It is especially important to make clear the authority and responsibilities of those in the organization who must identify nonconformities and require that corrective action be taken. This type of activity can involve anyone from senior managers to production workers, depending on the organization's size, complexity, and operating philosophy.

The minor change in wording of the first paragraph of clause 5.5.2, mentioned above, is intended to reinforce that the management representative needs to be someone who is a manager in the organization, not a consultant under contract. Consultants and other outsiders can help, but someone in the organization needs to be accountable for the activities of the management representative.

In today's organizations, great internal communications are more important than ever. It is also more critical than ever for all aspects of the quality management system to perform in an effective manner every day. Rapid communication mechanisms are needed so that all members of the organization regularly receive timely and accurate feedback on performance.

Questions to consider asking to assess conformity to this clause include:

- Are the organization's functions defined and communicated to facilitate effective quality management?
- Are responsibilities and authorities defined and communicated to facilitate effective quality management?
- Has top management appointed one or more management representatives as appropriate?
- Has top management defined the responsibilities and authority of the management representative?
- Does the management representative ensure that the processes of the quality management system are established and maintained? How?

- Does the management representative report to top management on the performance of the quality management system?
- Does the management representative promote awareness of customer requirements throughout the organization?
- Do discussions with employees at all levels indicate that the organization effectively communicates processes of the quality management system and their effectiveness?

## DEFINITIONS

*Customer* (3.3.5)—**organization** (3.3.1) or person that receives a **product** (3.4.2)

EXAMPLE Consumer, client, end-user, retailer, beneficiary and purchaser.

NOTE A customer can be internal or external to the organization.

*Requirement* (3.1.2)—need or expectation that is stated, generally implied or obligatory

NOTE 1 "Generally implied" means that it is custom or common practice for the **organization** (3.3.1), its **customers** (3.3.5) and other **interested parties** (3.3.7), that the need or expectation under consideration is implied.

NOTE 2 A qualifier can be used to denote a specific type of requirement, e.g. product requirement, quality management requirement, customer requirement.

NOTE 3 A specified requirement is one that is stated, for example in a **document** (3.7.2).

NOTE 4 Requirements can be generated by different **interested parties** (3.3.7).

NOTE 5 This definition differs from that provided in 3.12.1 of ISO/IEC Directives, Part 2:2004.

> **3.12.1**
> **requirement**
> expression in the content of a document conveying criteria to be fulfilled if compliance with the document is to be claimed and from which no deviation is permitted

*Top management* (3.2.7)—person or group of people who directs and controls an **organization** (3.3.1) at the highest level

*Source:* ANSI/ISO/ASQ Q9000-2005

## 5.6 Management review

### 5.6.1 General

Top management shall review the organization's quality management system, at planned intervals, to ensure its continuing suitability, adequacy and effectiveness. This review shall include assessing opportunities for improvement and the need for changes to the quality management system, including the quality policy and quality objectives.

Records from management reviews shall be maintained (see 4.2.4).

### 5.6.2 Review input

The input to management review shall include information on

a) results of audits,

b) customer feedback,

c) process performance and product conformity,

d) status of preventive and corrective actions,

e) follow-up actions from previous management reviews,

f) changes that could affect the quality management system, and

g) recommendations for improvement.

### 5.6.3 Review output

The output from the management review shall include any decisions and actions related to

a) improvement of the effectiveness of the quality management system and its processes,

b) improvement of product related to customer requirements, and

c) resource needs.

*Source:* ANSI/ISO/ASQ Q9001-2008

The requirements and text are the same as that found in ISO 9001:2000.

Management review of the quality system is the responsibility of top management. This is no different from the requirement of ISO 9001:1994, which also required review at defined intervals of the continuing suitability and effectiveness of the system.

ISO 9001:2000 introduced additional requirements by specifying minimum review input items and output actions. Inputs for the reviews are required to include customer feedback, process and product performance, status of preventive and corrective actions, changes that could affect the quality management system, and the results of audits. In addition, there is now a requirement to review follow-up actions from earlier management reviews.

Outputs of the management review are also specified and must include the following three types of actions:

- Management reviews are intended to identify opportunities to improve the quality management system and its processes. These could include actions to simplify or foolproof processes, to develop improved methods, to improve documentation, and so on.
- "Improvement of product related to customer requirements . . ." This phrase is important—there is no requirement to improve the product beyond the point where all customer requirements are met. Improvements related to customer requirements could be items related to improved conformity with known requirements. On the other hand, remember that the top management is required in clause 5.2 to ". . . ensure that customer requirements are determined and met with the aim of enhancing customer satisfaction. . ." It is important to recognize that these customer needs and expectations may change often so that organizations may also identify new customer requirements and establish actions to meet them.
- Actions related to resource needs, which would include ensuring that resources are provided as needed for continual operation and improvement of the quality management system.

## IMPLEMENTATION TIPS AND TYPICAL QUESTIONS TO ASK FOR CONFORMITY

The notion of management review is to stand back, look at the effectiveness of the quality management system, examine performance, and decide what changes are needed to further improve the system.

Many inputs to management review can be listed beyond those required by ISO 9001:2008. At the top of the list might be progress on measures related to meeting the quality objectives. But the keys to successful management reviews are things like:

- A top management attitude that the system *can and should be improved*. The objective of management review is to determine how. Management reviews are not celebrations of what went right; they are reviews to determine how to make more things go great!
- *Preparation* is essential. Someone needs to get all the inputs together and make sense of them before the review starts. This is so top managers can see issues from all relevant perspectives. For example, aggregation of internal process data with customer complaint information can paint a clear picture of an opportunity to improve customer satisfaction while simultaneously reducing costs.
- *Follow-up* is necessary to make certain that decisions are clear and action is taken. Progress needs to be reviewed frequently.

Robust management reviews can be effectively developed by starting them at the beginning of quality management system implementation and systematically improving the review process so that it becomes a key element of organizational success.

Questions to consider asking to assess conformity to this clause include:

- Does top management review the quality management system at planned intervals to ensure its continuing suitability, adequacy, and effectiveness?

- Do the management reviews include evaluation of the need for changes to the organization's quality management system, including quality policy and quality objectives?
- Does management review input include: results of audits, customer feedback, process performance, product conformity, status of preventive and corrective actions, follow-up actions from earlier management reviews, changes that could affect the quality management system, and recommendations for improvement?
- Do the outputs of management reviews include actions related to the improvement of the quality management system and its processes?
- Do the outputs of management reviews include actions related to the improvement of product related to customer requirements?
- Do the outputs of management reviews include resource needs?
- Are management review records maintained?

## DEFINITIONS

*Customer* (3.3.5)—**organization** (3.3.1) or person that receives a **product** (3.4.2)

EXAMPLE Consumer, client, end-user, retailer, beneficiary and purchaser.

NOTE A customer can be internal or external to the organization.

*Effectiveness* (3.2.14)—extent to which planned activities are realized and planned results achieved

*Product* (3.4.2)—result of a **process** (3.4.1)

NOTE 1 There are four generic product categories, as follows:

—services (e.g. transport);

—software (e.g. computer program, dictionary);

—hardware (e.g. engine mechanical part);

—processed materials (e.g. lubricant).

Many products comprise elements belonging to different generic product categories. Whether the product is then called service, software, hardware or processed material depends on the dominant element. For example, the offered product "automobile" consists of hardware (e.g. tyres), processed materials (e.g. fuel, cooling liquid), software (e.g. engine control software, driver's manual), and service (e.g. operating explanations given by the salesman).

NOTE 2 Service is the result of at least one activity necessarily performed at the interface between the **supplier** (3.3.6) and **customer** (3.3.5) and is generally intangible. Provision of a service can involve, for example, the following:

—an activity performed on a customer-supplied tangible product (e.g. automobile to be repaired);

—an activity performed on a customer-supplied intangible product (e.g. the income statement needed to prepare a tax return);

—the delivery of an intangible product (e.g. the delivery of information in the context of knowledge transmission);

—the creation of ambience for the customer (e.g. in hotels and restaurants).

Software consists of information and is generally intangible and can be in the form of approaches, transactions or **procedures** (3.4.5).

Hardware is generally tangible and its amount is a countable **characteristic** (3.5.1). Processed materials are generally tangible and their amount is a continuous characteristic. Hardware and processed materials often are referred to as goods.

NOTE 3 **Quality assurance** (3.2.11) is mainly focused on intended product.

*Requirement* (3.1.2)—need or expectation that is stated, generally implied or obligatory

NOTE 1 "Generally implied" means that it is custom or common practice for the **organization** (3.3.1), its **customers** (3.3.5) and other **interested parties** (3.3.7), that the need or expectation under consideration is implied.

NOTE 2 A qualifier can be used to denote a specific type of requirement, e.g. product requirement, quality management requirement, customer requirement.

NOTE 3 A specified requirement is one that is stated, for example in a **document** (3.7.2).

NOTE 4 Requirements can be generated by different **interested parties** (3.3.7).

NOTE 5 This definition differs from that provided in 3.12.1 of ISO/IEC Directives, Part 2:2004.

> **3.12.1**
> **requirement**
> expression in the content of a document conveying criteria to be fulfilled if compliance with the document is to be claimed and from which no deviation is permitted

*Review* (3.8.7)—activity undertaken to determine the suitability, adequacy and **effectiveness** (3.2.14) of the subject matter to achieve established objectives

NOTE Review can also include the determination of **efficiency** (3.2.15).

EXAMPLE Management review, design and development review, review of customer requirements and nonconformity review.

*Source:* ANSI/ISO/ASQ Q9000-2005

# CHAPTER 4

# Human and Other Resources

## 6 Resource management

### 6.1 Provision of resources

The organization shall determine and provide the resources needed

a) to implement and maintain the quality management system and continually improve its effectiveness, and

b) to enhance customer satisfaction by meeting customer requirements.

*Source:* ANSI/ISO/ASQ Q9001-2008

The requirements and text are the same as that found in ISO 9001:2000. ISO 9001:2008 addresses resources that are needed for the entire quality management system—for implementation and improvement of the effectiveness of the quality management system and for enhancing customer satisfaction. Organizations are required to provide the resources needed to assure that product meets customer requirements. This is broader than just the quality function personnel or those people who do audits and inspections.

This clause covers all resources needed to meet the requirements of ISO 9001:2008. By defining the scope of this clause in these terms, the standard embraces the resource requirements of the entire quality management system.

The organization is required to identify what needs to be done to implement this standard. In determining the resource requirements, the organization should be specific to a level of detail that is appropriate. This usually includes detailing job responsibilities, authority, and interrelationships. Note that this is not a universal mandate. It may be an overwhelming bureaucratic burden for a small service organization to write out every job responsibility. For larger companies, however, effective operation requires the recording of job responsibilities and decision-making authority.

The term "resource" is often used in reference to personnel. In fact, this clause covers all resources needed to meet the requirements of the standard and to meet customer and statutory and regulatory requirements as well. Although the standard is not specific as to what makes up these resources for each organization, normally this includes personnel, time, buildings, equipment, utilities, materials, supplies, instruments, software, and transport facilities.

The standard does not address the timeliness with which resources are to be provided, but in any event, the organization is required to provide resources in a reasonable time frame. Just because a position has been defined or the need for a piece of equipment has been justified and approved for purchase does not mean that the organization has met its responsibilities. For example, jobs should not be left unfilled for indeterminate periods, and purchase orders should not be left open if there is a recognized need that has to be filled.

## IMPLEMENTATION TIPS AND TYPICAL QUESTIONS TO ASK FOR CONFORMITY

It is important to focus on resources needed to meet customer and statutory and regulatory requirements. We also need to meet the requirements of ISO 9001:2008. After all, effectively meeting requirements is one of the basic ideas behind ISO 9001:2008. The organization might start by making a list of the types of resources that are required in three categories:

- *People*—determine what parts of the organization, what groups of people, perhaps even what individuals are needed to ensure conformity to requirements. Your objective is to understand the people required to develop and operate the quality management system so that customer requirements are consistently met and statutory and regulatory compliance is achieved.
- *Facilities*—determine what buildings, equipment, utilities, materials, supplies, instruments and transport facilities are needed to meet requirements.

- *Information infrastructure*—determine what mechanisms you will need to communicate the system, its processes, procedures, work instructions, and other information to those needing it. Consider all aspects of communication technology, computers, networks, software, printed material, and so on required to meet requirements.

You should make your initial list without consideration of whether or not you already have the listed resources. But be careful; you are not making a "wish list." Instead, you are preparing an input to the quality system planning process, which was covered in Chapter 3 when we discussed clause 5.4.2, *Quality management system planning*. Mark your list up to show which resources you have and which need to be acquired or developed. There will normally be both short- and longer-term needs. Be sure to include the short-term items in appropriate budgets. Integrate longer-term needs with strategic plans and capital expense programs as appropriate. Remember, there is always competition for resources. Resource needs should be defined and presented in terms top managers can easily understand—the return on that investment. The completed resource listings will help top managers understand the scope of the quality management system so that they can become comfortable with the expected return on investment for any new or reassigned resources.

Questions to consider asking to assess conformity to this clause include:

- Has the organization determined the resources necessary to implement the quality management system?
- Has the organization provided the resources necessary to implement the quality management system?
- Has the organization determined the resources necessary to improve the effectiveness of the quality management system?
- Has the organization provided the resources necessary to improve the effectiveness of the quality management system?

- Has the organization determined the resources necessary to meet customer requirements?
- Has the organization determined the resources necessary to enhance customer satisfaction?
- Has the organization provided the resources necessary to enhance customer satisfaction?

## DEFINITIONS

*Customer satisfaction* (3.1.4)—customer's perception of the degree to which the customer's **requirements** (3.1.2) have been fulfilled

NOTE 1 Customer complaints are a common indicator of low customer satisfaction but their absence does not necessarily imply high customer satisfaction.

NOTE 2 Even when customer requirements have been agreed with the customer and fulfilled, this does not necessarily ensure high customer satisfaction.

*Process* (3.4.1)—set of interrelated or interacting activities which transforms inputs into outputs

NOTE 1 Inputs to a process are generally outputs of other processes.

NOTE 2 Processes in an **organization** (3.3.1) are generally planned and carried out under controlled conditions to add value.

NOTE 3 A process where the **conformity** (3.6.1) of the resulting **product** (3.4.2) cannot be readily or economically verified is frequently referred to as a "special process".

*Quality management system* (3.2.3)—**management system** (3.2.2) to direct and control an **organization** (3.3.1) with regard to **quality** (3.1.1)

*Source:* ANSI/ISO/ASQ Q9000-2005

## CONSIDERATIONS FOR DOCUMENTATION

The records that are created by the activities to meet the requirements of this clause may need to be controlled in accordance with clause 4.2.4, *Control of records*. The organization determines, in this case, whether records need to be controlled.

> ## 6.2 Human resources
>
> ### 6.2.1 General
>
> Personnel performing work affecting conformity to product requirements shall be competent on the basis of appropriate education, training, skills and experience.
>
> NOTE Conformity to product requirements can be affected directly or indirectly by personnel performing any task within the quality management system.

*Source:* ANSI/ISO/ASQ Q9001-2008

The requirements of this clause have not changed. The text has been clarified. Previously, the clause referred to personnel "performing work affecting product quality," while ISO 9001:2008's text uses the words "affecting conformity to product requirements" to more directly align with the scope of ISO 9001. (See Chapter 1, clause 1.1) ISO 9001:2008, like ISO 9001:2000, includes all personnel who perform any work that affects that conformity either directly or indirectly, and a note has been added to the text to emphasize this. Because each organization is different, ISO 9001:2008 does not attempt to list all of these separate tasks that will need to be addressed. Experience with ISO 9001:1994 revealed that such a listing would inevitably be incomplete and open to misunderstanding. So, this clause contains a broad requirement that includes all of these personnel.

Written job requirements are usually needed in order to properly assign personnel. The requirement in clause 6.2.1 is that personnel are competent. Before the competency of employees can be ensured, the organization needs to identify job requirements.

Although the quality management system extends throughout an organization, this clause does not include all personnel—even though, in principle, everyone's work affects the quality of the products supplied by the organization. With the quality management system structured in four main clauses, it is clear that the intent of the standard is to relate this requirement to the personnel "performing work affecting conformity to product requirements" either directly or indirectly. This clause includes personnel involved in top management, resource management, product realization, and measurement-analysis-improvement processes. All of these personnel are required to be competent based on education, training, skills, and experience.

## IMPLEMENTATION TIPS AND TYPICAL QUESTIONS TO ASK FOR CONFORMITY

Defining job requirements and determining the competencies people need is a critical activity for conformity with ISO 9001:2008. It is not sufficient only to understand what human resources are required; it is even more important to understand these needed competencies and to what extent current personnel have them. Clause 6.2.1 works together with 6.2.2 to help the organization develop its competencies. It is safe to say that few organizations have every needed competency in each person all the time, And that is not the point. The point is that organizations need to understand where they are and work to improve those areas where there are gaps. One approach is to develop an improvement cycle, as follows:

- Identify competencies required.
- Identify gaps between the required competencies and actual competencies held by the organization.
- Determine the impacts of the gaps and determine what should change when the gaps are closed.
- Act to close the competency gaps.
- Determine if the expected improvements actually occur after you take action.
- Repeat the cycle as needed.

With a cycle like this, achieving competency improvement is a real, value-added activity, not just abstract action taken to satisfy ISO 9001:2008. It also becomes part of the continual improvement plans.

Questions to consider asking to assess conformity to this clause include:

- Are personnel who perform work affecting product quality competent based on education, training, skills, and experience? How do we know?

## DEFINITIONS

*Competence* (3.1.6)—demonstrated ability to apply knowledge and skills

NOTE The concept of competence is defined in a generic sense in this International Standard. The word usage can be more specific in other ISO documents.

*Source:* ANSI/ISO/ASQ Q9000-2005

## CONSIDERATIONS FOR DOCUMENTATION

The records that are created by the activities to ensure competency may need to be controlled per clause 4.2.4, *Control of records.* In this case, the organization determines whether records need to be controlled.

### 6.2.2 Competence, training and awareness

The organization shall

a) determine the necessary competence for personnel performing work affecting conformity to product requirements,

b) where applicable, provide training or take other actions to achieve the necessary competence,

c) evaluate the effectiveness of the actions taken,

d) ensure that its personnel are aware of the relevance and importance of their activities and how they contribute to the achievement of the quality objectives, and

e) maintain appropriate records of education, training, skills and experience (see 4.2.4).

*Source:* ANSI/ISO/ASQ Q9001-2008

The requirements of this clause are the same as in ISO 9001:2000. The text has been slightly edited for clarity. This clause requires the determination of needed competencies, emphasizes taking whatever action is needed to close competency gaps, and requires evaluation of the effectiveness of the actions taken to close competency gaps. There is also a requirement to ensure that employees are aware of the importance of their work.

The concept of determining competencies required and closing identified competency gaps was new in ISO 9001:2000 and is retained. While training is mentioned as a means of accomplishing this, ISO 9001:2008 recognizes that there are other possibilities. For example, organizations may hire new employees who have the needed competencies.

Having competent people is essential for the achievement of organizational objectives. This clause pertains to all personnel at all levels within the scope of this standard. It addresses all training and other actions needed to ensure competency for accomplishing assigned tasks.

The organization needs to identify what classroom training, seminars, on-the-job, or other training is necessary so that every employee involved in the quality management system is competent. This is not the same thing as determining job requirements. Competency may be determined by comparisons between the job requirements that define what employees are required to do and the qualifications of the employee. Where training is needed, it must be provided. The training process should address the competency needs of employees so that they either can become competent or can stay competent.

The training should include provisions to establish and maintain employee awareness of the importance of their work and how they contribute to the quality objectives of the organization. This training should be specific so that it relates to the responsibilities of each employee.

*Evaluation of the effectiveness of the actions (including training) is required.* It is common practice to conduct training evaluations in the following three parts:

- Evaluation of the training immediately upon completion

- Evaluation of the training received several weeks after the training
- Evaluation of the skills developed several months after the training

One approach is to have the student's supervisor evaluate the work performance related to the training, both in the short term and over several months. This provides input for evaluating the adequacy of the training. If means other than training are used to close competency gaps, the effectiveness of these other actions is required to be evaluated as well. For example, if new personnel are hired, their performance could be evaluated periodically during the early stages of their employment.

## IMPLEMENTATION TIPS AND TYPICAL QUESTIONS TO ASK FOR CONFORMITY

Some training is needed but training alone is often not enough. In fact, if competency gaps are not caused by a lack of training, money spent on training can be a waste. So do not get caught in the training trap—conducting training only for the sake of meeting clause 6.2.2. Training alone may not solve your competency issues, and you may spend a lot of training money only to realize this. Instead, determine your competency gaps first. Then explore the real causes of the gaps. If personnel lack needed basic education, on-the-job training is not likely to help. Once you know why each competency gap exists, develop an action plan to close that gap. Be creative. Then execute your plan and determine the effectiveness of your actions in terms of improved competence. Find ways to determine if the competency gaps have been closed. *Measure the effects of your actions and act on real measurable results*. Don't bother much about measuring how well you conducted the training or how efficient your other actions were. Instead, measure results.

Questions to consider asking to assess conformity to this clause include:

- Does the organization identify the competency needs of the individual personnel performing activities affecting quality, including additional training needs?

- Does the organization provide training or take other actions to satisfy these needs?
- Does the organization evaluate the effectiveness of the training provided or of other actions taken to ensure competency?
- Does the organization ensure that employees are aware of the relevance and importance of their activities and how they contribute to the achievement of the quality objectives?
- Does the organization maintain records of education, experience, training, and qualifications?

## DEFINITIONS

*Quality* (3.1.1)—degree to which a set of inherent **characteristics** (3.5.1) fulfils **requirements** (3.1.2)

NOTE 1 The term "quality" can be used with adjectives such as poor, good or excellent.

NOTE 2 "Inherent", as opposed to "assigned", means existing in something, especially as a permanent characteristic.

*Effectiveness* (3.2.14)—extent to which planned activities are realized and planned results achieved

*Quality objective* (3.2.5)—something sought, or aimed for, related to **quality** (3.1.1)

NOTE 1 Quality objectives are generally based on the organization's **quality policy** (3.2.4).

NOTE 2 Quality objectives are generally specified for relevant functions and levels in the **organization** (3.3.1).

*Source:* ANSI/ISO/ASQ Q9000-2005

## CONSIDERATIONS FOR DOCUMENTATION

Often organizations will document a formal, annual training plan to address the training needs of personnel. Records are also required where personnel need to demonstrate specific skills or demonstrate specific competencies based on skills, training, education, and experience. The records dealing with personnel education, experience, training, and qualifications that are created by the activities to meet the requirements of this clause need to be controlled per clause 4.2.4, *Control of records.*

> **6.3 Infrastructure**
>
> The organization shall determine, provide and maintain the infrastructure needed to achieve conformity to product requirements. Infrastructure includes, as applicable,
>
> a) buildings, workspace and associated utilities,
>
> b) process equipment (both hardware and software), and
>
> c) supporting services (such as transport, communication or information systems).

*Source:* ANSI/ISO/ASQ Q9001-2008

The requirements of this clause have not changed. One small addition has been made in c), where "information systems" has been added to the end of the parenthetical list of examples. Adding an obvious example does not change the requirement. As in ISO 9001:2000, there is a clear statement that facilities and associated infrastructure elements are within the domain of this standard. Although ISO 9001:1994 did not explicitly state requirements for facilities and workspace, even with that standard it was widely understood that these were at least partially addressed. Common sense dictates that physical resources need to be provided for achieving the product.

Quality management system records should indicate that the requirements of this clause have been considered and addressed.

This clause encompasses all of the physical resources needed to create the product and to provide it to the customer, except personnel. The requirements for personnel are covered in the preceding clause on human resources. Included in this clause are requirements to identify, provide, and maintain the infrastructure needed to achieve conformity of product. Infrastructure is broadly defined to encompass the buildings, workspace, equipment, and support services.

Infrastructure is one of the clauses under resource management. The significance of separating it from the old process control clause should be recognized. The organization is required to identify, provide, and maintain appropriate infrastructure for all of the processes within the quality management system. This goes beyond production and service operations and beyond even the realization processes to include the management processes; other resource processes (training, in particular); and the measurement, analysis, and improvement processes.

## IMPLEMENTATION TIPS AND TYPICAL QUESTIONS TO ASK FOR CONFORMITY

Remember that this requirement covers anything that can be involved in creating, maintaining, or delivering conforming product—anything needed to support the operation of the quality management system. Most organizations have little trouble with the equipment, buildings, workspace, computers, and other physical things in the workplace. Other things, like services provided by outside contractors or obscure computer applications, can be a bit tricky.

For *hardware, processed materials, and software,* physical resources provide the foundation for the work that is required to implement the quality management system. Design and development of new software requires appropriate workrooms, appropriate programming tools, and appropriate processors. Manufacturing computer chips requires special clean rooms. Sterilizing medical devices requires special equipment and equipment controls. Special transports are required for the delivery of products such as fuel, oil, or milk. This clause adds clarity of focus for a critical area that previously was assumed to be so obvious that it did not need to be identified as a unique requirement of the quality system.

For *service,* the availability of appropriate physical resources is equally important. For a warehousing organization, successful performance is highly dependent on the availability of warehouses in the right location and with the right capabilities. Does the warehouse require air conditioning, for example? For a delivery service, the availability of delivery vehicles is critical. For a repair facility, appropriate diagnostic and repair instruments are needed. For a food service, appropriate kitchens, handling equipment, and vehicles are needed. In each case, successful service realization requires the appropriate identification, provision, and maintenance of physical resources.

Questions to consider asking to assess conformity to this clause include:

- Does the organization identify, provide, and maintain the workspace and associated facilities it needs to achieve the conformity of product?
- Does the organization identify, provide, and maintain the equipment, hardware, and software it needs to achieve the conformity of product?
- Does the organization identify, provide, and maintain the supporting services it needs to achieve the conformity of product?

## DEFINITIONS

*Conformity* (3.6.1)—fulfilment of a **requirement** (3.1.2)

NOTE The term "conformance" is synonymous but deprecated.

*Infrastructure* (3.3.3)—⟨organization⟩ **system** (3.2.1) of facilities, equipment and services needed for the operation of an **organization** (3.3.1)

*Source:* ANSI/ISO/ASQ Q9000-2005

## CONSIDERATIONS FOR DOCUMENTATION

The records that are created by the activities to meet the requirements of this clause may need to be controlled per clause 4.2.4, *Control of records.* In this case, the organization determines whether records need to be controlled.

### 6.4 Work environment

The organization shall determine and manage the work environment needed to achieve conformity to product requirements.

NOTE The term "work environment" relates to those conditions under which work is performed including physical, environmental and other factors (such as noise, temperature, humidity, lighting or weather).

*Source:* ANSI/ISO/ASQ Q9001-2008

The requirement and wording of Clause 6.4 is identical to ISO 9001:2000. The note has been added to explain further that work environment refers to the environment under which work is performed such as noise, temperature, and so on.

The work environment of an organization can be considered to be a combination of human and physical factors. Examples of human factors in the work environment that may affect conformity of product include the following:

- Work methods
- Safety rules and guidance, including use of protective equipment
- Ergonomics

Physical factors can also affect the ability to achieve conforming product. It is important to control those factors that affect product quality characteristics, since they have a direct impact on the ability of the product to conform to specifications.

Examples of physical factors affecting the work environment may include the following:

- Heat
- Noise
- Light
- Hygiene
- Humidity
- Cleanliness
- Vibration
- Pollution
- Air flow

## IMPLEMENTATION TIPS AND TYPICAL QUESTIONS TO ASK FOR CONFORMITY

Remember that it is the work environment as it relates to conformity of product that matters here. There are other aspects of work environment controls, including the comfort and safety of the personnel in the area, that may be beyond the scope of this clause. In actual implementation it is useful to consider all of these conditions simultaneously so that the personnel and product conformity are both protected by the measures adopted. But don't forget, just taking care of worker safety, well-being, or comfort does not guarantee conformity of product. Additional measures may be required to accomplish that.

If the organization determines that it is necessary to control work areas for physical factors, it is common to consider actions such as the following:

- Identify standards to be maintained.
- Ensure that the facility meets the standards.
- Train personnel on standards pertaining to their work.
- Prohibit unauthorized access to the work area.
- Implement and maintain desired physical conditions.
- Maintain records of the conditions as a means of demonstrating compliance to the standards.

For *hardware and processed materials,* physical factors of the work environment include factors such as ambient humidity and temperature in a paint shop. Control of these factors is necessary to obtain a conforming painted surface. To achieve high performance of electronic components, particle contamination needs to be kept extremely low during fabrication.

For *service,* good personal hygiene of food service and pharmacy employees, for example, is important to prevent the contamination of customer product. Such factors are often tightly controlled by regulatory standards.

Questions to consider asking to assess conformity to this clause include:

- Does the organization identify the conditions in the work environment that need to be controlled to achieve conformity of product?
- Does the organization manage the human and physical factors of the work environment needed to achieve conformity of product?

## DEFINITIONS

*Work environment* (3.3.4)—set of conditions under which work is performed

NOTE Conditions include physical, social, psychological and environmental factors (such as temperature, recognition schemes, ergonomics and atmospheric composition).

*Conformity* (3.6.1)—fulfilment of a **requirement** (3.1.2)

NOTE The term "conformance" is synonymous but deprecated.

*Source:* ANSI/ISO/ASQ Q9000-2005

## CONSIDERATIONS FOR DOCUMENTATION

The records that are created by the activities to meet the requirements of this clause may need to be controlled per clause 4.2.4, *Control of records.* In this case, the organization determines whether records need to be controlled.

# CHAPTER 5

# Planning of Product Realization and Customer-Related Processes

## 7 Product realization

### 7.1 Planning of product realization

The organization shall plan and develop the processes needed for product realization. Planning of product realization shall be consistent with the requirements of the other processes of the quality management system (see 4.1).

In planning product realization, the organization shall determine the following, as appropriate:

a) quality objectives and requirements for the product;

b) the need to establish processes and documents, and to provide resources specific to the product;

c) required verification, validation, monitoring, measurement, inspection and test activities specific to the product and the criteria for product acceptance;

d) records needed to provide evidence that the realization processes and resulting product meet requirements (see 4.2.4).

The output of this planning shall be in a form suitable for the organization's method of operations.

NOTE 1 A document specifying the processes of the quality management system (including the product realization processes) and the resources to be applied to a specific product, project or contract can be referred to as a quality plan.

NOTE 2 The organization can also apply the requirements given in 7.3 to the development of product realization processes.

*Source:* ANSI/ISO/ASQ Q9001-2008

The requirements of this clause are essentially the same as in ISO 9001:2000. A minor addition was made for clarity. In planning product realization, the organization needs to determine required measurement activities as well as required verification, validation, monitoring, inspection, and test activities. Most of us recognize measurement activities as being included in the set of activities originally listed. Adding the term "measurement" to the listing under item 7.1.c) clarifies the intent that measurement activities specific to the product need to be determined. Although clause 7.1 consists of only three short paragraphs, it is one of the most important clauses in ISO 9001:2008. Along with clause 4.1 and clause 8.1, clause 7.1 provides the essence of the use of the process approach. It requires organizations to think about and plan all of the processes that, when linked together, will result in the delivery of products that will conform to customer requirements, create customer satisfaction, and foster continual improvement. The planning of realization processes also must be consistent with the other requirements of the quality management system and must be documented in a form that is appropriate for the organization.

The planning activity required by clause 7.1 may not be a trivial exercise. Fewer documented procedures may be required than in the past, and no specific format is dictated, but ISO 9001:2008 demands that the organization understand the processes needed to deliver conforming products to customers. These processes must be understood not only with respect to the products themselves but also in the broader context of the objectives of the organization and any other requirements of the quality management system. The planning activity for realization processes must address the quality objectives and requirements for the product; the need to establish appropriate processes and documentation; the need to provide resources and facilities specific to the product; required verification, validation, monitoring, measurement, inspection, and test activities; and the criteria for acceptability of the product. The organization is also required to determine what records are necessary to provide confidence that the processes and resulting product conform to requirements.

In note 1 to this clause, a product quality plan is described, the implication being that a quality plan can be one way to document the quality planning for a product.

Note 2 explains that an organization could consider using the same planning approach when designing product realization processes as is required by ISO 9001:2008, clause 7.3, to design new hardware or service products. From the viewpoint of operating effectiveness, it is strongly suggested that organizations control the design of their realization processes with the same rigor that they dedicate to products, even though this is not a specific requirement of ISO 9001:2008.

## IMPLEMENTATION TIPS AND TYPICAL QUESTIONS TO ASK FOR CONFORMITY

Many organizations will have little trouble conforming to these requirements, because processes and documentation already exist to address them. For others, this will require some careful thought. Perhaps flowcharts or process mapping will be appropriate to ensure that all process steps are addressed in terms of the availability of documentation, facilities, personnel, and any other required resources.

It may be advisable to:

- Create a quality plan for a product to describe how the quality management system will be modified and applied to the design and development of that product.
- Consider using the product design and development process approach for designing processes. This is a requirement in the automotive industry. It has become a best demonstrated practice in many organizations.
- Identify key performance measures for both products and processes. Align these key measures with your quality and business objectives.

Questions to consider asking to assess conformity to this clause include:

- Is there evidence of planning of production processes?
- Does the planning extend beyond production processes to encompass all product realization processes?
- Is the planning consistent with other elements of the quality management system?
- Does product realization documentation exist?
- Are product realization resources and facilities defined during the planning process, and do they appear to be adequate?
- Does the planning define the records that must be prepared to provide confidence in the conformity of the processes and resulting product?

## DEFINITIONS

*Requirement* (3.1.2)—need or expectation that is stated, generally implied or obligatory

NOTE 1 "Generally implied" means that it is custom or common practice for the **organization** (3.3.1), its **customers** (3.3.5) and other **interested parties** (3.3.7), that the need or expectation under consideration is implied.

NOTE 2 A qualifier can be used to denote a specific type of requirement, e.g. product requirement, quality management requirement, customer requirement.

NOTE 3 A specified requirement is one that is stated, for example in a **document** (3.7.2).

NOTE 4 Requirements can be generated by different **interested parties** (3.3.7).

NOTE 5 This definition differs from that provided in 3.12.1 of ISO/IEC Directives, Part 2:2004.

> **3.12.1**
> **requirement**
> expression in the content of a document conveying criteria to be fulfilled if compliance with the document is to be claimed and from which no deviation is permitted

*Capability* (3.1.5)—ability of an **organization** (3.3.1), **system** (3.2.1) or **process** (3.4.1) to realize a **product** (3.4.2) that will fulfil the **requirements** (3.1.2) for that product

NOTE Process capability terms in the field of statistics are defined in ISO 3534-2.

*Quality planning* (3.2.9)—part of **quality management** (3.2.8) focused on setting **quality objectives** (3.2.5) and specifying necessary operational **processes** (3.4.1) and related resources to fulfil the quality objectives

NOTE Establishing **quality plans** (3.7.5) can be part of quality planning.

*Process* (3.4.1)—set of interrelated or interacting activities which transforms inputs into outputs

NOTE 1 Inputs to a process are generally outputs of other processes.

NOTE 2 Processes in an **organization** (3.3.1) are generally planned and carried out under controlled conditions to add value.

NOTE 3 A process where the **conformity** (3.6.1) of the resulting **product** (3.4.2) cannot be readily or economically verified is frequently referred to as a "special process".

*Product* (3.4.2)—result of a **process** (3.4.1)

NOTE 1 There are four generic product categories, as follows:

—services (e.g. transport);

—software (e.g. computer program, dictionary);

—hardware (e.g. engine mechanical part);

—processed materials (e.g. lubricant).

Many products comprise elements belonging to different generic product categories. Whether the product is then called service, software, hardware or processed material depends on the dominant element. For example, the offered product "automobile" consists of hardware (e.g. tyres), processed materials (e.g. fuel, cooling liquid), software (e.g. engine control software, driver's manual), and service (e.g. operating explanations given by the salesman).

NOTE 2 Service is the result of at least one activity necessarily performed at the interface between the **supplier** (3.3.6) and **customer** (3.3.5) and is generally intangible. Provision of a service can involve, for example, the following:

—an activity performed on a customer-supplied tangible product (e.g. automobile to be repaired);

—an activity performed on a customer-supplied intangible product (e.g. the income statement needed to prepare a tax return);

—the delivery of an intangible product (e.g. the delivery of information in the context of knowledge transmission);

—the creation of ambience for the customer (e.g. in hotels and restaurants).

Software consists of information and is generally intangible and can be in the form of approaches, transactions or **procedures** (3.4.5).

Hardware is generally tangible and its amount is a countable **characteristic** (3.5.1). Processed materials are generally tangible and their amount is a continuous characteristic. Hardware and processed materials often are referred to as goods.

NOTE 3 **Quality assurance** (3.2.11) is mainly focused on intended product.

*Source:* ANSI/ISO/ASQ Q9000-2005

## CONSIDERATIONS FOR DOCUMENTATION

The organization should consider preparing a documented procedure to describe how the planning is accomplished. Alternatively, the planning of product realization could be described in the quality manual. Where a documented procedure is developed, it is recommended that standard checklists and other planning formats be developed and incorporated into the document. This clause also has a specific requirement that the planning define the records required to provide confidence of conformity to requirements.

> ## 7.2 Customer-related processes
>
> ### 7.2.1 Determination of requirements related to the product
>
> The organization shall determine
>
> a) requirements specified by the customer, including the requirements for delivery and post-delivery activities,
>
> b) requirements not stated by the customer but necessary for specified or intended use, where known,
>
> c) statutory and regulatory requirements applicable to the product, and
>
> d) any additional requirements considered necessary by the organization.
>
> NOTE Post-delivery activities include, for example, actions under warranty provisions, contractual obligations such as maintenance services, and supplementary services such as recycling or final disposal.

*Source:* ANSI/ISO/ASQ Q9001-2008

The requirements of this clause are essentially the same as in ISO 9001:2000. Minor additions were made for clarity. For example, now the standard states that *any additional requirements "considered necessary" by the organization* shall be identified rather than *any additional requirements that are "determined" by the organization*. This is fairly minor but we all have seen auditors insist that the organization must determine additional requirements even though the tone and intent has always been that the organization determines additional requirements only that it considers necessary. The note is new. Notes are not requirements of the standard but serve as explanations or provide clarifications. This note provides examples of post-delivery activities.

How important to an organization is the process of determining customer requirements? It is so important that it demands attention as a survival issue by every part of the organization. The quotation and order process has an enormous impact on ultimate customer satisfaction; if customer requirements are not bilaterally understood, the probability of achieving ultimate customer satisfaction is seriously diminished. Therefore, it is a business necessity to have an effective process established and implemented to identify customer requirements. Additionally, it is important for the organization to address product requirements that have not been specified by the customer but are necessary for the intended or specified use of the product.

## IMPLEMENTATION TIPS AND TYPICAL QUESTIONS TO ASK FOR CONFORMITY

Conformity is not difficult for organizations providing off-the-shelf catalog products manufactured to published specifications or standardized services with normal delivery requirements. However, if customers are purchasing complex systems with custom engineering and software according to a complex set of commercial terms, it is essential to obtain a clear understanding of customer requirements by whatever means possible, including activities such as holding face-to-face meetings and attending pre-bid meetings.

Full determination of customer requirements is often an iterative process. Often there are known issues that may evolve into real requirements at a later stage. In such cases, documentation of the open issues and providing for the attendant business risk may prove to be an acceptable approach to meeting the requirements of this clause.

Questions to consider asking to assess conformity to this clause include:

- Does the organization determine customer requirements?
- Does the process include the determination of requirements needed but not specified?
- Are records available that provide evidence that customer requirements have been determined?

## DEFINITIONS

*Customer* (3.3.5)—**organization** (3.3.1) or person that receives a **product** (3.4.2)

EXAMPLE Consumer, client, end-user, retailer, beneficiary and purchaser.

NOTE A customer can be internal or external to the organization.

*Requirement* (3.1.2)—need or expectation that is stated, generally implied or obligatory

NOTE 1 "Generally implied" means that it is custom or common practice for the **organization** (3.3.1), its **customers** (3.3.5) and other **interested parties** (3.3.7), that the need or expectation under consideration is implied.

NOTE 2 A qualifier can be used to denote a specific type of requirement, e.g. product requirement, quality management requirement, customer requirement.

NOTE 3 A specified requirement is one that is stated, for example in a **document** (3.7.2).

NOTE 4 Requirements can be generated by different **interested parties** (3.3.7).

NOTE 5 This definition differs from that provided in 3.12.1 of ISO/IEC Directives, Part 2:2004.

**3.12.1**
**requirement**
expression in the content of a document conveying criteria to be fulfilled if compliance with the document is to be claimed and from which no deviation is permitted

*Source:* ANSI/ISO/ASQ Q9000-2005

## CONSIDERATIONS FOR DOCUMENTATION

The determination of customer requirements is a critical activity and generally involves several functions and levels in an organization. It is wise to have a documented procedure to determine all aspects of customer requirements. The documented procedure should include determining product requirements specified by the customer and product requirements not specified by the customer but necessary for intended or specified use. Also, unique regulatory and statutory requirements should be considered. This procedure could be included in a broader document addressing customer communications. (See clause 7.2.3.)

Clause 7.2.1 also does not require any specific records. The planning for realization processes covered in clause 7.1 should define the records the organization will keep during the process of determining customer requirements. Organizations should consider keeping records of the written requirements and any documentation of conversations in which orally transmitted requirements are discussed.

### 7.2.2 Review of requirements related to the product

The organization shall review the requirements related to the product. This review shall be conducted prior to the organization's commitment to supply a product to the customer (e.g. submission of tenders, acceptance of contracts or orders, acceptance of changes to contracts or orders) and shall ensure that

a) product requirements are defined,

b) contract or order requirements differing from those previously expressed are resolved, and

c) the organization has the ability to meet the defined requirements.

Records of the results of the review and actions arising from the review shall be maintained (see 4.2.4).

Where the customer provides no documented statement of requirement, the customer requirements shall be confirmed by the organization before acceptance.

Where product requirements are changed, the organization shall ensure that relevant documents are amended and that relevant personnel are made aware of the changed requirements.

NOTE In some situations, such as internet sales, a formal review is impractical for each order. Instead the review can cover relevant product information such as catalogues or advertising material.

*Source:* ANSI/ISO/ASQ Q9001-2008

The requirements of this clause are identical to those of the same clause in ISO 9001:2000.

Like clause 7.2.1, this clause applies to all product types, to all market sectors, and to organizations of all sizes.

The acceptance of an order or the submission of a quote or a tender by an organization creates an obligation on the organization to meet the conditions stated in the order or to provide the goods and services included in the scope of the quotation or tender. The obligation assumed by the organization includes not only the products defined but also ancillary items such as conformance to stated delivery dates, adherence to referenced external standards, and compliance with the commercial terms and conditions applicable to the order, contract, quote, or tender.

The complexity of the order/quote review process depends on the business of the organization. A process for reviewing orders for off-the-shelf products with 24-hour delivery (for example, software packages) will differ considerably from a process for reviewing a large order for a one-of-a-kind product with a two-year delivery (for example, an order for a control system for an electric power generating station). The review process must also accommodate, as applicable, electronic orders, blanket orders with periodic releases, unsolicited orders, orders through distributors or representatives, faxed orders, and an almost infinite combination of these and other possibilities. The note to this clause, for example, recognizes that Internet transactions will require creative thinking on the part of organizations to efficiently review customer requirements.

## IMPLEMENTATION TIPS AND TYPICAL QUESTIONS TO ASK FOR CONFORMITY

With such a spectrum of possibilities, what is an organization expected to do to conform to the requirements? The first step should be to develop a clear understanding of the nature of the various kinds of customer requirements. If, for example, an organization publishes a catalog and accepts only written orders for catalog-listed items to standard delivery times, then a quotation and order or contract-review procedure can be as simple as a one-paragraph statement that a designated individual (for example, a manager, a clerk, or a president) shall review the written order and initial and date the order, indicating that its requirements can be met. If an organization must address possibilities that only occur rarely, the organization could simply note in a procedure that any circumstances different from standard terms and conditions will be addressed via a specific quality plan—which can be generated as the unique occasions arise.

Thus, for a simple order-entry situation, there can be a very brief and effective contract-review process. For the large, complex contracts or quotations, the review process may involve many organizational entities such as engineering, manufacturing, legal, finance, and quality assurance. Accordingly, the procedures governing such reviews can be complex and lengthy.

A good guideline to keep in mind when developing a process to address the specific requirements of clause 7.2.2 is to balance the risks to the organization with the effort expended in a review of customer requirements. The review is to add value, not to create a bureaucratic morass.

Clause 7.2.2c) requires that the organization have the ability to meet requirements. Often with advanced products there is a need to advance the state of the art as product development progresses. Such situations should be clearly identified so that the business risks are understood. In such cases, the defined requirement could be the development of the needed technological advance.

When changes to product requirements, orders, contracts, or quotations occur, it is a requirement that the organization ensure that relevant documentation is amended and communicated, as appropriate, within the organization.

Questions to consider asking to assess conformity to this clause include:

- Does a process exist to require the review of identified customer requirements before commitment to supply a product to the customer?
- Does a process exist to require the review of quotes and orders to ensure that requirements are adequately defined?
- Is there a process for handling the review of verbal orders?
- Is there a process to handle the resolution of differences between quotations and orders?
- Does a process exist for handling changes to product requirements?
- Are records maintained of the results of reviews and actions taken?

## CONSIDERATIONS FOR DOCUMENTATION

Organizations should consider documenting a process for the review of customer requirements and how these requirements can be met, as well as the consideration of additional requirements that may be appropriate.

This clause has a specific requirement for records that is self-explanatory—keep adequate records of reviews. It is worthwhile to establish minimum retention times for review documents (for example, three years or seven years). Some organizations have a cultural bias to retain such documents forever; however, it is usually not a good idea to create such a requirement by procedure unless required by a contract.

> **7.2.3 Customer communication**
>
> The organization shall determine and implement effective arrangements for communicating with customers in relation to
>
> a) product information,
>
> b) enquiries, contracts or order handling, including amendments, and
>
> c) customer feedback, including customer complaints.

*Source:* ANSI/ISO/ASQ Q9001-2008

The requirements of this clause are identical to those of the same clause in ISO 9001:2000. The basic requirements of this clause are not new. Customer communication has always been a requirement. The requirements for implementing arrangements with customers for communication on issues such as general feedback or specific complaints are broad in scope and explicit. An effective communications process contributes to the success of any organization's quality management system and to the success of the organization. Many problems experienced by an organization with its customers can be attributed directly to inadequate communications.

The arrangements identified and implemented should be appropriate for the organization in terms of its products, its orders or contracts, and the approaches to be used to obtain customer feedback.

## IMPLEMENTATION TIPS AND TYPICAL QUESTIONS TO ASK FOR CONFORMITY

Effective customer communications are critical for achieving customer satisfaction. ISO 9000:2005 defines "customer" as the recipient of the product. It further gives examples of customers including the "end user." Verify the effectiveness of your customer communications by considering the status of the organization's approaches for areas such as:

- The organization's general communication to existing or potential customers—such as advertisements and product literature
- Customer enquiries, contracts, and orders
- Customer complaints as well as customer feedback

If you employ dealers and retailers, consider the mechanisms for connecting to the end users. The needs of the dealers and retailers may at times be different from those of the end users.

Questions to consider asking to assess conformity to this clause include:

- Are there effective processes in place to communicate with customers about product information, inquiries, contracts, and order handling (including amendments), and customer feedback, including customer complaints?
- Do your customer communication channels promote an adequate awareness of the process by which customers can provide feedback?
- Do the inputs to the customer feedback process include relevant, representative, and reliable data?
- Are data analyzed effectively?
- Are complaints tracked, investigated, and resolved?
- Are complaints summarized and reported during management review?

## CONSIDERATIONS FOR DOCUMENTATION

Determination of customer requirements is a critical activity and generally involves several functions and levels in an organization. Organizations should consider having a process to assure adequate communications with customers relating to product information, inquiries, contracts, order handling (including amendments), and customer feedback, including customer complaints. The extent to which the process should be documented will depend upon the size of the organization and the variety of customer communication links.

# CHAPTER 6

# Design and Development

### 7.3 Design and development

#### 7.3.1 Design and development planning

The organization shall plan and control the design and development of product.

During the design and development planning, the organization shall determine

a) the design and development stages,

b) the review, verification and validation that are appropriate to each design and development stage, and

c) the responsibilities and authorities for design and development.

The organization shall manage the interfaces between different groups involved in design and development to ensure effective communication and clear assignment of responsibility.

Planning output shall be updated, as appropriate, as the design and development progresses.

NOTE Design and development review, verification and validation have distinct purposes. They can be conducted and recorded separately or in any combination, as suitable for the product and the organization.

*Source:* ANSI/ISO/ASQ Q9001-2008

The requirements of this clause are essentially the same as in ISO 9001:2000. A note was added to provide insight into the meaning of the requirements during design and development planning for review, verification, and validation activities.

The intent of clause 7.3.1 is to make sure that the organization plans and controls design and development projects. The key reason for this emphasis on planning is to maximize the probability that the project will meet defined requirements. If the design and development processes are planned and controlled well, an additional benefit should be that projects will be completed on time and within budget.

Planning is required to the level of detail needed to achieve the design and development objectives—not to generate an excessive amount of paperwork. Stages of the project need to be determined, and responsibilities, authority, and interfaces need to be defined. Requirements need to be established for the incorporation of review, verification, and validation into the design and development project. The organization needs to determine how communications will be structured (for example, weekly meetings, periodic reports, or other methods).

## IMPLEMENTATION TIPS AND TYPICAL QUESTIONS TO ASK FOR CONFORMITY

A typical approach is to generate some form of project flowchart that incorporates the pertinent personnel, timing, and interrelationship information. Examples include Gantt charts, PERT charts, and CPM charts. The important effort is the thinking and discussion required to determine how the project will proceed from inception to completion. Widely available software can be a useful tool in meeting the planning requirements of the standard.

Questions to consider asking to assess conformity to this clause include:

- Are the stages of the design and development project defined? Where?
- Are verification and validation addressed? Are these activities appropriate?
- Is it clear who is responsible for what?
- Are the communications channels and interfaces defined and managed? Is there evidence that communication on projects is occurring and that it is effective?

## DEFINITIONS

*Design and development* (3.4.4)—set of **processes** (3.4.1) that transforms **requirements** (3.1.2) into specified **characteristics** (3.5.1) or into the **specification** (3.7.3) of a **product** (3.4.2), **process** (3.4.1) or **system** (3.2.1)

NOTE 1 The terms “design” and “development” are sometimes used synonymously and sometimes used to define different stages of the overall design and development process.

NOTE 2 A qualifier can be applied to indicate the nature of what is being designed and developed (e.g. product design and development or process design and development).

*Process* (3.4.1)—set of interrelated or interacting activities which transforms inputs into outputs

NOTE 1 Inputs to a process are generally outputs of other processes.

NOTE 2 Processes in an **organization** (3.3.1) are generally planned and carried out under controlled conditions to add value.

NOTE 3 A process where the **conformity** (3.6.1) of the resulting **product** (3.4.2) cannot be readily or economically verified is frequently referred to as a "special process".

*Project* (3.4.3)—unique **process** (3.4.1), consisting of a set of coordinated and controlled activities with start and finish dates, undertaken to achieve an objective conforming to specific **requirements** (3.1.2), including the constraints of time, cost and resources

NOTE 1 An individual project can form part of a larger project structure.

NOTE 2 In some projects the objectives are refined and the product **characteristics** (3.5.1) defined progressively as the project proceeds.

NOTE 3 The outcome of a project can be one or several units of **product** (3.4.2).

NOTE 4 Adapted from ISO 10006:2003.

*Characteristic* (3.5.1)—distinguishing feature

NOTE 1 A characteristic can be inherent or assigned.

NOTE 2 A characteristic can be qualitative or quantitative.

NOTE 3 There are various classes of characteristic, such as the following:
—physical (e.g. mechanical, electrical, chemical or biological characteristics);
—sensory (e.g. related to smell, touch, taste, sight, hearing);
—behavioral (e.g. courtesy, honesty, veracity);
—temporal (e.g. punctuality, reliability, availability);
—ergonomic (e.g. physiological characteristic, or related to human safety);
—functional (e.g. maximum speed of an aircraft).

*System* (3.2.1)—set of interrelated or interacting elements

*Source:* ANSI/ISO/ASQ Q9000-2005

## CONSIDERATIONS FOR DOCUMENTATION

Considerations should include a documented procedure that states the expectations for formal project plans, including the minimum level of detail for each project. The planning and documentation requirements are often a function of the size of the project. Note that the clause requires that the planning be updated as the project progresses. This clause also does not require any specific records. Organizations should determine which design and development planning records should be retained.

> **7.3.2 Design and development inputs**
>
> Inputs relating to product requirements shall be determined and records maintained (see 4.2.4). These inputs shall include
>
> a) functional and performance requirements,
>
> b) applicable statutory and regulatory requirements,
>
> c) where applicable, information derived from previous similar designs, and
>
> d) other requirements essential for design and development.
>
> The inputs shall be reviewed for adequacy. Requirements shall be complete, unambiguous and not in conflict with each other.

*Source:* ANSI/ISO/ASQ Q9001-2008

The requirements of this clause are the same as in ISO 9001:2000. One of the often quoted, if ludicrous, criticisms of ISO 9001 is that it can be used to ensure that a process is in place to produce conforming concrete life preservers. Whoever proffered this criticism did not understand the meaning of clause 7.3.2 (or its equivalent in ISO 9001:1994). This clause is intended to ensure the development and documentation of a requirements specification or an equivalent statement of the general and specific characteristics of a product to be developed, including the suitability of the product to meet marketplace and customer needs.

## IMPLEMENTATION TIPS AND TYPICAL QUESTIONS TO ASK FOR CONFORMITY

There are many areas to consider when defining product requirements. Examples include statutory and regulatory requirements; environmental considerations such as ISO 14000;

industry standards; national and international standards; organizational standards; safety regulations; customer wants and needs; cost; past experiences; and, for designs that are related to specific customer orders, contract commitments.

The result of the consideration of such items is the documentation of a complete and unambiguous statement of product requirements, sometimes called a requirements specification. Development work should not begin until such a document exists in a form acceptable to all who have responsibility for contributing to the product specification (at least to those who must bring the product to the marketplace as well as to those who must do the design and development). Concurrence with the requirements document by all parties is not required explicitly by clause 7.3.1, but it should be considered to avoid misunderstandings during project implementation. It is especially worthwhile to obtain closure, where appropriate, between marketing or sales and those who will be doing the development work. A requirements specification signed by the involved parties is one way to ensure that concerned parties in an organization are in agreement regarding the product requirements. Such a document can provide the objective evidence of compliance with the requirements of this clause.

Questions to consider asking to assess conformity to this clause include:

- Are requirements for new products defined and records maintained?
- Are the requirements complete?
- Are the requirements unambiguous?
- Are the requirements without conflict?

## DEFINITIONS

*Product* (3.4.2)—result of a **process** (3.4.1)

NOTE 1 There are four generic product categories, as follows:

—services (e.g. transport);

—software (e.g. computer program, dictionary);

—hardware (e.g. engine mechanical part);

—processed materials (e.g. lubricant).

Many products comprise elements belonging to different generic product categories. Whether the product is then called service, software, hardware or processed material depends on the dominant element. For example, the offered product "automobile" consists of hardware (e.g. tyres), processed materials (e.g. fuel, cooling liquid), software (e.g. engine control software, driver's manual), and service (e.g. operating explanations given by the salesman).

NOTE 2 Service is the result of at least one activity necessarily performed at the interface between the **supplier** (3.3.6) and **customer** (3.3.5) and is generally intangible. Provision of a service can involve, for example, the following:

—an activity performed on a customer-supplied tangible product (e.g. automobile to be repaired);

—an activity performed on a customer-supplied intangible product (e.g. the income statement needed to prepare a tax return);

—the delivery of an intangible product (e.g. the delivery of information in the context of knowledge transmission);

—the creation of ambience for the customer (e.g. in hotels and restaurants).

Software consists of information and is generally intangible and can be in the form of approaches, transactions or **procedures** (3.4.5).

Hardware is generally tangible and its amount is a countable **characteristic** (3.5.1). Processed materials are generally tangible and their amount is a continuous characteristic. Hardware and processed materials often are referred to as goods.

NOTE 3 **Quality assurance** (3.2.11) is mainly focused on intended product.

*Requirement* (3.1.2)—need or expectation that is stated, generally implied or obligatory

NOTE 1 "Generally implied" means that it is custom or common practice for the **organization** (3.3.1), its **customers** (3.3.5) and other **interested parties** (3.3.7), that the need or expectation under consideration is implied.

NOTE 2 A qualifier can be used to denote a specific type of requirement, e.g. product requirement, quality management requirement, customer requirement.

NOTE 3 A specified requirement is one that is stated, for example in a **document** (3.7.2).

NOTE 4 Requirements can be generated by different **interested parties** (3.3.7).

NOTE 5 This definition differs from that provided in 3.12.1 of ISO/IEC Directives, Part 2:2004.

> **3.12.1**
> **requirement**
> expression in the content of a document conveying criteria to be fulfilled if compliance with the document is to be claimed and from which no deviation is permitted

*Source:* ANSI/ISO/ASQ Q9000-2005

## CONSIDERATIONS FOR DOCUMENTATION

Design and development inputs must be recorded. Later the design and development outputs must be provided in a form that permits verification against these inputs. This means careful thought should be given to the methods for determining and providing design and development inputs. Considerations should include:

- Creating a documented procedure that defines what will be recorded to ensure that product requirements are adequately defined and who will participate in the definition of product requirements
- Creating a procedure that defines the process for the review of product requirements for completeness and adequacy

This clause requires specific records of the design and development inputs. The planning for realization processes covered in clause 7.1 should include defining the records that the organization will keep during the process of developing the design and development inputs.

### 7.3.3 Design and development outputs

The outputs of design and development shall be in a form suitable for verification against the design and development input and shall be approved prior to release.

Design and development outputs shall

a) meet the input requirements for design and development,

b) provide appropriate information for purchasing, production and service provision,

c) contain or reference product acceptance criteria, and

d) specify the characteristics of the product that are essential for its safe and proper use.

NOTE Information for production and service provision can include details for the preservation of product.

*Source:* ANSI/ISO/ASQ Q9001-2008

The requirements of this clause are essentially the same as in ISO 9001:2000. Minor changes were made for clarity. A note has been added to explain that information for production and service provision can include details for the preservation of product.

This provision of the standard requires that design and development output be provided in a way that can be used for subsequent verification. This generally means there must be objective evidence that the design and development has been executed in accordance with the requirements that were defined at the inception of the project. The objective evidence can be in the form of development reports that contain data to show that the requirements have been satisfied, test results, or any other formal documentation of the results of the effort to develop a product with the specified characteristics. In some cases the output may include mock-ups, models, or other means to communicate the intent of the design and development team.

In addition to documenting that the output results meet the input requirements, the standard requires that information be provided to facilitate product production. For hardware products this means that the design and development team or individual should provide appropriate information to facilitate the production of the product to specified requirements. For software products it is generally not necessary or pertinent to address item 7.3.3b)—"provide appropriate information for purchasing, production and for service provision." For service products, however, it may be necessary to provide guidance to those in the organization who are responsible for producing collateral material that will be used in the delivery of the service (for example, training manuals).

Item 7.3.3c) requires a clear and unambiguous statement of the requirements that a product must meet in order to be acceptable to customers. Such requirements will typically be incorporated into the test or inspection of the product to ensure that the product will conform to defined customer needs. Providing clear product acceptance criteria from product design and development is essential for hardware, service, processed materials, and software products.

The output from the design and development process must "specify the characteristics of the product that are essential to its safe and proper use." The output from the design and development process is expected to include any information that relates to producing or using the product safely and properly. Organizations should pay particular attention to this issue. It not only addresses ultimate customer satisfaction with the product or service, but it also provides objective evidence that the organization considered the safe and proper use of products. The availability of such information could be important to demonstrating prudent judgment if there are liability issues related to the product or service. Conversely, not having such records could be viewed as evidence of a flawed design and development process.

Finally, the standard requires that the output from a design and development project be approved before the product is released. This requirement is included to ensure that all aspects of the project have been executed in accordance with documented plans and applicable procedures before the product is launched into production or delivered to a customer.

## IMPLEMENTATION TIPS AND TYPICAL QUESTIONS TO ASK FOR CONFORMITY

The conventional documentation of the results of a design and development project demonstrate that the product will do what it is expected to do. A more difficult issue to address with regard to design and development output is how to document that the product will not do what it should not do. It is especially important, for example, to ensure that a software product will not interfere with the operation of other software.

The documentation of the results of a development project is typically the responsibility of the team or person who performed the work on the project.

Questions to consider asking to assess conformity to this clause include:

- Is the output of design and development projects in a form suitable for verification against inputs?

- Does the design and development output satisfy input requirements (for example, as stated in a functional requirements specification)?
- Does output provide, as appropriate, information for purchasing, production operations, and service provision?
- Are product acceptance criteria clearly stated?
- Are product safety and use characteristics identified?
- Is there an approval process for the release of products from the design and development process?

## DEFINITIONS

*Objective evidence* (3.8.1)—data supporting the existence or verity of something

NOTE Objective evidence may be obtained through observation, measurement, **test** (3.8.3), or other means.

*Source:* ANSI/ISO/ASQ Q9000-2005

## CONSIDERATIONS FOR DOCUMENTATION

The design and development outputs are normally documented, but whatever form the output takes, it must be in a form that can be used for subsequent design and development verification. Considerations should include defining in a documented procedure the expectations of developers about the form and content of the design and development output.

This clause does not require any specific records. But records in some form should exist to demonstrate compliance and to provide evidence of the use of prudent judgment in the design and development process.

### 7.3.4 Design and development review

At suitable stages, systematic reviews of design and development shall be performed in accordance with planned arrangements (see 7.3.1)

a) to evaluate the ability of the results of design and development to meet requirements, and

b) to identify any problems and propose necessary actions.

Participants in such reviews shall include representatives of functions concerned with the design and development stage(s) being reviewed. Records of the results of the reviews and any necessary actions shall be maintained (see 4.2.4).

*Source:* ANSI/ISO/ASQ Q9001-2008

The requirements of this clause are identical to those in the same clause of ISO 9001:2000. Design and development review is used to ensure the timely release of a new product that fully meets the needs of the customers. It can also contribute significantly to reduced cost. The intent of the standard is to involve all appropriate individuals in the development of a new product as early as is feasible so that they can understand and address life-cycle issues early in the design and development process. Design and development review is intended to address more than just the question of whether the product will meet specified requirements. Design and development review is intended to address the "abilities" associated with a new product—manufacturability, deliverability, testability, inspectability, shipability, serviceability, repairability, availability, and reliability, as well as issues related to inventory and production planning and the purchase of components and subassemblies. Design and development reviews are intended to identify issues, to discuss possible resolutions, and to determine appropriate follow-up.

Design and development review is equally applicable to hardware, processed materials, software, and service projects. In fact, it is a critical element of the software design and development process. When robust design and development reviews are held for software projects, including design and development reviews of software test plans, development cycles are typically reduced and life-cycle costs are lower.

Records of design and development reviews must be maintained. The form of the documentation should suit the circumstances, but at a minimum it should include records of issues and proposed actions.

## IMPLEMENTATION TIPS AND TYPICAL QUESTIONS TO ASK FOR CONFORMITY

An important design and development review issue is to assure the design community that design review will not interfere with the creativity and innovation of the designers or slow down the development process. Rather, it is a process step intended to provide confidence that the spectrum of internal and external customer needs has been considered as early as possible and addressed with the aim of ultimately assusuring external customer satisfaction.

The standard does not prescribe the number of design and development reviews that should be conducted. This should be determined during the design and development planning process and should be modified, as appropriate, during the course of a project. Certainly one design and development review is a minimum.

Questions to consider asking to assess conformity to this clause include:

- Are design and development reviews being performed?
- Are they indicated in the project planning documents?
- Who attends?
- Is the attendance appropriate?
- Are results documented?
- Are follow-up actions taken?
- Are appropriate records maintained?

## DEFINITIONS

*Review* (3.8.7)—activity undertaken to determine the suitability, adequacy and **effectiveness** (3.2.14) of the subject matter to achieve established objectives

NOTE Review can also include the determination of **efficiency** (3.2.15).

EXAMPLE Management review, design and development review, review of customer requirements and nonconformity review.

*Effectiveness* (3.2.14)—extent to which planned activities are realized and planned results achieved

*Efficiency* (3.2.15)—relationship between the result achieved and the resources used

*Source:* ANSI/ISO/ASQ Q9000-2005

## CONSIDERATIONS FOR DOCUMENTATION

Considerations should include defining a documented procedure for conducting design and development reviews, including who calls the reviews, who will attend, requirements for documenting the reviews, and requirements for follow-up on issues raised during reviews.

This clause requires records to be kept of design and development reviews. The clause has specific reference to clause 4.2.4 for control of the records generated. These records must include the results of the reviews and follow-up actions. Organizations should also consider including a description of what was included in each review and who conducted the review.

> **7.3.5 Design and development verification**
>
> Verification shall be performed in accordance with planned arrangements (see 7.3.1) to ensure that the design and development outputs have met the design and development input requirements. Records of the results of the verification and any necessary actions shall be maintained (see 4.2.4).

*Source:* ANSI/ISO/ASQ Q9001-2008

The requirements of this clause are identical to those in the same clause of ISO 9001:2000. While this requirement is only two sentences long, it generates much misunderstanding. Verification is a distinct activity; it is different from validation. Both verification and validation are explicitly included in ISO 9001:2008.

Verification is a process step that can occur at various stages of the design and development process. It considers the product after the developers have completed work to ensure that the output meets specified requirements. Verification makes a determination, by any reasonable means, that the product does meet the stated requirements. Verification can be done by review and analysis of test data, by making alternative calculations, by additional testing of the product or its components, or by any other means that the organization chooses.

If issues arise during verification activities, they must be documented, and follow-up actions need to be identified. Such actions may require rechecking of the output results against the input specifications and requirements and revalidating the product before release.

## IMPLEMENTATION TIPS AND TYPICAL QUESTIONS TO ASK FOR CONFORMITY

An important point is that the capability of the product to meet specified requirements is verified and that objective evidence exists to demonstrate the basis for this assertion. This requirement applies equally to all product sectors. The service sector should be particularly attentive to conducting thoughtful product verification because the opportunity to address "nonconformity of product" after it is delivered to a customer usually does not exist. Service, even more than hardware or software, must be right the first time to maximize the probability of customer satisfaction.

Questions to consider asking to assess conformity to this clause include:

- Is a verification process in place?

- Is it effectively implemented?
- Are follow-up actions recorded?
- Are required records defined and maintained?

## DEFINITIONS

*Verification* (3.8.4)—confirmation, through the provision of **objective evidence** (3.8.1), that specified **requirements** (3.1.2) have been fulfilled

NOTE 1 The term "verified" is used to designate the corresponding status.

NOTE 2 Confirmation can comprise activities such as

—performing alternative calculations,

—comparing a new design **specification** (3.7.3) with a similar proven design specification,

—undertaking **tests** (3.8.3) and demonstrations, and

—reviewing documents prior to issue.

*Source:* ANSI/ISO/ASQ Q9000-2005

## CONSIDERATIONS FOR DOCUMENTATION

A documented procedure should be considered for defining the verification process, including the following:

- Who does verification?
- How should results be recorded?
- How should follow-up of verification issues and reverification be managed?

This clause requires records of design and development verification results and subsequent follow-up actions. There is also specific reference to clause 4.2.4 for control of the records generated.

> **7.3.6 Design and development validation**
>
> Design and development validation shall be performed in accordance with planned arrangements (see 7.3.1) to ensure that the resulting product is capable of meeting the requirements for the specified application or intended use, where known. Wherever practicable, validation shall be completed prior to the delivery or implementation of the product. Records of the results of validation and any necessary actions shall be maintained (see 4.2.4).

*Source:* ANSI/ISO/ASQ Q9001-2008

The requirements of this clause are identical to those in the same clause of ISO 9001:2000. The difference between validation and verification of design and development output has caused much confusion in the past, especially with new users of the standard. As was indicated previously for the verification clause, both verification and validation are explicitly included in ISO 9001:2008.

Design and development validation is intended to ensure that the design and development output conforms to defined user needs and "is capable of meeting the requirements for the specified application or intended use, where known." Design and development validation is usually performed after successful design and development verification. It is worthwhile to state again the difference between verification and validation. In simple language, verification addresses conformance to requirements, while validation addresses meeting defined user needs.

## IMPLEMENTATION TIPS AND TYPICAL QUESTIONS TO ASK FOR CONFORMITY

It is especially important to understand and address validation in the world of software product development because of the often mysterious interactions that occur deep in the workings of a computer. In addition to being an ISO 9001 requirement, and even though software designers complain that there is never enough time to perform robust validation, this is not an area to be ignored or given perfunctory treatment.

For software, if the output from a project to design a unit or module of a software product (for example, an SPC package) performed as specified in the SPC requirements specification but caused a word processor to crash when the SPC product was loaded into a system, then this product would "meet" the intent and requirement of the verification clause but not of the validation clause.

For hardware, if a water heater design meets all specified requirements but cannot be easily installed by a plumber, it would "meet" the intent and requirement of the verification clause but not of the validation clause.

For service, the primary requirements might be met but secondary factors can suddenly overshadow them. Validation helps to uncover incomplete service requirements. For example, an express mail service that guarantees overnight delivery might meet the schedule, but it is inadequate if the package is left in a doorway during inclement weather and is destroyed by rain. This service would meet the intent and requirement of the verification clause but not of the validation clause.

In addition to the customer-satisfaction implications, robust validation processes are critical to optimizing the life-cycle costs of software (the majority of which typically occur after product release) and to minimizing product-liability exposure. Thus, validation should receive careful attention, and the results should be recorded and retained as records.

Validation may be performed with or after verification, and in an environment that approximates as closely as possible the operating conditions that will exist in actual use. Also, whenever possible it should be performed before product is released for shipment. If it is not possible to perform a complete validation of a hardware, software, or service product before release and/or shipment to customers, then validation should be performed to the extent that is reasonable and final validation performed when and as appropriate.

In addition to customer-satisfaction issues, cost containment is a major reason for performing validation before a product is delivered to a customer. The resolution of issues after shipment can be very expensive.

Questions to consider asking to assess conformity to this clause include:

- Is design and development validation performed to confirm that the product is capable of meeting the requirements for intended use?
- Is validation completed prior to delivery, when applicable?
- Are suitable controls provided in cases where full validation cannot be performed prior to delivery?
- Are records of design and development validation maintained?

## DEFINITIONS

*Validation* (3.8.5)—confirmation, through the provision of **objective evidence** (3.8.1), that the **requirements** (3.1.2) for a specific intended use or application have been fulfilled

NOTE 1 The term "validated" is used to designate the corresponding status.

NOTE 2 The use conditions for validation can be real or simulated.

*Source:* ANSI/ISO/ASQ Q9000-2005

## CONSIDERATIONS FOR DOCUMENTATION

Considerations should include documenting a process for performing design and development validation. Clause 7.3.6 requires keeping records of the validation results, and of subsequent follow-up actions with specific reference to clause 4.2.4 on control of the records generated.

> **7.3.7 Control of design and development changes**
>
> Design and development changes shall be identified and records maintained. The changes shall be reviewed, verified and validated, as appropriate, and approved before implementation. The review of design and development changes shall include evaluation of the effect of the changes on constituent parts and product already delivered. Records of the results of the review of changes and any necessary actions shall be maintained (see 4.2.4).

*Source:* ANSI/ISO/ASQ Q9001-2008

The requirements of this clause are identical to those in the same clause of ISO 9001:2000. Any changes that occur in the design of a product, either during the design and development process, during production, or after the delivery of the product to a customer, "shall be identified and records maintained." This requirement applies to all product sectors and especially to software, where configuration control is a major issue.

Changes to a product should be viewed as miniprojects within a project. The reason for this is that any changes, even those perceived as "improvements," can have unforeseen adverse effects on other elements of a product or can result in unanticipated system performance when used in a real-life environment. Therefore, changes should be exercised through design and development review, verification, and validation processes.

This clause also requires evaluation of the effect of changes and follow-up actions, if necessary.

## IMPLEMENTATION TIPS AND TYPICAL QUESTIONS TO ASK TO ASSESS CONFORMITY OF PROCESSES

During the course of a design and development project, there are usually changes to the requirements that were defined at the input stage. Such changes occur for many reasons, including: (1) omissions that become apparent after design and development work starts, (2) errors or inconsistencies in the design or in a specification requirement, (3) changes requested by marketing or by a customer, (4) perceived improvement opportunities, (5) changing regulatory or statutory conditions, (6) issues raised in design and development review, (7) issues raised during the verification process, and (8) issues raised during the validation process. Changes to the design and development project for any one or combination of reasons need to be addressed in accordance with the requirements of this clause.

Questions to consider asking to assess conformity to this clause include:

- Are all design and development project changes documented and reviewed?
- Are design and development changes verified and validated, as appropriate?
- Is there evidence to demonstrate that changes are authorized?
- Do records include the results of reviews of changes?
- Have changes been communicated to interested parties?
- Do records include follow-up actions related to the review of changes?

## CONSIDERATIONS FOR DOCUMENTATION

Consideration should be given to documenting procedures to ensure that design and development project changes are communicated to all interested parties, that all changes are recorded, that document processing and control are adequate (see Chapter 2), and that appropriate authorization is documented for any changes.

This clause requires documentation of the results of the review of changes and subsequent follow-up. The clause also has a specific reference to clause 4.2.4 for control of the records generated. Design and development changes must be reflected in the design and development output documents. Records must also be kept of the design-change reviews themselves and follow-up actions taken.

# CHAPTER 7

# Purchasing

## 7.4 Purchasing

### 7.4.1 Purchasing process

The organization shall ensure that purchased product conforms to specified purchase requirements. The type and extent of control applied to the supplier and the purchased product shall be dependent upon the effect of the purchased product on subsequent product realization or the final product.

The organization shall evaluate and select suppliers based on their ability to supply product in accordance with the organization's requirements. Criteria for selection, evaluation and re-evaluation shall be established. Records of the results of evaluations and any necessary actions arising from the evaluation shall be maintained (see 4.2.4).

*Source:* ANSI/ISO/ASQ Q9001-2008

The requirement for the purchasing process is that the organization ensures that purchased product conforms to requirements. The content of this clause has not changed from ISO 9001:2000. The standard permits the organization to decide the "type and extent of control," which should be based on the effect of the purchased material on the product realization processes and on the products produced. If purchased material has little impact (for example, a bolt used inside a noncritical subassembly), then minimal control is needed. Generally speaking, minimal control is required for commodity-type purchased material.

If purchased material has high actual or high potential impact on either the final product or the realization processes, then more robust control is required. If, for example, the bolt is used for an aircraft engine mount, then the controls will be more extensive than if the bolt is used in a noncritical application inside a subassembly.

Determining the nature of the control is the responsibility of the organization as it considers customer, regulatory, industry, and other appropriate requirements. ISO 9001:2008 requires the organization to think about what makes sense from both a customer and a business perspective.

The standard requires the organization to evaluate suppliers and to define the criteria used to select and periodically evaluate suppliers. It also requires establishment criteria for the reevaluation of suppliers. However, the organization has broad flexibility regarding how to do this and can focus more on obtaining conforming material rather than on maintaining approved-supplier lists. The results of all evaluations and any required follow-up actions shall be documented and retained as records.

## IMPLEMENTATION TIPS AND TYPICAL QUESTIONS TO ASK FOR CONFORMITY

The organization needs to make sure that effective purchasing processes are defined and implemented for the selection and qualification of suppliers and for ongoing periodic evaluations of their performance. It is often useful to work from a list of potential suppliers developed with the input of staff from appropriate functions of the organization. The list of potential suppliers may be filtered and reduced to a few likely candidates using one or more of the following tools: request for quotation, supplier survey, supplier samples, and quality systems audit (where appropriate). Selection of suppliers should be based on review of each supplier's abilities to meet business requirements for quality, cost, delivery and other considerations important to the organization. Competitive comparisons of financial, business, and quality attributes should be considered where applicable.

Questions to consider asking to assess conformity to this clause include:

- Have criteria for the selection and periodic evaluation of suppliers been defined?
- Is there a process for selecting and evaluating suppliers?
- Are the results of evaluations documented and retained as records?

## DEFINITIONS

*Requirement* (3.1.2)—need or expectation that is stated, generally implied or obligatory

NOTE 1 "Generally implied" means that it is custom or common practice for the **organization** (3.3.1), its **customers** (3.3.5) and other **interested parties** (3.3.7), that the need or expectation under consideration is implied.

NOTE 2 A qualifier can be used to denote a specific type of requirement, e.g. product requirement, quality management requirement, customer requirement.

NOTE 3 A specified requirement is one that is stated, for example in a **document** (3.7.2).

NOTE 4 Requirements can be generated by different **interested parties** (3.3.7).

NOTE 5 This definition differs from that provided in 3.12.1 of ISO/IEC Directives, Part 2:2004.

> **3.12.1**
> **requirement**
> expression in the content of a document conveying criteria to be fulfilled if compliance with the document is to be claimed and from which no deviation is permitted

*Supplier* (3.3.6)—**organization** (3.3.1) or person that provides a **product** (3.4.2)

EXAMPLE Producer, distributor, retailer or vendor of a product, or provider of a service or information.

NOTE 1 A supplier can be internal or external to the organization.

NOTE 2 In a contractual situation, a supplier is sometimes called "contractor".

*Source:* ANSI/ISO/ASQ Q9000-2005

## CONSIDERATIONS FOR DOCUMENTATION

Organizations should consider documented procedures to describe processes for the selection and periodic evaluation of suppliers. Organizations should also carefully consider how they will communicate their processes for controlling purchased material that will affect customer satisfaction.

Typically, they will document the process to be used in the form of a written procedure to ensure that the requirements are understood and consistently implemented.

Clause 7.4.1 requires records of the results of supplier evaluations and subsequent follow-up actions, with specific reference to clause 4.2.4 for control of the records generated. These records would include reports of supplier evaluations, corrective actions requested of suppliers, and the actual corrective actions taken.

> **7.4.2 Purchasing information**
>
> Purchasing information shall describe the product to be purchased, including, where appropriate,
>
> a) requirements for approval of product, procedures, processes and equipment,
>
> b) requirements for qualification of personnel, and
>
> c) quality management system requirements.
>
> The organization shall ensure the adequacy of specified purchase requirements prior to their communication to the supplier.

*Source:* ANSI/ISO/ASQ Q9001-2008

This requirement is unchanged from 2000. The language used is general so that it can be applied to all product sectors. It states that purchasing documents (for example, purchase orders) should provide the information needed to clearly communicate to suppliers what the organization wants to purchase. The requirement indicates the various types of information that may be pertinent and indicates that these items shall be considered as appropriate.

This clause also requires a process to ensure that purchasing documents adequately state all of the requirements for the items to be purchased. This can be accomplished by a process as simple as a sign-off of a purchase order or by a more elaborate process that can involve several layers of review and approval, especially for high-value purchased items. Organizations that execute Web-based purchasing transactions will need to devise creative approaches to address the requirement for assuring the adequacy of purchase requirements. Perhaps a simple checkbox on the electronic transmission of an "order" indicating that the order has been reviewed before transmission would suffice.

## IMPLEMENTATION TIPS AND TYPICAL QUESTIONS TO ASK FOR CONFORMITY

At a minimum, purchasing information should include supplier quality and product requirements. Does your organization need confidentiality and nondisclosure agreements not otherwise contained in purchasing contracts? Do you need a statement of work? Based upon criticality of the supplied product, do you need a Supplier Quality Agreement? Keep it simple but consider what you need to agree upon in writing with your supplier to ensure effective and efficient conformity to requirements. To what extent do you need agreement with your suppliers on their processes? Do you need agreement on requirements to control supplier product changes and the expectations of suppliers to perform corrective and preventive action?

Questions to consider asking to assess conformity to this clause include:

- Do purchasing documents adequately describe the products being ordered?
- Do purchasing documents include, where appropriate, requirements for approval or qualification of product, procedures, processes, equipment, and personnel?
- Do purchasing documents include, where applicable, quality management system requirements?
- How does the organization ensure the adequacy of specified purchase requirements prior to communication to the supplier?

## DEFINITIONS

*Release* (3.6.13)—permission to proceed to the next stage of a **process** (3.4.1)

NOTE In English, in the context of computer software, the term "release" is frequently used to refer to a version of the software itself.

*Source:* ANSI/ISO/ASQ Q9000-2005

## CONSIDERATIONS FOR DOCUMENTATION

Considerations for documentation should include the development of a documented procedure that defines what to include in purchasing documents. Organizations should also consider the need for a written procedure that defines an approval process for review and approval of purchasing documents before release to suppliers. Clause 7.4.2 also does not require any specific records. The planning for realization processes covered in clause 7.1 should define the records the organization will keep. Consider keeping records of the purchased-material document review and copies of the purchase documents themselves.

### 7.4.3 Verification of purchased product

The organization shall establish and implement the inspection or other activities necessary for ensuring that purchased product meets specified purchase requirements.

Where the organization or its customer intends to perform verification at the supplier's premises, the organization shall state the intended verification arrangements and method of product release in the purchasing information.

*Source:* ANSI/ISO/ASQ Q9001-2008

The requirements of this clause are the same as in ISO 9001:2000. There are two distinct requirements in clause 7.4.3. The first is a requirement to ensure that purchased material conforms to requirements. The second requirement pertains to when verification activities are to be performed at the supplier's premises.

Verification of purchased product is directed at purchased product that will be incorporated into the products the organization delivers to customers, not the entire spectrum of products purchased by the organization (for example, pencils, rock salt, and so on would be outside the scope of this clause).

Performing verification activities at the supplier's premises is not common for many organizations. If this is the case, a simple statement in the quality management system documentation specifying that "this requirement does not apply and if such a situation ever arises, the organization shall prepare a unique quality plan to address the situation" will suffice to meet this requirement. If performing verification activities at the supplier's premises is an applicable requirement, then the purchasing documents should describe the procedures to be followed along with the criteria for the release of product by the supplier.

## IMPLEMENTATION TIPS AND TYPICAL QUESTIONS TO ASK FOR CONFORMITY

In the past, verifying that purchased product met specified purchase requirements was done through receiving inspection. The higher the quality the lower the inspection needed to have confidence in the quality of the supplied product. The process approach emphasizes that success with suppliers and obtaining products that flawlessly enter your product stream requires much more than this historical tollgate approach. Often this involves suppliers' demonstration of process capability. Many organizations focus on developing supplier relationships that treat suppliers as an extension of their own organizations. The eighth Quality Management Principle (ISO 9000:2005) states:

**Mutually beneficial supplier relationships** *an organization and its suppliers are interdependent and a mutually beneficial relationship enhances the ability of both to create value.*

Think of the total system and the other key processes of this standard. Supplier performance is more critical today than ever before. The performance of purchased goods and services needs to be included in your organization's overall system for managing quality including quality objectives, audit results, measurement and analysis of data, corrective and preventive actions, and management review. Consider what you need do to foster stronger supplier relationships. Often communication to suppliers of their performance and the results of your monitoring are key interface elements. These concepts should be considered for application to any outsourced processes as described in clause 4.1.

A process is required that can include approaches such as the following:

- Certifying suppliers (based on demonstrated performance or process capability) and requiring no inspection or test
- Conventional incoming inspection using sampling plans
- One hundred percent inspection (or more)
- Verification at the supplier's facility
- Any combination of these or other approaches

Whatever methods are used, the verification activities must be planned and effectively implemented.

Integration with other parts of your quality management system impact the effectiveness of maintaining high performing suppliers. Do not rely solely on verification activities. Product verification activities allow you to assess the acceptability of product. Use this information to evaluate suppliers and monitor performance. Conduct periodic supplier reviews and report to suppliers their performance. Performance can be measured based on quality systems assessments, quality performance, cost, delivery, service, and other commercial considerations.

Questions to consider asking to assess conformity to this clause include:

- Has the organization defined a process for verifying that purchased product conforms to defined requirements?
- Is the process effectively implemented?
- Does objective evidence exist of product acceptance?
- Is verification of purchased product performed at the supplier's premises? If so, are the arrangements specified and is there objective evidence of effective implementation?

## DEFINITIONS

*Verification* (3.8.4)—confirmation, through the provision of **objective evidence** (3.8.1), that specified **requirements** (3.1.2) have been fulfilled

NOTE 1 The term "verified" is used to designate the corresponding status.

NOTE 2 Confirmation can comprise activities such as

—performing alternative calculations,

—comparing a new design **specification** (3.7.3) with a similar proven design specification,

—undertaking **tests** (3.8.3) and demonstrations, and

—reviewing documents prior to issue.

*Source:* ANSI/ISO/ASQ Q9000-2005

## CONSIDERATIONS FOR DOCUMENTATION

Considerations should include the process for identifying and implementing the activities necessary to ensure conformance of purchased product. If verification activities are performed at the supplier's premises, consider preparing a documented procedure for performing this verification and for release of the product. This clause does not require any specific records. The planning for realization processes covered in clause 7.1 should define the records the organization will keep. Consideration should be given to keeping records of product verification and product release.

# CHAPTER

# 8

# Production and Service Provision

## 7.5 Production and service provision

### 7.5.1 Control of production and service provision

The organization shall plan and carry out production and service provision under controlled conditions. Controlled conditions shall include, as applicable,

a) the availability of information that describes the characteristics of the product,

b) the availability of work instructions, as necessary,

c) the use of suitable equipment,

d) the availability and use of monitoring and measuring equipment,

e) the implementation of monitoring and measurement, and

f) the implementation of product release, delivery and post-delivery activities.

*Source:* ANSI/ISO/ASQ Q9001-2008

The requirements of this clause are essentially the same as in ISO 9001:2000. A minor addition of referring to monitoring and measurement "equipment" instead of "devices" was made for clarity. The term "provision" is used in its common dictionary sense: the act of providing. This clause addresses the processes necessary for an organization to produce and deliver products and services.

Documentation requirements for the overall quality management system are stated in clause 4 and are not repeated here. Likewise, clause 7.1 addresses the planning of product realization processes and requires that they be documented in a manner suitable for the organization's method of operation. Process and product-measurement requirements are stated in clause 8.2.3 and clause 8.2.4. ISO 9001:2008 emphasizes the process approach for the entire quality management system. There is a clear need to view the entire interconnected quality management system, not a collection of individual, standalone elements.

The requirements are expressed in general terms that provide clarity as to their meaning for software and service providers. Although these appear in a general format, they should not be interpreted as lessened or weakened requirements for hardware producers or providers of processed materials.

The focus of clause 7.5.1, *Control of production and service provision,* is the key concept that processes need to be carried out under controlled conditions. "The organization shall plan and carry out production and service provision under controlled conditions." Considerations for achieving controlled conditions are presented. The requirements to determine the extent to which production and service operations are planned, established, documented, verified, and validated are presented in clause 7.1. Because clause 7.1 applies to all of the realization processes, these planning and development requirements are not repeated.

## IMPLEMENTATION TIPS AND TYPICAL QUESTIONS TO ASK FOR CONFORMITY

The organization should control process operations by considering a number of factors. This begins with understanding the specifications of the product that the processes need to produce or realize. The organization must determine the production and service processes that need to be controlled and the outputs that must be achieved at each stage of processing.

Also, the specific items of equipment that are needed to achieve the product specifications, including their sequence and operating conditions, need to be addressed. The organization needs to determine the criteria of acceptability for these processes and needs to perform evaluations against these criteria (see clause 7.1). One approach is to perform capability studies to demonstrate process suitability. From the determination of suitability, decisions can be made if additional process development effort is required to achieve the product specifications. Appropriate criteria and controls for these processes need to be determined and implemented to maintain process capability and to prevent nonconformities from occurring. The corresponding work instructions and the associated measurement equipment should be identified. In determining the extent of documentation needed, the organization should consider the criticality of the product, the competency of its people, and the complexity and size of the organization. Controls often include direct measurement of process parameters and characteristics. There may be inspection or test of the output of the process (for example, the product or service). In some cases, both may be used. Whichever combination of approaches is adopted, verification activities should be integrated to maximize both the efficiency of the verification and confidence in the product. Overall, this clause requires organizations to think about their operations.

*For services,* every organization should be aware of the requirements and conditions for the proper operation of its planned and offered services and should establish these in writing. One approach is to rank the offered services in the order of their importance, cost, and criticality. The task of the organization is to plan, monitor, and systematically supervise the fulfillment of services so that the quality objectives can be achieved. For some types of services, there is little or no process equipment to control, as the service consists of actions performed by the service personnel directly for or with the customer. In these cases, the requirements of this clause apply directly to the service personnel and to the processes that control their competence (see Chapter 4).

As appropriate, release methods need to be developed and implemented before providing the service to the customer. The release methods differ in form, timing, and application. For example, airline pilots use preflight checklists to verify that requirements have been met prior to takeoff. An automobile repair shop uses both test instruments and a test drive to verify the satisfactory completion of its service before releasing a repaired vehicle to the customer. Also, customer-contact employees can receive immediate feedback by asking customers if the services have been adequately provided.

*For hardware and processed materials,* raw materials, parts, and subassemblies should conform to appropriate specifications before being introduced into processing. In determining the amount of testing or inspection necessary, organizations should compare the cost of evaluation at various stages to the added value of subsequent activities. The economic impact of discarding or reworking product should be considered when planning the controls. In-process materials should be appropriately stored, segregated, handled, and protected to maintain their suitability. Special consideration should be given to shelf life and the potential for deterioration. Where in-plant traceability of material is important to quality, appropriate identification should be maintained throughout processing to ensure traceability to original material identification and quality status. Where important to quality characteristics, auxiliary materials and utilities such as water, compressed air, electric power, and chemicals used for processing should be controlled and verified periodically to ensure uniformity of effect on the process. Where a work environment (such as temperature, humidity, and cleanliness) is important to product and service quality, appropriate limits should be specified, controlled, and verified (see Chapter 4).

*For software,* the creation of code is usually part of the design and development process. Mass production of software involves replicating the code and may involve consulting services to tailor the software for specific customer needs. Nevertheless, it is essential to control the final stages of development through to code replication and subsequent installation and servicing processes.

In this area, configuration management is very important. The process controls should include documented procedures for configuration management to the extent appropriate. This discipline should have been initiated early in the design phase and should continue through the life cycle of the software. It assists in the control of design, development, provision, and use of the software, and it enables the organization to examine the state of the software during its life. Configuration management can include configuration identification, configuration control, configuration status accounting, and configuration audit.

It is not uncommon for organizations to provide a combination of hardware, processed materials, services, and software to customers. The controls for each product category may be different but their provision to a customer must be achieved in an integrated way.

Questions to consider asking to assess conformity to this clause include:

- Are specifications available that define quality characteristic requirements of the product or service?
- Has the organization determined the criteria of acceptability for demonstrating the suitability of equipment for production and service operations to meet product or service specifications?
- Has the organization demonstrated the suitability of equipment for production and service operations to meet product or service specifications?
- Has the organization defined all production and service provision activities that require control, including those that need ongoing monitoring, work instructions, or special controls?
- Are work instructions available and adequate to permit control of the appropriate operations so as to ensure conformity of the product or service?
- Have the requirements for the work environment needed to ensure the conformity of the product or service been defined and are these work environment requirements being met?
- Is suitable monitoring and measurement equipment available when and where necessary to ensure conformity of the product or service?
- Have monitoring and measurement activities been planned and are they carried out as required?
- For hardware, processed material, and software, have suitable processes been implemented for release of the product and for its delivery to the customer?
- Have suitable release mechanisms been put in place to ensure that product and service conforms to requirements?

## DEFINITIONS

*Capability* (3.1.5)—ability of an **organization** (3.3.1), **system** (3.2.1) or **process** (3.4.1) to realize a **product** (3.4.2) that will fulfil the **requirements** (3.1.2) for that product

NOTE Process capability terms in the field of statistics are defined in ISO 3534-2.

*Characteristic* (3.5.1)—distinguishing feature

NOTE 1 A characteristic can be inherent or assigned.

NOTE 2 A characteristic can be qualitative or quantitative.

NOTE 3 There are various classes of characteristic, such as the following:

—physical (e.g. mechanical, electrical, chemical or biological characteristics);

—sensory (e.g. related to smell, touch, taste, sight, hearing);

—behavioral (e.g. courtesy, honesty, veracity);

—temporal (e.g. punctuality, reliability, availability);

—ergonomic (e.g. physiological characteristic, or related to human safety);

—functional (e.g. maximum speed of an aircraft).

*Process* (3.4.1)—set of interrelated or interacting activities which transforms inputs into outputs

NOTE 1 Inputs to a process are generally outputs of other processes.

NOTE 2 Processes in an **organization** (3.3.1) are generally planned and carried out under controlled conditions to add value.

NOTE 3 A process where the **conformity** (3.6.1) of the resulting **product** (3.4.2) cannot be readily or economically verified is frequently referred to as a "special process".

*Quality characteristic* (3.5.2)—inherent **characteristic** (3.5.1) of a **product** (3.4.2), **process** (3.4.1) or **system** (3.2.1) related to a **requirement** (3.1.2)

NOTE 1 Inherent means existing in something, especially as a permanent characteristic.

NOTE 2 A characteristic assigned to a product, process or system (e.g. the price of a product, the owner of a product) is not a quality characteristic of that product, process or system.

*Release* (3.6.13)—permission to proceed to the next stage of a **process** (3.4.1)

NOTE In English, in the context of computer software, the term "release" is frequently used to refer to a version of the software itself.

*Requirement* (3.1.2)—need or expectation that is stated, generally implied or obligatory

NOTE 1 "Generally implied" means that it is custom or common practice for the **organization** (3.3.1), its **customers** (3.3.5) and other **interested parties** (3.3.7), that the need or expectation under consideration is implied.

NOTE 2 A qualifier can be used to denote a specific type of requirement, e.g. product requirement, quality management requirement, customer requirement.

NOTE 3 A specified requirement is one that is stated, for example in a **document** (3.7.2).

NOTE 4 Requirements can be generated by different **interested parties** (3.3.7).

NOTE 5 This definition differs from that provided in 3.12.1 of ISO/IEC Directives, Part 2:2004.

> **3.12.1**
> **requirement**
> expression in the content of a document conveying criteria to be fulfilled if compliance with the document is to be claimed and from which no deviation is permitted

*Specification* (3.7.3)—**document** (3.7.2) stating **requirements** (3.1.2)

NOTE A specification can be related to activities (e.g. procedure document, process specification and test specification), or **products** (3.4.2) (e.g. product specification, performance specification and drawing).

*Verification* (3.8.4)—confirmation, through the provision of **objective evidence** (3.8.1), that specified **requirements** (3.1.2) have been fulfilled

NOTE 1 The term "verified" is used to designate the corresponding status.

NOTE 2 Confirmation can comprise activities such as

—performing alternative calculations,

—comparing a new design **specification** (3.7.3) with a similar proven design specification,

—undertaking **tests** (3.8.3) and demonstrations, and

—reviewing documents prior to issue.

*Work environment* (3.3.4)—set of conditions under which work is performed

NOTE Conditions include physical, social, psychological and environmental factors (such as temperature, recognition schemes, ergonomics and atmospheric composition).

*Source:* ANSI/ISO/ASQ Q9000-2005

## CONSIDERATIONS FOR DOCUMENTATION

There is a specific requirement for the implementation of a defined process for release, delivery, and applicable post-delivery activities. An easy way of defining such processes is through the use of documented procedures. Considerations should include the development and documentation of needed procedures and work instructions.

## 7.5.2 Validation of processes for production and service provision

The organization shall validate any processes for production and service provision where the resulting output cannot be verified by subsequent monitoring or measurement and, as a consequence, deficiencies become apparent only after the product is in use or the service has been delivered.

Validation shall demonstrate the ability of these processes to achieve planned results.

The organization shall establish arrangements for these processes including, as applicable,

a) defined criteria for review and approval of the processes,

b) approval of equipment and qualification of personnel,

c) use of specific methods and procedures,

d) requirements for records (see 4.2.4), and

e) revalidation.

*Source:* ANSI/ISO/ASQ Q9001-2008

The requirements of this clause are the same as in ISO 9001:2000. When the processes are such that the achievement of the product specifications cannot be fully verified by the examination of finished product, either at an earlier stage of production or after finishing, process validation must be performed. Inability to fully verify every unit of product may be due to the nature of the testing (for example, when the testing is destructive). In such cases, the process must be validated. Records of validation need to be established and maintained, as appropriate.

There is a requirement for defining the conditions and criteria for revalidation. After being validated, processes must be maintained in a validated state. If changes are made to the process equipment, the product design, the materials used to produce the product, or to other significant factors such as new personnel, the process often requires revalidation. The organization therefore needs to define the conditions that require a revalidation to be performed. Even if no initiating events occur, common practice often requires revalidation after a minimum period of use, a number of operating cycles, or a period of time. In some industries, revalidation is required if a period of five years has elapsed without an intervening validation. Validation should be carried out at appropriate intervals to respond to changes in market requirements, regulations, or standards in addition to assuring the continued acceptable performance of processes.

## IMPLEMENTATION TIPS AND TYPICAL QUESTIONS TO ASK FOR CONFORMITY

Ultimately, the output of processes should provide finished product that meets the customer requirements. Many finished products do not present any difficulty for verification against end-user requirements through visual inspection, direct measurement of product characteristics, or testing of performance. For processes used to create these products, the extent to which all of the production and service processes require validation is based on practical and economic factors. It is always in the best interest of the organization to develop and implement processes that are fully capable of meeting finished-product requirements; by so doing, the organization minimizes or eliminates the creation of nonconforming product that would need to be reprocessed or discarded. To demonstrate that this has been achieved, organizations often validate all major processes. There is a common expression that it is always less expensive to make the product right the first time. From a practical standpoint, the organization must find the best balance between product verification and process validation.

*For services,* examples of processes requiring validation include those processes that create financial or legal documents and those that deal with professional advice. Validation includes considering a number of factors such as the need to qualify the processing method, the qualifying of service equipment, and having qualified personnel providing the service.

*For hardware and processed material,* examples of processes that require validation include welding, soldering, gluing, casting, forging, heat treating, and forming processes.

Products with quality characteristics that require certain test and inspection techniques for verification such as nondestructive examinations (e.g., radiographic, eddy current, or ultrasonic examination), environmental testing, or mechanical stress tests usually require process validation. Validation includes consideration of the qualification of equipment, personnel, and processes.

*For software,* the organization may not be able to verify even the simplest code through testing. The expectations are that all software needs to be created by controlled processes following the model described in clause 7.3. The methods and extent of the process validations will differ widely based on the criticality and use of the software. The qualification of personnel, equipment, and software development methodologies and procedures is an important aspect of assuring that software conforms to specified requirements.

Questions to consider asking to assess conformity to this clause include:

- Has the organization determined which production or service processes require validation? Have these processes been validated?
- Has the organization defined criteria for the review and approval of production or service processes? Have the reviews and approvals been performed?
- Has the organization determined what personnel need to be qualified and has it determined the qualification criteria? Have these personnel been qualified?
- Does the organization use defined methods and procedures to validate processes?
- Have the requirements for records of validated processes been defined?
- Are records of validated processes maintained?
- Have the processes requiring revalidation been defined?
- Have processes, as required, been revalidated?
- Do adequate records exist to assure that process validation is effectively implemented?

## DEFINITIONS

*Verification* (3.8.4)—confirmation, through the provision of **objective evidence** (3.8.1), that specified **requirements** (3.1.2) have been fulfilled

NOTE 1 The term "verified" is used to designate the corresponding status.

NOTE 2 Confirmation can comprise activities such as
—performing alternative calculations,
—comparing a new design **specification** (3.7.3) with a similar proven design specification,
—undertaking **tests** (3.8.3) and demonstrations, and
—reviewing documents prior to issue.

*Validation* (3.8.5)—confirmation, through the provision of **objective evidence** (3.8.1), that the **requirements** (3.1.2) for a specific intended use or application have been fulfilled

NOTE 1 The term "validated" is used to designate the corresponding status.

NOTE 2 The use conditions for validation can be real or simulated.

*Source:* ANSI/ISO/ASQ Q9000-2005

## CONSIDERATIONS FOR DOCUMENTATION

Clause 7.5.2 requires that the organization define the arrangements for the validation of processes. Organizations should consider defining these arrangements in a written procedure. This clause requires applicable records. The planning for realization processes covered in clause 7.1 should define the records the organization will keep. Clause 7.5.2 requires the organization to define any records that are to be kept as a part of process validation. Organizations should consider keeping records of personnel and equipment qualifications where such qualifications are required.

**7.5.3 Identification and traceability**

Where appropriate, the organization shall identify the product by suitable means throughout product realization.

The organization shall identify the product status with respect to monitoring and measurement requirements throughout product realization.

Where traceability is a requirement, the organization shall control the unique identification of the product and maintain records (see 4.2.4).

NOTE In some industry sectors, configuration management is a means by which identification and traceability are maintained.

*Source:* ANSI/ISO/ASQ Q9001-2008

The requirements of this clause are essentially the same as in ISO 9001:2000. Minor changes were made for clarity: the requirements are now unambiguous that product status needs to be maintained throughout product realization and records maintained.

Identification and traceability are separate but related issues. The degree of product identification that is needed must be determined, including any requirements for tracking purchased components, materials, and supplies that are uniquely related to the product. Appropriateness depends upon the nature of the product, the nature and complexity of the process, industry practice, and whether identification is required in a contract. Integral to product identification is its status in meeting requirements at various stages of production or service development, storage, and delivery as indicated by passing tests and inspections.

In order to trace a product, the organization must identify the product and its component parts in adequate detail. Thus, traceability is closely related to identification. Full traceability involves the ability to trace the history, application, or location of an item or activity. This is usually required when there is a need to trace a problem back to its source and when it is necessary to be able to isolate all parts of an affected batch. Records that are needed to ensure traceability should be defined. For example, traceability is typically a contract requirement for certain medical devices, for defense/space vehicle assemblies, and for devices used in nuclear power plants.

## IMPLEMENTATION TIPS AND TYPICAL QUESTIONS TO ASK FOR CONFORMITY

It may be important to identify specific personnel involved in each phase of a service delivery process. Different personnel may be involved in successive service functions, each of which is to be traceable. For example, the recording through signatures on serially numbered documents in banking operations is often required. In this case, there is no tangible product, but each person's identity needs to be traceable to provide the appropriate documentation trail. In a different application, signatures often serve as indications of processing status and approval to proceed with payment of, for example, an invoice.

*For hardware and processed materials,* product identification is often achieved by marking or tagging a product or its container. When products are visually identical but their functional characteristics are different, different markings or colors may be used. More often, quantities of product are segregated into batches with unique batch numbers. Batch definition may be determined by identifying potential sources of batch-to-batch variation. Sources of variation traditionally are the five Ms of man (operator), method (or procedure), material, measurement (measurement method and instrument), and machine (or processing step). New batches may be defined as these potential sources change. Traceability approaches vary widely and depend on the application regarding how the unique identification of product is accomplished.

*For software,* configuration management practices require that each version of a configuration item be identified by some appropriate means. Likewise, there is a need to maintain the status of the verification steps and tests that have been completed. The results achieved by the product or product components at each phase of the development cycle must also be maintained.

Questions to consider asking to assess conformity to this clause include:

- Has the product been identified by suitable means throughout production and service operations?
- Has the status of the product been identified at suitable stages with respect to monitoring and measurement requirements?
- Is traceability a requirement?
- Where traceability is a requirement, is the unique identification of the product recorded and controlled?

## DEFINITIONS

*Traceability* (3.5.4)—ability to trace the history, application or location of that which is under consideration

NOTE 1 When considering **product** (3.4.2), traceability can relate to
— the origin of materials and parts,
— the processing history, and
— the distribution and location of the product after delivery.

NOTE 2 In the field of metrology the definition in VIM:1993, 6.10, is the accepted definition.

*Source:* ANSI/ISO/ASQ Q9000-2005

## CONSIDERATIONS FOR DOCUMENTATION

Documentation considerations should include a documented procedure for maintaining identification and for control of product status. Where there are specific requirements for unique identity, the organization should consider preparing a documented procedure to describe how this is accomplished and recorded. This clause requires records of unique identification in cases where traceability is required.

> **7.5.4 Customer property**
>
> The organization shall exercise care with customer property while it is under the organization's control or being used by the organization. The organization shall identify, verify, protect and safeguard customer property provided for use or incorporation into the product. If any customer property is lost, damaged or otherwise found to be unsuitable for use, the organization shall report this to the customer and maintain records (see 4.2.4).
>
> NOTE Customer property can include intellectual property and personal data.

*Source:* ANSI/ISO/ASQ Q9001-2008

The requirements of this clause are essentially the same as in ISO 9001:2000. Very minor changes were made for clarity, readability, and presenting requirements in the active case. For example the previous "records maintained" now reads "maintain records."

Customer property is owned by the customer and furnished to the organization for use in meeting the requirements of the agreement between the two. Upon receipt of the property from the customer, the organization agrees to safeguard the property while it is in the organization's possession.

The requirements for the control of customer property include all property provided by the customer, including such items as tooling, information, test software, and shipping containers. It is fundamental that the customer will provide product that is acceptable for the purpose provided. However, if this is product that needs to be repaired, for example, it would need to be acceptable for repair. If not, the organization might return the product to the customer as not repairable. A contractual business relationship, written or understood, should deal with this situation.

The note makes it clear that information or other intellectual property is a type of customer property.

## IMPLEMENTATION TIPS AND TYPICAL QUESTIONS TO ASK FOR CONFORMITY

*For services,* this requirement entails a service provided by the organization to the customer. Repair of a piece of equipment requires clearly defining the responsibilities of both parties. An automotive repair shop must not damage a customer's car. On a much larger scale, shipowners contract for the repair of ships with private shipbuilders using owner-furnished equipment and owner-furnished material for a ship that often is to arrive at some future date. Equipment and material may be held in inventory before and after repairs are completed by the private shipbuilder. The storage and handling of supplied material must be considered.

*For hardware and processed material,* the organization should examine property received for identity, quantity, and damage. The property should be safeguarded and maintained. The organization may need to provide maintenance or use a maintenance contract with a third party. In such cases, the contractual agreements need to be clear as to responsibility.

*For software,* this clause can be a significant factor. An example is the case in which a customer provides source code to a contract programming organization for modification to incorporate additional features. The organization must exercise care in protecting the original functionality of the software. Detailed agreements typically define these relationships, including verification and validation requirements of the changes.

Questions to consider asking to assess conformity to this clause include:

- Has the organization identified, verified, protected, and maintained customer property that is provided for incorporation into the product?
- Does control extend to all customer property, including intellectual property?
- Does the organization have records that indicate when customer property has been lost, damaged, or otherwise found to be unsuitable?

- Is there evidence that when customer property has been lost, damaged, or otherwise found to be unsuitable that the customer has been informed? Are records maintained?

## DEFINITIONS

*Verification* (3.8.4)—confirmation, through the provision of **objective evidence** (3.8.1), that specified **requirements** (3.1.2) have been fulfilled

NOTE 1 The term "verified" is used to designate the corresponding status.

NOTE 2 Confirmation can comprise activities such as

—performing alternative calculations,

—comparing a new design **specification** (3.7.3) with a similar proven design specification,

—undertaking **tests** (3.8.3) and demonstrations, and

—reviewing documents prior to issue.

*Source:* ANSI/ISO/ASQ Q9000-2005

## CONSIDERATIONS FOR DOCUMENTATION

Whether or not a documented procedure is needed depends upon the nature of customer property, the control requirements (if any) laid out by the customer, and the nature and size of the organization. So, for example, it is not always necessary to have a documented procedure for the protection of confidential information provided verbally by a customer. Also, if the confidential information is provided in a few documents, it may not be necessary to have documented procedures if the organization is a small consulting firm with a single administrative assistant handling and storing all documents. If, on the other hand, the organization is a large corporation with many people potentially handling the documents, it may be appropriate to have documented procedures defining their control.

This clause requires records to be kept of customer property that is lost, damaged, or found to be unsuitable. The purpose for recording the loss, damage, or unsuitable condition is to report it to the customer. Organizations would be well advised to keep copies of these reports as controlled records.

**7.5.5 Preservation of product**

The organization shall preserve the product during internal processing and delivery to the intended destination in order to maintain conformity to requirements. As applicable, preservation shall include identification, handling, packaging, storage and protection. Preservation shall also apply to the constituent parts of a product.

*Source:* ANSI/ISO/ASQ Q9001-2008

The requirements of this clause are essentially the same as in ISO 9001:2000. A minor addition was made for clarity. The organization must safeguard and protect the product during and between all processing steps through to delivery. It should have a system for appropriately identifying, handling, packaging, storing, and delivering the product, including its components.

## IMPLEMENTATION TIPS AND TYPICAL QUESTIONS TO ASK FOR CONFORMITY

Marking and labeling should be readable, visually or by machine. Consideration should be given to documented procedures for segregating batches, stock rotation, and expiration dates. Packaging, containers, wraps, and pallets should be appropriate and durable for protecting the product from damage. Suitable storage facilities that include both physical security and protection from the environment should be provided. It may be necessary to check product periodically to detect deterioration. The organization should provide appropriate handling and transportation equipment, such as conveyors, vessels, tanks, pipelines, or vehicles to minimize harm due to handling or due to exposure to the environment.

*For services,* this clause can be viewed as an enhancement to the requirements of subclause 7.5.1. Examples include delivery of packages by air freight, trucking services, and food-delivery services.

Questions to consider asking to assess conformity to this clause include:

- Does the organization uniquely identify product during internal processing and delivery?
- Does the organization handle the product during internal processing and delivery so as to preserve conformity to customer requirements?
- Does the organization package the product during internal processing and delivery so as to preserve conformity to requirements?
- Does the organization store the product during internal processing and delivery so as to preserve conformity to requirements?
- Does the organization protect the product during internal processing and delivery so as to preserve conformity to requirements?

## DEFINITIONS

*Conformity* (3.6.1)—fulfilment of a **requirement** (3.1.2)

NOTE The term "conformance" is synonymous but deprecated.

*Source:* ANSI/ISO/ASQ Q9000-2005

## CONSIDERATIONS FOR DOCUMENTATION

Documentation considerations should include preparation of work instructions needed to ensure proper handling and preservation of product as appropriate.

## 7.6 Control of monitoring and measuring equipment

The organization shall determine the monitoring and measurement to be undertaken and the monitoring and measuring equipment needed to provide evidence of conformity of product to determined requirements.

The organization shall establish processes to ensure that monitoring and measurement can be carried out and are carried out in a manner that is consistent with the monitoring and measurement requirements.

Where necessary to ensure valid results, measuring equipment shall

a) be calibrated or verified, or both, at specified intervals, or prior to use, against measurement standards traceable to international or national measurement standards; where no such standards exist, the basis used for calibration or verification shall be recorded (see 4.2.4);

b) be adjusted or re-adjusted as necessary;

c) have identification in order to determine its calibration status;

d) be safeguarded from adjustments that would invalidate the measurement result;

e) be protected from damage and deterioration during handling, maintenance and storage.

In addition, the organization shall assess and record the validity of the previous measuring results when the equipment is found not to conform to requirements. The organization shall take appropriate action on the equipment and any product affected.

Records of the results of calibration and verification shall be maintained (see 4.2.4).

When used in the monitoring and measurement of specified requirements, the ability of computer software to satisfy the intended application shall be confirmed. This shall be undertaken prior to initial use and reconfirmed as necessary.

NOTE Confirmation of the ability of computer software to satisfy the intended application would typically include its verification and configuration management to maintain its suitability for use.

*Source:* ANSI/ISO/ASQ Q9001-2008

The requirements of this clause are essentially the same as in ISO 9001:2000. Minor changes to the text were made for clarity. The note in ISO 9001:2000 referring to ISO 10012-1 and ISO 10012-2 was removed because these standards were combined and revised as a single requirement standard, ISO 10012:2003, *Measurement management systems—Requirements for measurement processes and measuring equipment.* It no longer is appropriate generic guidance. The note in ISO 9001:2008 clarifies that when this clause applies to computer software, verification and configuration management need to be considered.

Measurements must be made to assure that product meets specifications. The necessary measurements need to be identified, along with any special instruments or monitoring and measurement devices needed for making them. This part of the standard is focused on assuring the quality of the measurements and of the monitoring and measurement devices. If the devices used to make measurements are not accurate, are unstable, are damaged in any way, or are inappropriate for making the measurement, then the product may not meet its requirements. Even worse, the organization will not know this. Monitoring and measurement devices need to be capable and their use needs to be controlled.

All monitoring and measurement instruments or equipment required to ensure the conformance of product to requirements fall within the scope of this clause.

Monitoring and measurement devices that are required to assure conformity of product need to be controlled. This includes devices used during design and development, those used for inspection and testing of raw materials, those used for in-process and final testing, and those used for monitoring quality once the product has been released to the customer.

The extent of the control to be exercised for the monitoring and measurement devices is listed in items a through e of clause 7.6. Although the concept of a measurement system is not specifically addressed in the standard, clause 7.6 provides the framework for the establishment and maintenance of a measurement system. When measuring equipment is found not to conform to requirements, the validity of any measurements made since it was last known to be in conformity needs to be investigated. Records of calibrations and verification measurements need to be kept.

## IMPLEMENTATION TIPS AND TYPICAL QUESTIONS TO ASK FOR CONFORMITY

This requirement encompasses two concepts: the concept of achieving and maintaining a stable measurement system (consistent performance) and the concept of achieving and maintaining a capable measurement system (measurement requirements must be met). Statistical methods may be useful for obtaining assurance that this requirement is met.

Software used in monitoring and measurement devices must be appropriate for the type of measurements to be made. This needs to be checked before initial use. Continuing suitability needs to be reconfirmed as necessary.

Questions to consider asking to assess conformity to this clause include:

- Has the organization identified the measurements to be made?
- Has the organization identified the monitoring and measurement devices required to ensure conformity of product to specified requirements?
- Are monitoring and measurement devices used to ensure measurement capability?
- Are monitoring and measurement devices calibrated and adjusted periodically or before use against devices traceable to international or national standards?
- Is the basis used for calibration recorded when traceability to international or national standards cannot be done, because no standards exist?
- Are monitoring and measurement devices safeguarded from adjustments that would invalidate the calibration?
- Are monitoring and measurement devices protected from damage and deterioration during handling, maintenance, and storage?
- Do monitoring and measurement devices have the results of their calibration recorded?
- Does the organization have the validity of previous results from monitoring and measurement devices reassessed if

they are subsequently found to be out of calibration? Is corrective action taken?

- Is the software used for monitoring and measurement of specified requirements confirmed as to its suitability before use?

## DEFINITIONS

*Measurement management system* (3.10.1)—set of interrelated and interacting elements necessary to achieve **metrological confirmation** (3.10.3) and continual control of **measurement processes** (3.10.2)

*Measuring equipment* (3.10.4)—measuring instrument, software, measurement standard, reference material or auxiliary apparatus or combination thereof necessary to realize a **measurement process** (3.10.2)

*Measurement process* (3.10.2)—set of operations to determine the value of a quantity

*Source:* ANSI/ISO/ASQ Q9000-2005

## CONSIDERATIONS FOR DOCUMENTATION

Documentation considerations should include a documented procedure for the control and calibration of monitoring and measurement devices. Work instructions should also be prepared for the actual work of performing the calibrations.

This clause requires records of calibration results with specific reference to clause 4.2.4 for control of the records generated.

# CHAPTER 9

# Measurement

## 8 Measurement, analysis and improvement

### 8.1 General

The organization shall plan and implement the monitoring, measurement, analysis and improvement processes needed

a) to demonstrate conformity to product requirements,

b) to ensure conformity of the quality management system, and

c) to continually improve the effectiveness of the quality management system.

This shall include determination of applicable methods, including statistical techniques, and the extent of their use.

*Source:* ANSI/ISO/ASQ Q9001-2008

The requirements and the text of this clause are essentially the same as contained in ISO 9001:2000. The only wording modification in ISO 9001:2008 is in 8.1.a), and it is intended to provide clarification. The change replaces "conformity of the product" to "conformity of the product to requirements" in clause 8.1.a).

The requirements of this clause apply to all product types (hardware, software, and services), to all market sectors, and to organizations of all sizes. Although this clause is only two sentences long, some feel that it is one of the most significant clauses in ISO 9001:2008. The other clauses of similar significance are clause 7.1 and clause 4.1. These three clauses contain the essential requirements for planning, developing, and deploying the process model to be used to address product realization, continual improvement, and customer satisfaction.

Clause 8.1 requires organizations to think about the processes used to achieve product realization and to assure that the necessary monitoring, measurement, analysis, and improvement activities are planned and implemented. It is the responsibility of the organization to decide what it needs to monitor and measure, where to monitor and measure, what analyses should be performed, and how the analysis of the data derived from monitoring and measurement should be used. It is worth repeating that the organization decides the "monitoring, measurement, analysis and improvement processes needed to demonstrate conformity of product, to ensure conformity of the quality management system and to continually improve the effectiveness of the quality management system." These decisions are not made by external auditors or consultants, or based on interpretations provided by external agencies (for example, by national bodies), or by relying on the contents of this book. They are made by the organization based on the objectives and needs of the organization. Herein lies the challenge of ISO 9001:2008. The organization must take ownership of monitoring and measurement of its processes to the extent needed to effectively manage conformity of its products, conformity to the requirements of its QMS, and to drive improvement.

Regarding the requirement for determining applicable methodologies, including statistical techniques and the extent of their use, the intent of the standard is to make clear that the use of statistical techniques is a stated requirement.

## IMPLEMENTATION TIPS AND TYPICAL QUESTIONS TO ASK FOR CONFORMITY

One approach that has proven to be effective and efficient for addressing the requirements of clause 8.1 is to first ensure that the key processes required for product realization, support, and improvement are identified as required by clause 4.1. Then, for each key process the inputs to and outputs from the process can be defined. Once the outputs of key processes are defined and understood, it is possible to contemplate the options for measuring the outputs and to implement the most favorable option to ensure that the outputs meet requirements. While considering outputs and how to measure them, it is advisable to also consider any records that may be required as objective evidence of conformity to requirements.

Such an approach can be implemented using a template consisting of a 3x2 matrix of blocks. The upper left block can be used for listing the process inputs, the top middle block for listing the activity characteristics, and the upper right block for listing the process outputs. The lower left block can be used for listing the interfaces with the activity being analyzed, the lower middle block for listing the records required, and the lower right block for listing the metrics to be used to ensure that the output meets requirements.

A simplified example of such a template completed for the corrective action process could look as follows:

| **Inputs**<br>Undesirable process or condition<br>Customer complaint | **Process**<br>Review request<br>Proceed with corrective action<br>If yes, develop CA plan<br>Implement plan<br>Check effectiveness | **Outputs**<br>Implemented CA<br>Documentation to management review file |
|---|---|---|
| **Interactions**<br>Depends on CA; could be purchasing department, design engineering, training department, etc. | **Records**<br>CA plan<br>CA effectiveness | **Metrics**<br>CA log<br>CA closeout<br>Time to close out the CA |

The planning and implementing of monitoring, measurement, analysis, and improvement processes can be accomplished by any means the organization chooses. We have found that having a model and a defined approach for addressing these requirements ensures appropriate attention especially to the planning of the monitoring, measurement, analysis, and improvement processes. The completion of a matrix as described above for key processes is one approach that ensures that we are addressing the requirements of this clause.

Questions to consider asking to assess conformity to clause 8.1 include:

- Is objective evidence available to demonstrate that the organization has defined, planned, and implemented the monitoring and measurement activities needed to ensure conformity and to achieve improvement?

- Is objective evidence available to demonstrate that the organization has determined the need for and use of applicable methodologies, including statistical techniques?

## DEFINITIONS

*Conformity* (3.6.1)—fulfilment of a **requirement** (3.1.2)

NOTE The term "conformance" is synonymous but deprecated.

*Source:* ANSI/ISO/ASQ Q9000-2005

## CONSIDERATIONS FOR DOCUMENTATION

No specific documentation is advised or necessary to address the requirements of this clause.

### 8.2 Monitoring and measurement

#### 8.2.1 Customer satisfaction

As one of the measurements of the performance of the quality management system, the organization shall monitor information relating to customer perception as to whether the organization has met customer requirements. The methods for obtaining and using this information shall be determined.

NOTE Monitoring customer perception can include obtaining input from sources such as customer satisfaction surveys, customer data on delivered product quality, user opinion surveys, lost business analysis, compliments, warranty claims and dealer reports.

*Source:* ANSI/ISO/ASQ Q9001-2008

The requirement of this clause is identical to ISO 9001:2000. The note has been added to enhance clarity.

An often-voiced early criticism of ISO 9001 subsequent to its initial release was that it focused on paper and written procedures rather than on ensuring the delivery of products that would address customer satisfaction by meeting customer requirements. A primary thrust of ISO 9001:2000 was to increase the emphasis on customer satisfaction, which should be a primary reason for the existence of most organizations. Increased emphasis on customer satisfaction was explicitly and clearly identified as a marketplace need in the market research that was performed by ISO before the development of ISO 9001:2000.

During the development of ISO 9001:2000, the issue of how to address customer satisfaction was hotly debated. Many wanted very aggressive measures as requirements. Others wanted no reference to customer satisfaction, in spite of the "voice of the customer." In addition, the auditability of "soft requirements" was a concern. The final resolution of these conflicting viewpoints was language that requires the organization to "monitor information relating to customer perception as to whether the organization has met customer requirements."

## IMPLEMENTATION TIPS AND TYPICAL QUESTIONS TO ASK FOR CONFORMITY

In ISO 9001:2008 the requirements contained in this clause have remained essentially unchanged. Only a note has been added to offer guidance on approaches that can be considered to monitor customer perception, because the approaches that an organization may use to comply with this requirement are not defined. In ISO 9001:2008 it is still the organization's responsibility to decide what customer perception information it will monitor and measure. For example, organizations that function in regulated markets may choose to monitor customer reports of product deficiencies. A large automobile manufacturer might measure customer satisfaction as reflected in surveys mailed to owners of new cars. Service providers may choose to use focus groups to probe customers' perceptions. Software suppliers could monitor reported bugs from field installations. The important point is that the organization decides what to monitor and what methods to use.

It is worthwhile to recognize the order of "monitoring and measurement." Previous drafts of ISO 9001:2000 presented these action verbs in the order "measure and monitor." Now the order of these terms is reversed. Monitoring usually provides less information than measuring. The results of monitoring may indicate a need to gather more information through measuring. An organization might monitor or measure or do both for similar types of data.

A few examples of sources of customer satisfaction information that could be used to meet the requirements of this clause include the following:

- Customer complaints
- Returns
- Warranty information
- Customer-satisfaction studies
- Results from focus group meetings
- Customer tracking studies
- Questionnaires and surveys
- Reports from consumer organizations
- Direct customer communication
- Benchmarking data
- Industry group information
- Trade association information

Although many sources of information about customer satisfaction and dissatisfaction are typically available, this information is often poorly organized and even more poorly used. This requirement of the standard should encourage organizations to better use the "gold mine" of information readily available to them.

The organization also must decide the extent to which its processes go beyond mere conformance to requirements to meet the unstated needs and expectations of customers. This should include price and delivery considerations. It is up to the organization to decide how far to go in this direction, which should be related to the organization's quality policy and objectives.

The standard takes one additional step in the area of customer satisfaction—it includes a requirement that the methods for obtaining and using customer information must be determined. This means that the organization must think about how to gather information and what will be done with the information after it is gathered. Many organizations gather information, and some make an effort to understand what the information means, but few actually do something to improve the organization and its processes. The intent of the standard is to encourage organizations to plan what to gather, to gather the information, to analyze and understand it, and to take appropriate action.

For regulated products such as medical devices, this involves, at a minimum, the evaluation of product use or misuse and the evaluation of customer complaints.

Questions to consider asking to assess conformity to this clause include:

- Is customer satisfaction information monitored?
- Are methods for gathering and using customer information determined and deployed throughout the organization?
- Is our process really effective for monitoring information relating to customer perception as to whether the organization has met or is meeting customer requirements?

## DEFINITIONS

*Conformity* (3.6.1)—fulfilment of a **requirement** (3.1.2)

NOTE The term "conformance" is synonymous but deprecated.

*Measurement process* (3.10.2)—set of operations to determine the value of a quantity

*Source:* ANSI/ISO/ASQ Q9000-2005

## CONSIDERATIONS FOR DOCUMENTATION

While no specific documented procedure is needed to address this clause, several processes may be needed to address the requirements for customer-satisfaction measurement. Consideration should be given to documentation of what customer information should be gathered, who should gather it, how often it should be gathered, in what form it should be gathered, who will analyze the information, and what will be done with the results of the analysis.

**8.2.2 Internal audit**

The organization shall conduct internal audits at planned intervals to determine whether the quality management system

a) conforms to the planned arrangements (see 7.1), to the requirements of this International Standard and to the quality management system requirements established by the organization, and

b) is effectively implemented and maintained.

An audit programme shall be planned, taking into consideration the status and importance of the processes and areas to be audited, as well as the results of previous audits. The audit criteria, scope, frequency and methods shall be defined. The selection of auditors and conduct of audits shall ensure objectivity and impartiality of the audit process. Auditors shall not audit their own work.

A documented procedure shall be established to define the responsibilities and requirements for planning and conducting audits, establishing records and reporting results.

Records of the audits and their results shall be maintained (see 4.2.4).

The management responsible for the area being audited shall ensure that any necessary corrections and corrective actions are taken without undue delay to eliminate detected nonconformities and their causes. Follow-up activities shall include the verification of the actions taken and the reporting of verification results (see 8.5.2).

NOTE See ISO 19011 for guidance.

*Source:* ANSI/ISO/ASQ Q9001-2008

There have been modest changes to clause 8.2.2 in ISO 9001:2008, but these changes do not alter requirements or intent. They clarify, provide emphasis, or indicate a changed reference (ISO 19011 is referenced in the note vs. ISO 10011–1, 2, 3 in ISO 9001:2000 document).

Paragraph 4 of ISO 9001:2000 has been deleted and replaced with a new paragraph that clearly indicates the requirement for a documented procedure. Although this requirement was clear before, it is perhaps more clear in the ISO 9001:2008 wording. Sometimes standards writers seem to focus on distinctions that may not really be differences.

Also there are new words related to records (". . . Records of the audits and their results shall be maintained . . ."). It is not really a new requirement but rather an emphasis on the need to maintain audit records.

Internal audit of the quality management system remains grouped with clauses for monitoring information relating to customer perception as to whether the organization has met customer requirements and to monitoring and measurement of processes and product. The message of the placement of this requirement in the standard should be clear, but it deserves emphasis—the internal audit process is a form of measurement specifically focused on the quality management system and the products of the organization. It should be deployed to drive improvement of product realization and of the ability of the organization to meet customer expectations.

## IMPLEMENTATION TIPS AND TYPICAL QUESTIONS TO ASK FOR CONFORMITY

Even as we recognize internal audit of the quality management system as a form of measurement, it continues to be an essential process to provide confidence in the effective implementation of the quality management system. To better understand the role of internal audit, it is useful to consider its role as complementary to that of two other forms of quality management system evaluation—management review and self-assessment.

The evaluation of a quality management system can vary in scope, and it typically encompasses the following three major approaches:

- Auditing, an aspect of which is the subject of this section, ISO 9001:2008, clause 8.2.2, *Internal audit*.

- Reviewing the quality management system, the subject of ISO 9001:2008, clause 5.6, *Management review.*
- Self-assessment is also addressed in the text and an Annex in ISO 9004.

Audits are used to evaluate the adequacy of quality management system documentation, conformance to quality management system requirements, and the effectiveness of system implementation. The results of audits can be used to identify opportunities for improvement. ISO 9001:2008 continues to require auditors to determine the effectiveness of implementation. Determination of overall system suitability and effectiveness is left to top management, who use audit results and other data to make that evaluation.

In auditing language, internal audits are considered to be first-party audits—audits conducted by or on behalf of the organization for internal purposes that, incidentally, can form the basis for an organization's self-declaration of conformity. Second-party audits are conducted by customers of the organization or by other persons on behalf of a customer. Third-party audits are conducted by external independent audit service organizations (e.g., a registrar). Registrars can verify conformity with the requirements of ISO 9001:2008. See the formal definitions below for a description of these audit types.

One role of top management is to carry out regular, systematic evaluations of the suitability, adequacy, effectiveness, and efficiency of the quality management system with respect to the quality policy and objectives. This review (see ISO 9001:2008, clause 5.6) can include consideration of the need to adapt the quality policy and objectives in response to the changing needs and expectations of interested parties. The review includes determination of the need for actions. Among other sources of information, audit reports are used for management review of the quality management system.

An organization's self-assessment is a comprehensive and planned review of the organization's activities and results referenced against the quality management system or a model of excellence. The use of self-assessment methodology can provide an overall view of the performance of the organization and the degree of maturity of the quality management system. It can also help identify areas requiring improvement in the organization and to determine priorities. Such self-assessments typically go beyond auditing to assess conformance to requirements. They look for opportunities for the organization to improve its efficiency and performance and may even consciously attempt to identify best practices that may be portable to other areas of the organization. A robust self-assessment process is a valuable companion to the internal audit process of an organization

ISO 9001:2008 requires internal quality audits to be conducted periodically. These audits should be used to determine conformity to the requirements of ISO 9001:2008 and the degree to which the quality management system has been effectively implemented and maintained. An indicator of problems with the effectiveness of the quality management system is the occurrence of high numbers of customer complaints or of high levels of scrap and rework within the organization. As stated in clause 8.2.1, organizations are expected to monitor customers' perceptions. Internal auditors often use this information to identify product realization processes that require further investigation regarding the extent to which they have been effectively implemented and maintained. In a similar fashion, scrap and rework information may be of value for identifying subject areas for internal audits.

Whatever factors and methods are used, internal quality audits may be performed on processes of the quality management system or on the entire system. Whatever approach is used, details need to be established in plans, and quality system processes should be investigated in order of their priority. Previous audit results should be used in developing the prioritization. The scope of each audit should be clear, and the frequency of audits within the audit program and the audit methodology should be identified.

One aspect of internal auditing that is frequently underaddressed is the competence of internal auditors. Just because an individual is a subject matter expert does not mean that such an individual will be a competent internal auditor. Internal auditors should be qualified as auditors. This is particularly necessary for "guest" auditors or technical experts from other functions who are used to provide product or process technical expertise to the effort to evaluate effectiveness but who tend to be inexperienced at auditing. As is true about all work that is performed by an organization, those that perform the work are required to be competent. One approach to ensuring competence of internal auditors is to establish minimum requirements in terms of training and/or experience and/or working with experienced auditors until competence has been demonstrated by some method or combination of methods to a member of management.

Audit results should be documented in a written report, and records should indicate deficiencies. Target dates should be established for responding to audit findings and organizations should take timely corrective action. Audit results are required to be inputs to management reviews. It is also helpful if audit reports also indicate opportunities for improvement and best practices observed.

Follow-up actions should be evaluated to assure the effectiveness of the corrective actions.

☑ Questions to consider asking to assess conformity to this clause include:

- Does the organization conduct periodic audits of the quality management system?
- Do the periodic audits evaluate the conformity of the quality management system to the requirements of ISO 9001:2008?
- Do the periodic audits evaluate the degree to which the quality management system has been effectively implemented and maintained?
- Does the organization plan the audit program taking into consideration the status and importance of areas to be audited?
- Does the organization plan the audit program taking into consideration the results of previous audits?
- Are the audit scope, frequency, and methodologies defined?
- Does the audit process and auditor assignment ensure objectivity and impartiality?
- Is there a documented procedure that includes the responsibilities and requirements for conducting audits?

- Is there a documented procedure that describes how to ensure the independence of auditors?
- Is there a documented procedure for reporting results and maintaining records?
- Is timely corrective action taken on deficiencies found during the audit?
- Is the process identified and appropriately described?
- Are process output requirements clearly defined?
- Are responsibilities assigned?
- Are personnel competent?
- Are required processes implemented and maintained?
- Are the metrics of process performance adequate to determine if the process output is conforming to requirements?
- Is objective evidence available to demonstrate conformity to requirements (i.e. records)?
- Are the interfaces to other processes understood?
- Is the process effective in achieving the required results?

The collective answers to these questions can be very helpful to the auditor who is evaluating whether the process meets requirements and is planned and operating under controlled conditions.

## DEFINITIONS

*Audit* (3.9.1)—systematic, independent and documented **process** (3.4.1) for obtaining **audit evidence** (3.9.4) and evaluating it objectively to determine the extent to which **audit criteria** (3.9.3) are fulfilled

NOTE 1 Internal audits, sometimes called first-party audits, are conducted by, or on behalf of, the **organization** (3.3.1) itself for management review and other internal purposes, and may form the basis for an organization's declaration of **conformity** (3.6.1). In many cases, particularly in smaller organizations, independence can be demonstrated by the freedom from responsibility for the activity being audited.

NOTE 2 External audits include those generally termed second- and third-party audits. Second-party audits are conducted by parties having an interest in the organization, such as **customers** (3.3.5), or by other persons on their behalf. Third-party audits are conducted by external, independent auditing organizations, such as those providing certification/registration of conformity to ISO 9001 or ISO 14001.

NOTE 3 When two or more **management systems** (3.2.2) are audited together, this is termed a combined audit.

NOTE 4 When two or more auditing organizations cooperate to audit a single **auditee** (3.9.8), this is termed a joint audit.

*Audit client* (3.9.7)—**organization** (3.3.1) or person requesting an **audit** (3.9.1)

NOTE The audit client may be the **auditee** (3.9.8) or any other **organization** (3.3.1) that has the regulatory or contractual right to request an audit

*Audit conclusion* (3.9.6)—outcome of an **audit** (3.9.1) provided by the **audit team** (3.9.10) after consideration of the audit objectives and all **audit findings** (3.9.5)

*Audit criteria* (3.9.3)—set of policies, **procedures** (3.4.5) or **requirements** (3.1.2)

NOTE Audit criteria are used as a reference against which **audit evidence** (3.9.4) is compared.

*Auditee* (3.9.8)—**organization** (3.3.1) being audited

*Audit evidence* (3.9.4)—**records** (3.7.6), statements of fact or other **information** (3.7.1) which are relevant to the **audit criteria** (3.9.3) and verifiable

NOTE Audit evidence can be qualitative or quantitative.

*Audit findings* (3.9.5)—results of the evaluation of the collected **audit evidence** (3.9.4) against **audit criteria** (3.9.3)

NOTE Audit findings can indicate either **conformity** (3.6.1) or **nonconformity** (3.6.2) with audit criteria or opportunities for improvement.

*Audit programme* (3.9.2)—set of one or more **audits** (3.9.1) planned for a specific time frame and directed towards a specific purpose

NOTE An audit programme includes all activities necessary for planning, organizing and conducting the audits.

*Auditor* (3.9.9)—person with the demonstrated personal attributes and **competence** (3.1.6 and 3.9.14) to conduct an **audit** (3.9.1)

NOTE The relevant personal attributes for an auditor are described in ISO 19011.

*Corrective action* (3.6.5)—action to eliminate the cause of a detected **nonconformity** (3.6.2) or other undesirable situation

NOTE 1 There can be more than one cause for a nonconformity.

NOTE 2 Corrective action is taken to prevent recurrence whereas **preventive action** (3.6.4) is taken to prevent occurrence.

NOTE 3 There is a distinction between **correction** (3.6.6) and corrective action.

*Management* (3.2.6)—coordinated activities to direct and control an **organization** (3.3.1)

NOTE In English, the term "management" sometimes refers to people, i.e. a person or group of people with authority and responsibility for the conduct and control of an organization. When "management" is used in this sense, it should always be used with some form of qualifier to avoid confusion with the concept "management" defined above. For example, "management shall . . . " is deprecated whereas "**top management** (3.2.7) shall . . . " is acceptable.

*Procedure* (3.4.5)—specified way to carry out an activity or a **process** (3.4.1)

NOTE 1 Procedures can be documented or not.

NOTE 2 When a procedure is documented, the term "written procedure" or "documented procedure" is frequently used. The **document** (3.7.2) that contains a procedure can be called a "procedure document".

*Record* (3.7.6)—**document** (3.7.2) stating results achieved or providing evidence of activities performed

NOTE 1 Records can be used, for example, to document **traceability** (3.5.4) and to provide evidence of **verification** (3.8.4), **preventive action** (3.6.4) and **corrective action** (3.6.5).

NOTE 2 Generally records need not be under revision control.

*Technical expert* (3.9.11)—⟨audit⟩ person who provides specific knowledge or expertise to the **audit team** (3.9.10)

NOTE 1 Specific knowledge or expertise relates to the **organization** (3.3.1), the **process** (3.4.1) or activity to be audited, or language or culture.

NOTE 2 A technical expert does not act as an **auditor** (3.9.9) in the audit team.

*Verification* (3.8.4)—confirmation, through the provision of **objective evidence** (3.8.1), that specified **requirements** (3.1.2) have been fulfilled

NOTE 1 The term "verified" is used to designate the corresponding status.

NOTE 2 Confirmation can comprise activities such as

—performing alternative calculations,

—comparing a new design **specification** (3.7.3) with a similar proven design specification,

—undertaking **tests** (3.8.3) and demonstrations, and

—reviewing documents prior to issue.

*Source:* ANSI/ISO/ASQ Q9000-2005

## CONSIDERATIONS FOR DOCUMENTATION

A documented procedure is required that describes the responsibilities and requirements for planning and conducting audits, establishing records, and reporting results.

This clause does not require any specific records, only that they be maintained (see also 4.2.4). It would usually be expected of the organization to have records of audit plans and descriptions of audits, including their scope, frequency, and methodologies used. Records should be available to provide evidence that audit findings were reported (e.g., an audit report) and that there was timely corrective action on deficiencies found during the audit. There should also be records that verification was performed for the implementation of corrective action and that the verification results were reported.

> **8.2.3 Monitoring and measurement of processes**
>
> The organization shall apply suitable methods for monitoring and, where applicable, measurement of the quality management system processes. These methods shall demonstrate the ability of the processes to achieve planned results. When planned results are not achieved, correction and corrective action shall be taken, as appropriate.
>
> NOTE When determining suitable methods, it is advisable that the organization consider the type and extent of monitoring or measurement appropriate to each of its processes in relation to their impact on the conformity to product requirements and on the effectiveness of the quality management system.

*Source:* ANSI/ISO/ASQ Q9001-2008

Clause 8.2.3 contains no new requirements. The only changes from ISO 9001:2000 were to delete the words "to ensure conformity of the product" from the last sentence of the first paragraph. Also, a note was added to clarify what to consider when determining what suitable methods to apply.

The monitoring and measurement activities of ISO 9001:2008 apply to all relevant processes of the quality management system, not just those that deal with product realization.

## IMPLEMENTATION TIPS AND TYPICAL QUESTIONS TO ASK FOR CONFORMITY

This clause contains broad requirements. Each organization must determine, plan, and implement the monitoring and measurement activities needed to achieve the planned results of all quality management system processes. This includes, as appropriate, the processes of management responsibility, the resource processes, the measurement and improvement processes, and the product realization processes.

Realistically, not all processes or all process parameters can be monitored or measured. The number of even the most basic processes and process parameters that are candidates for monitoring can be overwhelming. Clause 8.4, *Analysis of data,* of ISO 9001:2008 can be a source of information in identifying the key processes to monitor. Data from capability studies commonly are used to help determine what processes have high inherent variation and require tight control versus processes that are both capable and relatively stable. It may also be useful to use data from capability studies, where they are available, to help determine which processes have high inherent variation and require tight control versus what processes are both capable and relatively stable.

Also remember that clause 8.2.3 links to 8.5.2, *Corrective action*. When process monitoring or measurements indicate that the desired results are not being achieved, the process may need correction or corrective action to identify and eliminate root causes.

Questions to consider asking to assess conformity to this clause include:

- Have the key quality management system processes, especially the product realization processes, needed to meet planned results been identified?
- Are suitable methods used to measure and monitor these key processes?
- Are the intended purposes of the key processes quantified by process parameter specifications, by specifications for the product output of the process, or by some other means?

- Are the monitoring and measurement methods for processes of the quality management system adequate for confirming the continuing suitability of each process to satisfy its intended purpose and achieve its planned result?

## DEFINITIONS

*Measurement process* (3.10.2)—set of operations to determine the value of a quantity

*Process* (3.4.1)—set of interrelated or interacting activities which transforms inputs into outputs

NOTE 1 Inputs to a process are generally outputs of other processes.

NOTE 2 Processes in an **organization** (3.3.1) are generally planned and carried out under controlled conditions to add value.

NOTE 3 A process where the **conformity** (3.6.1) of the resulting **product** (3.4.2) cannot be readily or economically verified is frequently referred to as a "special process".

*Record* (3.7.6)—**document** (3.7.2) stating results achieved or providing evidence of activities performed

NOTE 1 Records can be used, for example, to document **traceability** (3.5.4) and to provide evidence of **verification** (3.8.4), **preventive action** (3.6.4) and **corrective action** (3.6.5).

NOTE 2 Generally records need not be under revision control.

*Requirement* (3.1.2)—need or expectation that is stated, generally implied or obligatory

NOTE 1 "Generally implied" means that it is custom or common practice for the **organization** (3.3.1), its **customers** (3.3.5) and other **interested parties** (3.3.7), that the need or expectation under consideration is implied.

NOTE 2 A qualifier can be used to denote a specific type of requirement, e.g. product requirement, quality management requirement, customer requirement.

NOTE 3 A specified requirement is one that is stated, for example in a **document** (3.7.2).

NOTE 4 Requirements can be generated by different **interested parties** (3.3.7).

NOTE 5 This definition differs from that provided in 3.12.1 of ISO/IEC Directives, Part 2:2004.

> **3.12.1**
> **requirement**
> expression in the content of a document conveying criteria to be fulfilled if compliance with the document is to be claimed and from which no deviation is permitted

*Source:* ANSI/ISO/ASQ Q9000-2005

## CONSIDERATIONS FOR DOCUMENTATION

Objective evidence confirming the effective operation and control of processes needs to be available. This will vary depending upon the size and type of organization, the complexity and interaction of processes, and the competence of personnel. Objective evidence may be in the form of procedures and records, particularly where manual measurement processes are used. This may be demonstrated through observation of these monitoring and measurement processes, particularly when online sensors and electromechanical, closed-loop feedback systems are employed.

> **8.2.4 Monitoring and measurement of product**
>
> The organization shall monitor and measure the characteristics of the product to verify that product requirements have been met. This shall be carried out at appropriate stages of the product realization process in accordance with the planned arrangements (see 7.1). Evidence of conformity with the acceptance criteria shall be maintained.
>
> Records shall indicate the person(s) authorizing release of product for delivery to the customer (see 4.2.4).
>
> The release of product and delivery of service to the customer shall not proceed until the planned arrangements (see 7.1) have been satisfactorily completed, unless otherwise approved by a relevant authority and, where applicable, by the customer.

*Source:* ANSI/ISO/ASQ Q9001-2008

The requirements of ISO 9001:2000 for monitoring and measuring product have not significantly changed. The requirements for monitoring and measuring of product, whether they are for software, hardware, processed material, or a service, are stated in this generic clause. The text in the third paragraph was modified to clarify that the requirements of this clause refer only to final delivery.

## IMPLEMENTATION TIPS AND TYPICAL QUESTIONS TO ASK FOR CONFORMITY

The scope of this clause includes all measurement activities associated with materials, components, assemblies, and product from receiving inspection to product delivery. It covers the actual measurements used to verify that requirements are met for the materials that go into the product as well as the product itself at appropriate stages of the product-realization process.

Compliance with the requirements of this clause often needs to involve people working in several areas in the organization, including test engineers, design engineers, production engineers, and quality engineers as well as individuals in support operations such as purchasing.

For purchased material, clause 7.4.3, *Verification of purchased product,* requires the organization to identify and implement verification activities. The requirements for the associated measures are contained in clause 8.2.4, *Monitoring and measurement of product.* For in-process and final product, clause 7.5.1, *Operations control,* requires the organization to implement defined processes for monitoring, measurement, release, and delivery. And issues relating to monitoring and measuring of product are often of high interest during design review for a product or process.

Conformity to requirements needs to be documented. Records need to indicate who within the organization has the authority to release final product. Analysis of the data for release and also for improvement is detailed in clause 8.4, *Analysis of data.* This includes the use of applicable methodologies, including statistical techniques (see clause 8.1) to determine the type of data to collect and the decision rules for release.

Product release and service delivery require that all specified activities be accomplished unless release is otherwise approved by a relevant authority or by the customer. This usually means that some form of record should be available to document that specified activities have been accomplished.

Questions to consider asking to assess conformity to this clause include:

- Does the organization measure and monitor product characteristics to verify that product requirements are met?
- Does the organization measure and monitor product characteristics at appropriate stages of the product realization process?
- Is there objective evidence that acceptance criteria for product have been met?
- Do records identify the person authorizing release of the product?
- Are all specified activities performed before product release and service delivery?
- If there are instances in which all specified activities have not been performed before product release or service delivery, has a relevant authority, or as appropriate the customer, been informed and approved of the action?

## DEFINITIONS

*Characteristic* (3.5.1)—distinguishing feature

NOTE 1 A characteristic can be inherent or assigned.

NOTE 2 A characteristic can be qualitative or quantitative.

NOTE 3 There are various classes of characteristic, such as the following:
—physical (e.g. mechanical, electrical, chemical or biological characteristics);
—sensory (e.g. related to smell, touch, taste, sight, hearing);
—behavioral (e.g. courtesy, honesty, veracity);
—temporal (e.g. punctuality, reliability, availability);
—ergonomic (e.g. physiological characteristic, or related to human safety);
—functional (e.g. maximum speed of an aircraft).

*Measurement process* (3.10.2)—set of operations to determine the value of a quantity

*Objective evidence* (3.8.1)—data supporting the existence or verity of something

NOTE Objective evidence may be obtained through observation, measurement, **test** (3.8.3), or other means.

*Product* (3.4.2)—result of a **process** (3.4.1)

NOTE 1 There are four generic product categories, as follows:

—services (e.g. transport);

—software (e.g. computer program, dictionary);

—hardware (e.g. engine mechanical part);

—processed materials (e.g. lubricant).

Many products comprise elements belonging to different generic product categories. Whether the product is then called service, software, hardware or processed material depends on the dominant element. For example, the offered product "automobile" consists of hardware (e.g. tyres), processed materials (e.g. fuel, cooling liquid), software (e.g. engine control software, driver's manual), and service (e.g. operating explanations given by the salesman).

NOTE 2 Service is the result of at least one activity necessarily performed at the interface between the **supplier** (3.3.6) and **customer** (3.3.5) and is generally intangible. Provision of a service can involve, for example, the following:

—an activity performed on a customer-supplied tangible product (e.g. automobile to be repaired);

—an activity performed on a customer-supplied intangible product (e.g. the income statement needed to prepare a tax return);

—the delivery of an intangible product (e.g. the delivery of information in the context of knowledge transmission);

—the creation of ambience for the customer (e.g. in hotels and restaurants).

Software consists of information and is generally intangible and can be in the form of approaches, transactions or **procedures** (3.4.5).

Hardware is generally tangible and its amount is a countable **characteristic** (3.5.1). Processed materials are generally tangible and their amount is a continuous characteristic. Hardware and processed materials often are referred to as goods.

NOTE 3 **Quality assurance** (3.2.11) is mainly focused on intended product.

*Quality characteristic* (3.5.2)—inherent **characteristic** (3.5.1) of a **product** (3.4.2), **process** (3.4.1) or **system** (3.2.1) related to a **requirement** (3.1.2)

NOTE 1 Inherent means existing in something, especially as a permanent characteristic.

NOTE 2 A characteristic assigned to a product, process or system (e.g. the price of a product, the owner of a product) is not a quality characteristic of that product, process or system.

*Requirement* (3.1.2)—need or expectation that is stated, generally implied or obligatory

NOTE 1 "Generally implied" means that it is custom or common practice for the **organization** (3.3.1), its **customers** (3.3.5) and other **interested**

**parties** (3.3.7), that the need or expectation under consideration is implied.

NOTE 2 A qualifier can be used to denote a specific type of requirement, e.g. product requirement, quality management requirement, customer requirement.

NOTE 3 A specified requirement is one that is stated, for example in a **document** (3.7.2).

NOTE 4 Requirements can be generated by different **interested parties** (3.3.7).

NOTE 5 This definition differs from that provided in 3.12.1 of ISO/IEC Directives, Part 2:2004.

**3.12.1**
**requirement**
expression in the content of a document conveying criteria to be fulfilled if compliance with the document is to be claimed and from which no deviation is permitted

*Source:* ANSI/ISO/ASQ Q9000-2005

## CONSIDERATIONS FOR DOCUMENTATION

Consideration should be given to the work instructions needed to ensure that measurement of product is conducted as planned. Records are required to provide objective evidence that the product acceptance criteria have been met. They should also indicate the authority responsible for release of the product. This clause contains specific reference to clause 5.5.7 for control of the records generated.

# CHAPTER 10

# Control of Nonconforming Product

> **8.3 Control of nonconforming product**
>
> The organization shall ensure that product which does not conform to product requirements is identified and controlled to prevent its unintended use or delivery. A documented procedure shall be established to define the controls and related responsibilities and authorities for dealing with nonconforming product.
>
> Where applicable, the organization shall deal with nonconforming product by one or more of the following ways:
>
> a) by taking action to eliminate the detected nonconformity;
>
> b) by authorizing its use, release or acceptance under concession by a relevant authority and, where applicable, by the customer;
>
> c) by taking action to preclude its original intended use or application;
>
> d) by taking action appropriate to the effects, or potential effects, of the nonconformity when nonconforming product is detected after delivery or use has started.
>
> When nonconforming product is corrected it shall be subject to re-verification to demonstrate conformity to the requirements.
>
> Records of the nature of nonconformities and any subsequent actions taken, including concessions obtained, shall be maintained (see 4.2.4).

*Source:* ANSI/ISO/ASQ Q9001-2008

The essence of these requirements, and in fact even the title of the clause, have been included in ISO 9001 since the initial release in 1987. The intent was, from the beginning, to prevent inadvertent use or instillation of nonconforming product. Many old-timers will remember Material Review Boards that were frequently convened to handle the disposition of nonconforming material. As our organizations have migrated to more service-oriented products, some of the relevance of this clause has been diminished, although the intent is still applicable to hardware. For example, how does an organization control the delivery of a nonconforming service? Often this is not possible.

The only changes from the ISO 9001:2000 edition relate to modest rewording in the first paragraph to provide clarity that a documented procedure is required, addition of the words "Where applicable" at the beginning of the second paragraph to recognize that it is not always possible to deal with nonconforming product (see comments above), changing the order of paragraphs 3 and 4 to enhance clarity (no change in the words) and deletion of the last paragraph of the ISO 9001:2000 edition while inserting the essence of this text into item d of the clause.

The specific requirements of this clause include establishing processes to ensure that product that does not conform to requirements is identified and controlled to prevent unintended use or delivery. These activities shall be defined in a documented procedure.

Also the organization needs to ensure that nonconforming product is corrected and subject to reverification after correction to demonstrate conformity, where applicable.

Finally, when nonconforming product is detected after delivery or use has started, the organization needs to address how it will take appropriate action regarding the consequences of the nonconformity.

It will often be required that the proposed rectification of nonconforming product be reported for concession to the customer, the end user, regulatory body, or other body.

## IMPLEMENTATION TIPS AND TYPICAL QUESTIONS TO ASK FOR CONFORMITY

A primary requirement of clause 8.3 is to ensure the effective implementation of processes that prevent unintended use or delivery of product that does not conform to requirements. This is a simple requirement that makes business sense. The challenge to an organization is to devise processes to accomplish this objective in a way that encourages personnel to address nonconformity of product rather than to find ways to avoid identification and control of such product.

This clause also requires the organization to take appropriate action when the organization delivers product that is subsequently determined to be nonconforming. Records of such action should be maintained, if only to document the use of prudent judgment in addressing such situations. And finally, when it is required (for example, by contract or by internal procedures) to report a proposed rectification of nonconforming product to the customer, the end user, a regulatory body, or any other body, the organization should have processes in place to ensure that such reporting to the customer occurs.

Typically, organizations will establish processes that provide for review of nonconformity by appropriate individuals in the organization. Such processes may have different levels of approval depending on the nature of the decision regarding the action to be taken for the nonconformity. A decision to "use as is," for example, may require engineering approval, because such a decision is effectively a "change in design" with liability implications, while manufacturing management may be permitted to approve a rework or scrap disposition.

Note that the second and third paragraphs of this clause require that, where applicable, all nonconforming products be corrected and that when corrections are made, the organization must reverify the product to demonstrate conformity. There are frequently circumstances where organizations will not correct nonconforming product. Products that meet functional requirements are often used "as is," without taking action to make the product fully conform with all requirements, especially if such a decision will not affect the conformance of the end product ultimately delivered to a customer. Also, nonconforming product may be scrapped or regraded, or for purchased material, it may be returned to a supplier.

For *service,* the clause only subtly recognizes the fact that nonconforming service often cannot be controlled. If a bank has a requirement that tellers be courteous to all customers and a teller "insults" a customer, how can the "insult," the nonconforming service, be controlled. Like the fairy-tale genie that could not be stuffed back into the magic lamp, once the nonconforming service is delivered there is no way to control this nonconforming product. Corrective action may be appropriate or even possible. Clause 8.5.2 may be applicable, but not clause 8.3. So if services are the product of an organization, clause 8.3 may have limited applicability.

Questions to consider asking to assess conformity to this clause include:

- Is there a documented procedure to ensure that product that does not conform to requirements is identified and controlled to prevent unintended use or delivery? Is the procedure implemented and maintained?
- Is there evidence of appropriate action being taken when nonconforming product has been detected after delivery or use has started?
- Is it required that any proposed rectification of nonconforming product be reported for concession to the customer, the end user, or a regulatory body?
- Is there objective evidence of appropriate communication with a customer, where applicable, when the organization proposes use or acceptance of nonconforming product?

## DEFINITIONS

*Conformity* (3.6.1)—fulfilment of a **requirement** (3.1.2)

NOTE The term "conformance" is synonymous but deprecated.

*Nonconformity* (3.6.2)—non-fulfilment of a **requirement** (3.1.2)

*Correction* (3.6.6)—action to eliminate a detected **nonconformity** (3.6.2)

NOTE 1 A correction can be made in conjunction with a **corrective action** (3.6.5).

NOTE 2 A correction can be, for example, **rework** (3.6.7) or **regrade** (3.6.8).

*Concession* (3.6.11)—permission to use or release a **product** (3.4.2) that does not conform to specified **requirements** (3.1.2)

NOTE A concession is generally limited to the delivery of a product that has nonconforming **characteristics** (3.5.1) within specified limits for an agreed time or quantity of that product.

*Release* (3.6.13)—permission to proceed to the next stage of a **process** (3.4.1)

NOTE In English, in the context of computer software, the term "release" is frequently used to refer to a version of the software itself.

*Defect* (3.6.3)—non-fulfilment of a **requirement** (3.1.2) related to an intended or specified use

NOTE 1 The distinction between the concepts defect and **nonconformity** (3.6.2) is important as it has legal connotations, particularly those associated with product liability issues. Consequently the term "defect" should be used with extreme caution.

NOTE 2 The intended use as intended by the **customer** (3.3.5) can be affected by the nature of the information, such as operating or maintenance instructions, provided by the **supplier** (3.3.6).

*Repair* (3.6.9)—action on a nonconforming **product** (3.4.2) to make it acceptable for the intended use

NOTE 1 Repair includes remedial action taken on a previously conforming product to restore it for use, for example as part of maintenance.

NOTE 2 Unlike **rework** (3.6.7), repair can affect or change parts of the nonconforming product.

*Rework* (3.6.7)—action on a nonconforming **product** (3.4.2) to make it conform to the **requirements** (3.1.2)

NOTE Unlike rework, **repair** (3.6.9) can affect or change parts of the nonconforming product.

*Regrade* (3.6.8)—alteration of the **grade** (3.1.3) of a nonconforming **product** (3.4.2) in order to make it conform to **requirements** (3.1.2) differing from the initial ones

*Scrap* (3.6.10)—action on a nonconforming **product** (3.4.2) to preclude its originally intended use

EXAMPLE Recycling, destruction.

NOTE In a nonconforming service situation, use is precluded by discontinuing the service.

*Source:* ANSI/ISO/ASQ Q9000-2005

## CONSIDERATIONS FOR DOCUMENTATION

A documented procedure is required to ensure that product that does not conform to requirements is identified and controlled to prevent unintended use or delivery. The organization should consider documenting a process for addressing the disposition of nonconforming product and, where appropriate, reverifying the product. This documentation could be a separate procedure or a part of a comprehensive nonconformity procedure.

The organization should also consider documenting a process for addressing situations in which nonconforming product is detected after delivery to or use by a customer has occurred.

For organizations whose primary products are services, it may be appropriate to document the actions that are required when nonconforming services are delivered to customers. Such a procedure would demonstrate an understanding of the requirements of this clause, while recognizing that under certain circumstances, it may not be applicable or possible to apply the requirements of this clause. Typically organizations will indicate addressing this occurrence of nonconformity via the corrective action process.

Finally, documenting a process for communication with customers, where appropriate, of circumstances that involve proposed rectification of product nonconformity should be considered. This documentation could be in the form of separate procedures or as a part of a comprehensive nonconformity procedure.

# CHAPTER

# 11

# Analysis of Data

> **8.4 Analysis of data**
>
> The organization shall determine, collect and analyse appropriate data to demonstrate the suitability and effectiveness of the quality management system and to evaluate where continual improvement of the effectiveness of the quality management system can be made. This shall include data generated as a result of monitoring and measurement and from other relevant sources.
>
> The analysis of data shall provide information relating to
>
> a) customer satisfaction (see 8.2.1),
>
> b) conformity to product requirements (see 8.2.4),
>
> c) characteristics and trends of processes and products, including opportunities for preventive action (see 8.2.3 and 8.2.4), and
>
> d) suppliers (see 7.4).

*Source:* ANSI/ISO/ASQ Q9001-2008

The requirements of this clause have remained essentially unchanged from the ISO 9001:2000 standard. The only difference in the text is the clarification of references to other clauses.

So this clause requires the organization to collect and analyse appropriate data to determine the suitability and effectiveness of the quality management system and to identify improvements that can be made. This includes data generated by measuring and monitoring activities and other relevant sources.

Furthermore, the clause requires analysis of data to provide information on:

- customer satisfaction;
- conformity to product requirements;
- characteristics of processes, product and their trends;
- suppliers;
- opportunities for preventive action.

The intent of this clause remains focused on requiring the organization to manage by fact. It clearly and forcefully mandates the organization to collect and analyze data to guide the prioritization of activities that will result in improvement of customer satisfaction and efficiency and effectiveness of internal operations. It also, if only indirectly, forces the organization and its management to convert the data to information which will not only guide selection and prioritization of improvement initiatives, but also provide a basis for justifying the investments, both human and capital, required to implement the improvement projects.

## IMPLEMENTATION TIPS AND TYPICAL QUESTIONS TO ASK FOR CONFORMITY

An organization dedicated to continual improvement will view the requirements of clauses 5, 7, and 8 as linked in the sense that the organization should function on a closed-loop basis. This means continually measuring processes and products, analyzing data, and using the facts derived from analysis to improve both the QMS system and products of the organization.

The gathering and analysis of data is a powerful tool for driving continual improvement. The organization should seriously consider documenting expectations for this activity at least in the areas of data related to customer satisfaction (see 8.2.1), conformity to product requirements (see 8.2.4), characteristics and trends of processes and products, including opportunities for preventive action (see 8.2.3 and 8.2.4), and suppliers.

Information from analysis of data should be used as part of the management review input. Analysis may also be conducted as a part of the management review itself. Clause 8.4 requires analysis to determine the suitability and effectiveness of the quality management system, and clause 5.6.1 requires that top management review the quality management system to ensure its suitability, adequacy, and effectiveness. Top management has a good deal of flexibility in complying with these requirements. Options for top management include the following:

- Data may be analyzed "off-line," and information from the analysis may be provided as input to top management for use in determining suitability and effectiveness of the system. This may be typical of larger organizations or organizations with dedicated analytical staff.

- The data may be provided to top management; in this case, top managers could conduct or direct the analysis as a part of the management review. This may be more typical for a small organization.

The organization is required to analyze data to identify areas in which improvements can be made. The analysis must provide information in four specific areas: (a) customer satisfaction and/or dissatisfaction; (b) conformance to customer requirements; (c) characteristics of processes, product, and their trends; and (d) suppliers. The specific information that is appropriate may differ based on the type and size of the organization as well as on the product category.

Customer satisfaction and/or dissatisfaction information is different from the information related to meeting customer requirements. It is possible for customers to be satisfied with product that is nonconforming or to be highly dissatisfied with product that fully conforms with requirements. In either case, identification of the situation offers an opportunity to change requirements to reflect actual customer needs. Measurement of customer information may include such items as issues of importance to customers, gaps in meeting customer expectations, customers' desires for changes in characteristics or features of the product, the relative satisfaction of customers with the organization and its competitors, and/or the organization's most significant customer-complaint areas. The appropriate information on customer satisfaction and/or dissatisfaction may depend upon the nature of an organization's relationships with its customers. For example, large organizations selling products to consumers through multiple distribution channels may need information related to several tiers of customers in their value chain. This may include information on the several distribution channels and on consumers as well. This could be the case for toy manufacturers (hardware), home computer software providers (software), and airlines (service). At another extreme, organizations with a single customer and day-to-day personal customer contact may have significantly different information needs.

Information related to conformance to customer requirements is information that describes how well the customer's requirements are being met. It includes information related to requirements, needs, and expectations not specifically stated by the customer. Customer inspections/tests, field problem reports, and warranty returns are typical of customer information related to conformance to requirements that should be considered for analysis.

Information on characteristics of processes, products, and their trends can be derived from analysis of product and process data obtained from the measurement process. This may also include information from aggregation and analysis of both internal operational data and feedback from customers.

Information on suppliers is information that can be developed from analysis of supplier performance data. It may include information on both excellent and poor performing suppliers. Because purchased material is often a significant percentage of total cost of goods sold, it makes business sense to invest appropriately in ensuring excellent performance by suppliers (for example, zero defects or 100 percent on-time delivery).

Sales personnel are often a good source of input data related to customer satisfaction and product conformity to customer requirements and expectations.

Collection of data without developing the data into useful information is a waste of organizational resources. The purpose of analysis is to convert data into usable information. One of the most important considerations in establishing data-collection methods is to determine how the data will be used. When a data collection scheme has been well designed, the analysis effort is simplified. Data-collection systems that are poorly designed cannot only be inefficient, but they can also yield misleading information.

*For hardware and processed materials,* information related to conformance to customer requirements that should be considered for analysis may include such items as the most numerous/significant nonconformities reported by the customer, costs of customer returns, and significant design changes resulting from customer feedback. Information on characteristics of processes, products, and their trends may include manufacturing process capabilities, types of significant assembly defects, order entry error rates, cost of quality data and statistical process control data. It may also include such items as line balance information, cell cycle times, and other information needed to improve scheduling and cycle time.

*For services,* information related to conformance to customer requirements that may be considered for analysis may include such items as nonconformities related to service delivery by customer-contact employees and/or service deliverers. The information may also include causes of late service performance, most significant reasons for service outages, unavailability of service due to overcapacity scheduling, inadequate documentation, and billing and other accounting errors.

Information on characteristics of processes, product, and their trends may include significant causes of process backlogs, ability of key service processes to deliver required services when requested by the customer, time needed to respond to service requests, satisfaction with delivered training, acceptability of consulting service, late delivery of service, and late and/or over-budget development projects. Any and perhaps all of these causes of service delivery nonconformity or customer dissatisfaction can be considered for analysis.

For *software,* the organization should consider gathering and analyzing information related to the most numerous/significant nonconformities reported by the customer, the cost to correct a nonconformity, and issues related to installation, start-up and integration of software modules. Because the majority of the cost of ownership of software occurs after purchase or product release, gathering and analysis of nonconformity costs can prolong the lifetime of software products. Alternatively, not addressing life-cycle costs can render software products untenable.

Information on characteristics of processes, product, and their trends may include rate of decline of bugs found, on-time release, acceptability of design reviews, and controlling change.

Questions to consider asking to assess conformity to this clause include:

- Has the organization determined the appropriate data to be collected?
- Does the organization analyze the appropriate data to determine the suitability and effectiveness of the quality management system?
- Does the organization analyze appropriate data to identify improvements that can be made?
- Does the organization analyze appropriate data to provide information on customer satisfaction and/or dissatisfaction?
- Does the organization analyze appropriate data to provide information on conformance to customer requirements?
- Does the organization analyze appropriate data to provide information on characteristics of processes, product, and their trends?
- Does the organization analyze appropriate data to provide information on suppliers?

## DEFINITIONS

*Characteristic* (3.5.1)—distinguishing feature

NOTE 1 A characteristic can be inherent or assigned.

NOTE 2 A characteristic can be qualitative or quantitative.

NOTE 3 There are various classes of characteristic, such as the following:

—physical (e.g. mechanical, electrical, chemical or biological characteristics);

—sensory (e.g. related to smell, touch, taste, sight, hearing);

—behavioral (e.g. courtesy, honesty, veracity);

—temporal (e.g. punctuality, reliability, availability);

—ergonomic (e.g. physiological characteristic, or related to human safety);

—functional (e.g. maximum speed of an aircraft).

*Customer* (3.3.5)—**organization** (3.3.1) or person that receives a **product** (3.4.2)

EXAMPLE Consumer, client, end-user, retailer, beneficiary and purchaser.

NOTE A customer can be internal or external to the organization.

*Customer satisfaction* (3.1.4)—customer's perception of the degree to which the customer's **requirements** (3.1.2) have been fulfilled

NOTE 1 Customer complaints are a common indicator of low customer satisfaction but their absence does not necessarily imply high customer satisfaction.

NOTE 2 Even when customer requirements have been agreed with the customer and fulfilled, this does not necessarily ensure high customer satisfaction.

*Effectiveness* (3.2.14)—extent to which planned activities are realized and planned results achieved

*Management system* (3.2.2)—**system** (3.2.1) to establish policy and objectives and to achieve those objectives

NOTE A management system of an **organization** (3.3.1) can include different management systems, such as a **quality management system** (3.2.3), a financial management system or an environmental management system.

*Process* (3.4.1)—set of interrelated or interacting activities which transforms inputs into outputs

NOTE 1 Inputs to a process are generally outputs of other processes.

NOTE 2 Processes in an **organization** (3.3.1) are generally planned and carried out under controlled conditions to add value.

NOTE 3 A process where the **conformity** (3.6.1) of the resulting **product** (3.4.2) cannot be readily or economically verified is frequently referred to as a "special process".

*Measurement process* (3.10.2)—set of operations to determine the value of a quantity

*Product* (3.4.2)—result of a **process** (3.4.1)

NOTE 1 There are four generic product categories, as follows:

—services (e.g. transport);

—software (e.g. computer program, dictionary);

—hardware (e.g. engine mechanical part);

—processed materials (e.g. lubricant).

Many products comprise elements belonging to different generic product categories. Whether the product is then called service, software, hardware or processed material depends on the dominant element. For example, the offered product "automobile" consists of hardware (e.g. tyres), processed materials (e.g. fuel, cooling liquid), software (e.g. engine control software, driver's manual), and service (e.g. operating explanations given by the salesman).

NOTE 2 Service is the result of at least one activity necessarily performed at the interface between the **supplier** (3.3.6) and **customer** (3.3.5) and is generally intangible. Provision of a service can involve, for example, the following:

—an activity performed on a customer-supplied tangible product (e.g. automobile to be repaired);

—an activity performed on a customer-supplied intangible product (e.g. the income statement needed to prepare a tax return);

—the delivery of an intangible product (e.g. the delivery of information in the context of knowledge transmission);

—the creation of ambience for the customer (e.g. in hotels and restaurants).

Software consists of information and is generally intangible and can be in the form of approaches, transactions or **procedures** (3.4.5).

Hardware is generally tangible and its amount is a countable **characteristic** (3.5.1). Processed materials are generally tangible and their amount is a continuous characteristic. Hardware and processed materials often are referred to as goods.

NOTE 3 **Quality assurance** (3.2.11) is mainly focused on intended product.

*Quality characteristic* (3.5.2)—inherent **characteristic** (3.5.1) of a **product** (3.4.2), **process** (3.4.1) or **system** (3.2.1) related to a **requirement** (3.1.2)

NOTE 1 Inherent means existing in something, especially as a permanent characteristic.

NOTE 2 A characteristic assigned to a product, process or system (e.g. the price of a product, the owner of a product) is not a quality characteristic of that product, process or system.

*Requirement* (3.1.2)—need or expectation that is stated, generally implied or obligatory

NOTE 1 "Generally implied" means that it is custom or common practice for the **organization** (3.3.1), its **customers** (3.3.5) and other **interested parties** (3.3.7), that the need or expectation under consideration is implied.

NOTE 2 A qualifier can be used to denote a specific type of requirement, e.g. product requirement, quality management requirement, customer requirement.

NOTE 3 A specified requirement is one that is stated, for example in a **document** (3.7.2).

NOTE 4 Requirements can be generated by different **interested parties** (3.3.7).

NOTE 5 This definition differs from that provided in 3.12.1 of ISO/IEC Directives, Part 2:2004.

*Source:* ANSI/ISO/ASQ Q9000-2005

# CHAPTER 12

# Improvement

> ## 8.5 Improvement
>
> ### 8.5.1 Continual improvement
>
> The organization shall continually improve the effectiveness of the quality management system through the use of the quality policy, quality objectives, audit results, analysis of data, corrective and preventive actions and management review.

*Source:* ANSI/ISO/ASQ Q9001-2008

The key requirements for continual improvement in ISO 9001:2008 are identical to the ISO 9001:2000 requirements. Prior to 2000, many practitioners argued that ISO 9001 did not deal with continual improvement because there was not a separate section titled as such. To end this debate and to clearly communicate the mechanism for achieving an important quality principle, clause 8.5 was created in ISO 9001:2000 and titled *Improvement.* Clause 8.5 has remained essentially unchanged in ISO 9001:2008.

ISO 9001:2000 makes it clear that continual improvement must be planned and implemented (see clause 8.1). The key elements for continual improvement are listed in 8.5.1 and are identified as constituting the major items that, working together, serve as the primary means of continually improving the effectiveness of the quality management system. Indeed, it should be apparent that, if an organization invokes robust processes for establishing a quality policy, setting quality objectives, analysis of data, pursues corrective action, preventive action, internal audit and management review it would be difficult *not* to improve.

While clause 8.5 contains the requirements for corrective and preventive actions, the other key elements for improvement of the quality management system are located elsewhere in the standard. To be clear about what is expected of organizations, the requirement remains that the quality policy must include a commitment to continual improvement. Clause 5.3b) still requires that the policy include ". . . commitment to . . . continual improvement." Objectives must be used as an element of continual improvement. The setting of objectives consistent with a quality policy containing a commitment to continual improvement of the effectiveness of the quality management system (see clause 5.3) is required in clause 5.4.1. In addition, audit results (see Chapter 9) form a key input in determining where opportunities lie for continual improvement.

As discussed in clause 8.4 (Chapter 11), analysis of data must be performed to provide information for identifying opportunities for continual improvement. Management reviews required by clause 5.6 provide a mechanism to ensure that top management reviews the status of corrective and preventive actions and acts to improve the quality management system and its processes.

The practices required to comply with clause 8.5.1 are essentially identical regardless of the category of product.

## IMPLEMENTATION TIPS AND TYPICAL QUESTIONS TO ASK FOR CONFORMITY

When considering the development and deployment of processes to address the improvement requirements of ISO 9001:2000, it is important to recognize that improvement is critical to the sustainability of the organization. If the organization is not improving its products and services to its customers and the efficiency of the processes employed to realize the products and services, its long-term survival is threatened. Certainly competitors will not be standing still, and expectations of customers are likely to become higher. Clause 8.5.1 requires the organization to improve the effectiveness of the organization through the use of the quality policy, quality objectives, audit results, analysis of data, corrective and preventive actions, and management review. Is it really necessary to consider all these factors in the planning and implementation of the improvement processes?

We strongly believe it is not only necessary to consider all these aspects of the quality management system, but that it is vital to do so. An improvement attitude needs to permeate the culture and the behavior of the entire organization if the organization wants to survive. Clause 8.5.1 is requiring attention to align the improvement processes to be complementary to other quality management system activities. To meet absolute minimum requirements, it may be sufficient to write a simple corrective action and preventive action procedure and have the quality activity create objective evidence that such procedures are actually followed occasionally. Such an approach may get or keep an organization certified, but is not sufficient to ensure the survival of the organization. The intent of clause 8.5.1 is to achieve an integrated improvement mentality throughout the organization. This means using as many avenues as possible and ensuring the intention is clear to all in the organization that improvement is a core value. The ideal is to achieve a state in which everyone in the organization is a contributor to continual improvement.

When the improvement process has been developed, documented, and deployed it can be helpful to ask questions to ensure that the organization is meeting at least the minimum requirements of ISO 9001:2008. A much broader set of questions can be developed for self-assessment that will highlight the degree of maturity of the improvement process, which can range from barely complying with minimum requirements to having an improvement process in place that is making ongoing and significant contributions to improving organizational performance.

Questions to consider asking to assess conformity to this clause include:

- Does the organization plan and manage processes necessary for the continual improvement of the quality management system?
- Does the organization use quality policy, quality objectives, and data analysis to facilitate the continual improvement of the quality management system?
- Does the organization use audit results, corrective action, and preventive action to facilitate the continual improvement of the quality management system?

# DEFINITIONS

*Continual improvement* (3.2.13)—recurring activity to increase the ability to fulfil **requirements** (3.1.2)

NOTE The **process** (3.4.1) of establishing objectives and finding opportunities for improvement is a continual process through the use of **audit findings** (3.9.5) and **audit conclusions** (3.9.6), analysis of data, management **reviews** (3.8.7) or other means and generally leads to **corrective action** (3.6.5) or **preventive action** (3.6.4).

*Organization* (3.3.1)—group of people and facilities with an arrangement of responsibilities, authorities and relationships

EXAMPLE Company, corporation, firm, enterprise, institution, charity, sole trader, association, or parts or combination thereof.

NOTE 1 The arrangement is generally orderly.

NOTE 2 An organization can be public or private.

NOTE 3 This definition is valid for the purposes of quality management system (3.2.3) standards. The term "organization" is defined differently in ISO/IEC Guide 2.

*Process* (3.4.1)—set of interrelated or interacting activities which transforms inputs into outputs

NOTE 1 Inputs to a process are generally outputs of other processes.

NOTE 2 Processes in an **organization** (3.3.1) are generally planned and carried out under controlled conditions to add value.

NOTE 3 A process where the **conformity** (3.6.1) of the resulting **product** (3.4.2) cannot be readily or economically verified is frequently referred to as a "special process".

*Quality objective* (3.2.5)—something sought, or aimed for, related to **quality** (3.1.1)

NOTE 1 Quality objectives are generally based on the organization's **quality policy** (3.2.4).

NOTE 2 Quality objectives are generally specified for relevant functions and levels in the **organization** (3.3.1).

*Quality policy* (3.2.4)—overall intentions and direction of an **organization** (3.3.1) related to **quality** (3.1.1) as formally expressed by **top management** (3.2.7)

NOTE 1 Generally the quality policy is consistent with the overall policy of the organization and provides a framework for the setting of **quality objectives** (3.2.5).

NOTE 2 Quality management principles presented in this International Standard can form a basis for the establishment of a quality policy. (See 0.2.)

*Audit* (3.9.1)—systematic, independent and documented **process** (3.4.1) for obtaining **audit evidence** (3.9.4) and evaluating it objectively to determine the extent to which **audit criteria** (3.9.3) are fulfilled

NOTE 1 Internal audits, sometimes called first-party audits, are conducted by, or on behalf of, the **organization** (3.3.1) itself for management review and other internal purposes, and may form the basis for an organization's declaration of **conformity** (3.6.1). In many cases, particularly in smaller organizations, independence can be demonstrated by the freedom from responsibility for the activity being audited.

NOTE 2 External audits include those generally termed second- and third-party audits. Second-party audits are conducted by parties having an interest in the organization, such as **customers** (3.3.5), or by other persons on their behalf. Third-party audits are conducted by external, independent auditing organizations, such as those providing certification/registration of conformity to ISO 9001 or ISO 14001.

NOTE 3 When two or more **management systems** (3.2.2) are audited together, this is termed a combined audit.

NOTE 4 When two or more auditing organizations cooperate to audit a single **auditee** (3.9.8), this is termed a joint audit.

*Corrective action* (3.6.5)—action to eliminate the cause of a detected **nonconformity** (3.6.2) or other undesirable situation

NOTE 1 There can be more than one cause for a nonconformity.

NOTE 2 Corrective action is taken to prevent recurrence whereas **preventive action** (3.6.4) is taken to prevent occurrence.

NOTE 3 There is a distinction between **correction** (3.6.6) and corrective action.

*Preventive action* (3.6.4)—action to eliminate the cause of a potential **nonconformity** (3.6.2) or other undesirable potential situation

NOTE 1 There can be more than one cause for a potential nonconformity.

NOTE 2 Preventive action is taken to prevent occurrence whereas **corrective action** (3.6.5) is taken to prevent recurrence.

*Review* (3.8.7)—activity undertaken to determine the suitability, adequacy and **effectiveness** (3.2.14) of the subject matter to achieve established objectives

NOTE Review can also include the determination of **efficiency** (3.2.15).

EXAMPLE Management review, design and development review, review of customer requirements and nonconformity review.

*Audit findings* (3.9.5)—results of the evaluation of the collected **audit evidence** (3.9.4) against **audit criteria** (3.9.3)

NOTE Audit findings can indicate either **conformity** (3.6.1) or **nonconformity** (3.6.2) with audit criteria or opportunities for improvement.

*Document* (3.7.2)—**information** (3.7.1) and its supporting medium

EXAMPLE **Record** (3.7.6), **specification** (3.7.3), procedure document, drawing, report, standard.

NOTE 1 The medium can be paper, magnetic, electronic or optical computer disc, photograph or master sample, or a combination thereof.

NOTE 2 A set of documents, for example specifications and records, is frequently called "documentation".

NOTE 3 Some **requirements** (3.1.2) (e.g. the requirement to be readable) relate to all types of documents, however there can be different requirements for specifications (e.g. the requirement to be revision controlled) and records (e.g. the requirement to be retrievable).

*Source:* ANSI/ISO/ASQ Q9000-2005

## CONSIDERATIONS FOR DOCUMENTATION

No specific documentation is required to comply with the requirements of clause 8.5.1. Documentation required or advisable to comply with other clauses however directly impact the ability of the organization to meet the requirements of this clause. The organization should think through and consider documenting how quality policy, quality objectives, management review, corrective action, and preventive action are integrated to drive improvement throughout the organization.

### 8.5.2 Corrective action

The organization shall take action to eliminate the causes of nonconformities in order to prevent recurrence. Corrective actions shall be appropriate to the effects of the nonconformities encountered.

A documented procedure shall be established to define requirements for

a) reviewing nonconformities (including customer complaints),

b) determining the causes of nonconformities,

c) evaluating the need for action to ensure that nonconformities do not recur,

d) determining and implementing action needed,

e) records of the results of action taken (see 4.2.4), and

f) reviewing the effectiveness of the corrective action taken.

*Source:* ANSI/ISO/ASQ Q9001-2008

The corrective action concept has been a part of ISO 9001 from the beginning. It involves taking action to eliminate the causes of nonconformities. There is essentially no change in the requirements for corrective action in ISO 9001:2008.

Nonconformities must be identified in some manner so that the system can deal with them. This does not relate to the physical identification and disposition of nonconforming product covered in clause 8.3. Requirements for customer communications in clause 7.2.3 state that arrangements must be made with customers relating to complaints. Clause 8.5.2 requires the identification of nonconformities to include these customer complaints.

The requirements for determining the causes of nonconformities and complaints continue to need to be specified in a documented procedure. Organizations should focus the process on determining root causes. There must be a process to evaluate the need for actions to ensure that nonconformities do not recur. In some cases, action may neither be required nor appropriate. If the nonconformity is minor and an isolated condition, the risks or cost associated with taking corrective action may not be justified. Without this kind of determination, resources may be diverted from the identification and correction of the more important customer complaints and nonconformities. It is fundamental that the corrective actions taken be appropriate to the nature of the problem.

Nonconformities need to be evaluated, and the root causes of their occurrence need to be determined. Evaluations of the nonconformities should indicate what corrective actions to take to eliminate the root causes of the nonconformities.

Once action to correct the cause of the nonconformity has been determined, it needs to be implemented. The corrective action process must also provide for recording the results of the corrective actions taken. In many organizations, a sign-off by someone who reviews the action taken and judges its effectiveness has been used to meet this requirement.

If actual results are recorded, the review for effectiveness can be conducted in a more objective manner. Review is required to ensure that the corrective actions have been implemented and are effective in preventing the problem from recurring.

The practices required to comply with clause 8.5.2 are essentially identical regardless of the category of product.

## IMPLEMENTATION TIPS AND TYPICAL QUESTIONS TO ASK FOR CONFORMITY

Six items articulated in 8.5.2 require attention. They are all important. It is an unfortunate fact that in many organizations the difference between correction and corrective action is not understood or is routinely ignored. Correction of problems is common. Corrective action is not. So the challenge to organizations is to develop a process that requires the use of items a through f in clause 8.5.2 to solve problems. A bigger challenge is to ensure that all personnel understand the meaning of ***CORRECTIVE ACTION*** and to ensure that personnel are competent to follow the process.

It is an excellent investment of time to develop a broad set of questions to conduct a self-assessment of the corrective action process. Such an assessment will highlight the degree of maturity that can range from barely complying with minimum requirements to having a world-class corrective action process. Such information about the corrective action process robustness is very valuable when deciding where to invest resources to improve performance.

It is also our experience that personnel throughout the organization need to understand the difference between correction and corrective action, and also need to be competent to conduct analysis to determine and correct the cause of problems.

In some cases, action may neither be required nor appropriate. If the nonconformity is minor and an isolated condition, the risks or cost associated with taking corrective action may not be justified. Deciding not to take corrective action as a management decision is acceptable, as long as it is a conscious decision.

Questions to consider asking to assess conformity to this clause include:

- Does the organization take corrective action to eliminate the causes of nonconformities?
- Is the corrective action taken appropriate to the impact of the problems encountered?

- Do documented procedures for corrective action provide for identifying nonconformities, determining causes, evaluating the need for actions to prevent recurrence, determining the corrective action needed, and the implementation of the needed corrective action?
- Do documented procedures for corrective action provide for recording the results of corrective actions taken?
- Do the documented procedures for corrective action provide for reviewing the corrective action taken?

## DEFINITIONS

*Corrective action* (3.6.5)—action to eliminate the cause of a detected **nonconformity** (3.6.2) or other undesirable situation

NOTE 1 There can be more than one cause for a nonconformity.

NOTE 2 Corrective action is taken to prevent recurrence whereas **preventive action** (3.6.4) is taken to prevent occurrence.

NOTE 3 There is a distinction between **correction** (3.6.6) and corrective action.

*Customer* (3.3.5)—**organization** (3.3.1) or person that receives a **product** (3.4.2)

EXAMPLE Consumer, client, end-user, retailer, beneficiary and purchaser.

NOTE A customer can be internal or external to the organization.

*Nonconformity* (3.6.2)—non-fulfilment of a **requirement** (3.1.2)

*Requirement* (3.1.2)—need or expectation that is stated, generally implied or obligatory

NOTE 1 "Generally implied" means that it is custom or common practice for the **organization** (3.3.1), its **customers** (3.3.5) and other **interested parties** (3.3.7), that the need or expectation under consideration is implied.

NOTE 2 A qualifier can be used to denote a specific type of requirement, e.g. product requirement, quality management requirement, customer requirement.

NOTE 3 A specified requirement is one that is stated, for example in a **document** (3.7.2).

NOTE 4 Requirements can be generated by different **interested parties** (3.3.7).

NOTE 5 This definition differs from that provided in 3.12.1 of ISO/IEC Directives, Part 2:2004.

**3.12.1**
**requirement**
expression in the content of a document conveying criteria to be fulfilled if compliance with the document is to be claimed and from which no deviation is permitted

*Review* (3.8.7)—activity undertaken to determine the suitability, adequacy and **effectiveness** (3.2.14) of the subject matter to achieve established objectives

NOTE Review can also include the determination of **efficiency** (3.2.15).

EXAMPLE Management review, design and development review, review of customer requirements and nonconformity review.

*Source:* ANSI/ISO/ASQ Q9000-2005

## CONSIDERATIONS FOR DOCUMENTATION

Clause 8.5.2 specifically requires a documented procedure for corrective action, and the procedure must provide for specific listed activities. This clause requires the recording of the results of corrective action. There is also a specific reference to clause 4.2.4 for control of the records generated. Organizations should maintain records of corrective actions required, root causes found, actions taken, results of the actions, and review of the results to ensure that the action was effective.

### 8.5.3 Preventive action

The organization shall determine action to eliminate the causes of potential nonconformities in order to prevent their occurrence. Preventive actions shall be appropriate to the effects of the potential problems.

A documented procedure shall be established to define requirements for

a) determining potential nonconformities and their causes,

b) evaluating the need for action to prevent occurrence of nonconformities,

c) determining and implementing action needed,

d) records of results of action taken (see 4.2.4), and

e) reviewing the effectiveness of the preventive action taken.

*Source:* ANSI/ISO/ASQ Q9001-2008

There is no change in the requirements for preventive action in ISO 9001:2008.

The concept of preventive action was added to ISO 9001 in the 1994 revision, and the preventive action requirements in ISO 9001:2008 are identical to those in the 2000 version. Many organizations do not separate the concepts, using the same process for both corrective action and preventive action. Actually, the concepts are somewhat different and the techniques are different for each. While corrective action involves the solving of known problems, preventive action is intended to identify the potential causes of problems. In preventive action the organization is required to identify how it will eliminate the "causes" of potential nonconformities in order to prevent their occurrence. Some organizations also consider analysis of risk and the consideration of risk avoidance strategies to be a form of preventive action.

It is not intended that the organization identify every possible nonconformity that could be envisioned, but there must be a defined method to identify those for which the organization chooses to take preventive action. Organizations have the freedom to define this in a manner that best suits their business situation. There are a number of ways to identify potential problems and to assess their potential impact. Some examples include the following:

- When nonconformities are identified in one part of the organization and causes are addressed by the corrective action system, some organizations look for similar situations in other areas. For example, if action is taken to correct the cause of nonconformity for one product line, it may be wise to determine whether similar nonconformities are likely for other lines. If so, preventive action may be appropriate for the other lines.
- Risk analysis or failure modes and effects analysis (FMEA) may be used to identify potential problems, especially during the design phase of the product life cycle, and to assess their potential impacts.
- The analysis of data on process performance may identify process parameters that have a high probability of creating nonconformities.

- Management review may be used as a vehicle for discussing and evaluating areas for preventive actions.

The documented procedure required by this clause must also provide for determining and ensuring the implementation of preventive actions to eliminate the potential causes identified.

As with corrective action, ISO 9001:2008 requires that the results of the preventive actions taken be recorded. In many organizations, a sign-off by someone who reviews the action taken and judges the effectiveness has been used to meet this requirement.

This implies that there will be some information or data recorded to verify that the potential nonconformity has not occurred over some reasonable time period. Review is required to ensure that the preventive actions have been implemented and are effective in preventing the potential problem from occurring.

The practices required to comply with clause 8.5.3 are essentially identical regardless of the category of product.

## IMPLEMENTATION TIPS AND TYPICAL QUESTIONS TO ASK FOR CONFORMITY

The best implementation tip for preventive action is to actually develop, document, and deploy a real preventive action process—not a weak variation of the corrective action process. Our experience is that many organizations do not take preventive action processes seriously, or they migrate corrective actions to preventive actions to have some objective evidence of having addressed this requirement of the standard. The five items in 8.5.3—a) through e)—are not abstract or incomprehensible, and paying attention to them, really paying attention to them, can have dramatic impact on lowering quality costs. For example, avoiding one product liability lawsuit because of consideration of "what can go wrong" and taking action to avoid such a condition can justify the investment in an honest effort to address the preventive action requirement.

Some specific items to consider including in a preventive action process include:

- Consider performing FMECA analyses (failure modes, effects, and criticality analyses) in the design stage
- Consider performing Mean Time Between Failures analyses to make component reliability tradeoffs
- Consider fault tree analyses
- Consider data analysis of other areas of the organization to identify problems in one area that may become problems elsewhere
- Review corrective actions to determine if there is potential to expand the scope to embrace preventive measures also

When the preventive action process has been developed, documented, and deployed, it can be helpful to ask the following questions to ensure that the organization is meeting at least the minimum requirements of ISO 9001:2008. As was stated for corrective action, it is an excellent investment of time to develop a broad set of questions to conduct a self-assessment of the preventive action process that will highlight its degree of maturity.

Questions to consider asking to assess conformity to this clause include:

- Does the organization identify preventive actions needed to eliminate the potential causes of possible nonconformities?
- Is preventive action taken appropriate to the impact of potential problems?
- Do the documented procedures for preventive action provide for identifying potential nonconformities and their probable causes?
- Do the documented procedures for preventive action provide for determining the need for preventive action and the implementation of the preventive action needed?

- Do the documented procedures for preventive action provide for recording the results of the preventive actions taken?
- Do the documented procedures for preventive action provide for reviewing the preventive action taken?

## DEFINITIONS

*Nonconformity* (3.6.2)—non-fulfilment of a **requirement** (3.1.2)

*Preventive action* (3.6.4)—action to eliminate the cause of a potential **nonconformity** (3.6.2) or other undesirable potential situation

NOTE 1 There can be more than one cause for a potential nonconformity.

NOTE 2 Preventive action is taken to prevent occurrence whereas **corrective action** (3.6.5) is taken to prevent recurrence.

*Requirement* (3.1.2)—need or expectation that is stated, generally implied or obligatory

NOTE 1 "Generally implied" means that it is custom or common practice for the **organization** (3.3.1), its **customers** (3.3.5) and other **interested parties** (3.3.7), that the need or expectation under consideration is implied.

NOTE 2 A qualifier can be used to denote a specific type of requirement, e.g. product requirement, quality management requirement, customer requirement.

NOTE 3 A specified requirement is one that is stated, for example in a **document** (3.7.2).

NOTE 4 Requirements can be generated by different **interested parties** (3.3.7).

NOTE 5 This definition differs from that provided in 3.12.1 of ISO/IEC Directives, Part 2:2004.

> **3.12.1**
> **requirement**
> expression in the content of a document conveying criteria to be fulfilled if compliance with the document is to be claimed and from which no deviation is permitted

*Review* (3.8.7)—activity undertaken to determine the suitability, adequacy and **effectiveness** (3.2.14) of the subject matter to achieve established objectives

NOTE Review can also include the determination of **efficiency** (3.2.15).

EXAMPLE Management review, design and development review, review of customer requirements and nonconformity review.

*Source:* ANSI/ISO/ASQ Q9000-2005

## CONSIDERATIONS FOR DOCUMENTATION

As with corrective action, the organization is required to have a documented procedure to define specific activities. Clause 8.5.3 requires records of preventive action results with specific reference to clause 4.2.4 for control of the records generated. Organizations should consider maintaining records of preventive action projects undertaken, potential root causes found, actions taken, results of the actions, and review of the results to ensure that the action was effective.

# CHAPTER 13

# Implementation of a Quality Management System Conforming to ISO 9001:2008

ISO 9001:2008 contains requirements for the process and activities needed for an effective quality management system, but it does not tell the organization how to carry out those requirements or how to implement the system. The success or failure of the quality management system implementation depends most on how the requirements are implemented, the process used for implementation, and the mindset of top managers and other employees. As with many things in life, do it right and you succeed; do the same things in the wrong way and you fail!

Successful implementation of ISO 9001:2008 depends not only on technical conformity but also on the organization's people and their willingness to serve customers!

## KEY SUCCESS FACTORS

A few simple things are almost always important for successful implementation. They include:

- Learning about quality management systems—a good understanding of quality management systems and how the quality management systems approach can work in your organization to improve customer satisfaction and performance
- Engaging top managers and achieving top management leadership of quality management system implementation and operations
- Achieving and maintaining a clear understanding of why your organization needs to implement a quality management system in conformity with ISO 9001:2008
- Developing your organization's principles
- Aligning your organization's overall business objectives and the quality objectives
- Planning the implementation process
- Identifying the important processes and associated controls, particularly those related to ensuring your product consistently meets customer and other requirements
- Developing a focus on corrective action and continual improvement, particularly on improving those things important to customers

- Keeping the processes, documentation, and overall quality management system as simple and easy to understand as possible
- Auditing during and after implementation
- Making management reviews meaningful both to the organization and to each top manager

## LEARN ABOUT QUALITY MANAGEMENT SYSTEMS

A first step for the quality leader in any organization might be to attain an understanding of what a good quality management system is and how it functions. This starts with learning the quality management principles that are major underpinning ideas for ISO 9001:2008. Those principles are found in ISO 9000:2005 clause 0.2:

### 0.2 Quality management principles

To lead and operate an organization successfully, it is necessary to direct and control it in a systematic and transparent manner. Success can result from implementing and maintaining a management system that is designed to continually improve performance while addressing the needs of all interested parties. Managing an organization encompasses quality management amongst other management disciplines.

Eight quality management principles have been identified that can be used by top management in order to lead the organization towards improved performance.

a) **Customer focus**

Organizations depend on their customers and therefore should understand current and future customer needs, should meet customer requirements and strive to exceed customer expectations.

b) **Leadership**

Leaders establish unity of purpose and direction of the organization. They should create and maintain the internal environment in which people can become fully involved in achieving the organization's objectives.

*(Continued.)*

c) **Involvement of people**

People at all levels are the essence of an organization and their full involvement enables their abilities to be used for the organization's benefit.

d) **Process approach**

A desired result is achieved more efficiently when activities and related resources are managed as a process.

e) **System approach to management**

Identifying, understanding and managing interrelated processes as a system contributes to the organization's effectiveness and efficiency in achieving its objectives.

f) **Continual improvement**

Continual improvement of the organization's overall performance should be a permanent objective of the organization.

g) **Factual approach to decision making**

Effective decisions are based on the analysis of data and information.

h) **Mutually beneficial supplier relationships**

An organization and its suppliers are interdependent and a mutually beneficial relationship enhances the ability of both to create value.

These eight quality management principles form the basis for the quality management system standards within the ISO 9000 family.

*Source:* ANSI/ISO/ASQ Q9000-2005

The next step in your education is getting familiar with the fundamentals of quality management systems. This can be obtained from a study of ISO 9000:2005, clause 2. This means that the journey toward conformity with ISO 9001:2008 starts not with that standard but rather with ISO 9000:2005! From a close reading of ISO 9000:2005, clause 2, the quality leader can gain a good initial understanding of the concepts that underpin quality management: ISO 9000:2005, clause 2 covers:

- *Rationale for quality management systems*—how the quality management system can help improve customer satisfaction and organizational performance

- *Requirements for quality management system and requirements for products*—how requirements for products differ from requirements for the quality management system
- *Quality management system approach*—the basics of the management systems approach to achieving conformity of product and customer satisfaction
- *The process approach*—how the activities and resources of the organization can be managed as processes to more effectively meet requirements
- *Quality policy and quality objectives*—how policy and objectives form the basic focus for the organization on meeting requirements and achieving continual improvement
- *Role of top management within the quality management system*—how top managers can make a real difference by taking specific actions to drive the organizations success
- *Documentation*—the value and types of documentation needed to ensure effective implementation and operations of the quality management system
- *Evaluating the quality management system*—how the four techniques of process evaluation, audit, management review, and self-assessment can be used as tools to understand and improve quality management system implementation and effectiveness
- *Continual improvement*—the basic actions required to achieve continual improvement of products and of quality management system effectiveness
- *Role of statistical techniques*—how statistical techniques can help in understanding variability and aid in improvement
- *Quality management systems and other management system focuses*—the need for organizations to develop integrated management systems that address aspects such as product quality, employee safety, environmental performance, and financial controls
- *Relationship between quality management systems and excellence models*—how excellence models (such as the Malcolm Baldrige National Quality Award in the United States) differ from quality management system standards and how these two can be used together

We also recommend that the quality professional study ISO 9001:2008 in some detail. It may be useful to attend a course or seminar on it. But your learning will be enhanced significantly if it starts with ISO 9000:2005.

## ENGAGE TOP MANAGERS

This action item is what is commonly called a "no-brainer." Adopting a quality management system is a strategic decision for any organization. And no strategic decision can be made, nor the action required to execute that decision be carried out, without the full engagement, support, and participation of top managers. Engaging top managers in a dialogue on quality may be the first step. Show them the potential for improved products and services, explain how better satisfied customers will bring repeat business. *Make the case in language that top managers can easily understand: in terms of return on investment!*

Initial support can be achieved by making promises for results to be expected in the future, but as time goes on, top managers will want and deserve reports that show real results. These results need to illustrate how the system has increased customer satisfaction, how improved satisfaction has driven customers' buying decisions, and how costs have been reduced—in other words, results that have a positive effect on financial performance.

## ACHIEVE AND MAINTAIN A CLEAR UNDERSTANDING OF WHY YOU NEED A FORMAL QUALITY MANAGEMENT SYSTEM

Getting and retaining top managers' support can be greatly facilitated by having them define the reasons why the organization needs to implement a formal quality management system. Also, consider whether or not the organization will seek certification or registration of the quality management system. It is useful to hold a meeting or series of meetings with top managers in which they are asked to determine the problems the organization will face if it does not implement such a system and what business improvements such a system could bring. These two lists can be used to develop a clear understanding of top managers' expectations of the new system. The list should be maintained and updated as the system matures. The following questions should be part of each management review:

- Is our system completely living up to all our expectations?
- If any area is not meeting expectations, what changes should be made for improvement?

William F. Houser and Russ Bloom provide a detailed discussion of this technique they call the "push-pull" exercise in Chapter 1 of *The ASQ ISO 9000:2000 Handbook.*[1]

It is important to realize that there may often be members of top management who see little or no benefits coming from the quality management system. It is important to continually measure progress, show results, and address underperforming situations.

## DEVELOP YOUR ORGANIZATION'S PRINCIPLES

Some organizations call these key beliefs, core values, or other names. In effect, the idea is to answer for all employees the question: "What beliefs should everyone in the organization keep in mind as they make everyday decisions and take everyday action?"

## ALIGN YOUR ORGANIZATION'S OVERALL BUSINESS OBJECTIVES AND THE QUALITY OBJECTIVES

Next, we recommend that the organization establish a set of quality objectives and make certain they are aligned with the overall business objectives. These objectives will be reaffirmed or revised later as the quality management system is developed, but it is important to know up front what the organization expects the system to achieve.

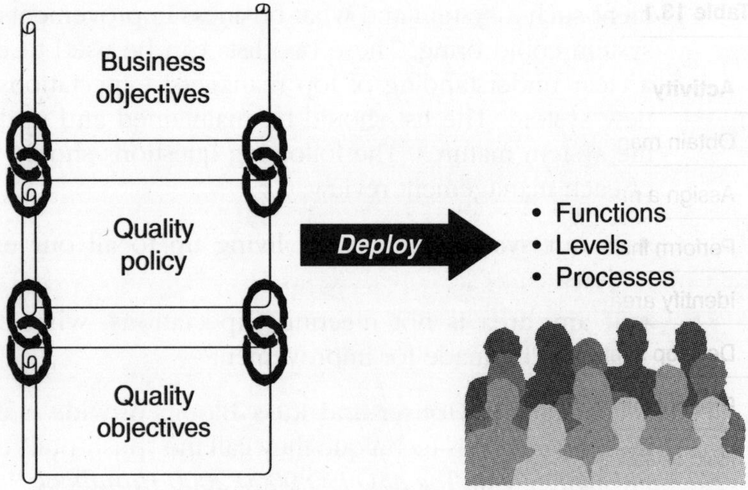


**Figure 13.1** Align quality objectives to business objectives.

Making a list of these basic objectives, along with the clear understanding of why the system is required, will help keep the implementation planning and execution on track.

The important concept here is to start—early on—a continual effort to achieve alignment of your organization's mission, future vision, business objectives, quality policy, and quality objectives. (See Figure 13.1.) Ultimately you want every employee's objectives to be aligned with these overall ideals. Your organization's future may depend on it.

We have already covered a lot of ground so far in this chapter on implementation. Actually, we authors think we have about exhausted the list of things critical to success. Yet we have just reached the point where most organizations start. The point? There is a lot to be done before you even start implementation planning.

## PLAN THE IMPLEMENTATION PROCESS

The easy part of implementation planning is developing a list of things to be done and timing for each. Table 13.1 gives an example of a listing and timing for an implementation project. This list was developed from one prepared by Leslie S. Schnoll

**Table 13.1 Sample implementation planning table.**[2]

| Activity | Timing (weeks) |
|---|---|
| Obtain management support/commitment. | 01–03 |
| Assign a management representative and deputy. | 03–05 |
| Perform initial system pre-assessment audit. | 08–09 |
| Identify areas for improvement. | 10–15 |
| Develop strategic quality plan and objectives. | 12–18 |
| Present internal seminars and workshops. | 14–16 |
| Hold review/progress meetings. | 14–52 |
| Identify key processes and interactions; develop quality manual. | 14–20 |
| Identify and map of flowchart processes, develop procedures. | 16–30 |
| Provide internal auditor training. | 16–17 |
| Develop work instructions. | 18–50 |
| Develop forms, tags, and labels (level 4 documents) | 20–50 |
| Implement quality system. | 20–52 |
| Establish measures of system performance. | 20–24 |
| Select registrar. | 21–35 |
| Perform internal audits. | 21–50 |
| Implement corrective actions. | 22–60 |
| Management review of quality system. | 22–60 |
| Perform second system pre-assessment audit. | 40–41 |
| Evaluate/perform corrective actions to quality manual. | 41–50 |
| Measure and evaluate system performance; take any corrective actions needed to ensure adequacy and value-added activities. | 45–66 |
| Submit quality manual and application to registrar. | 51–52 |
| Registrar pre-assessment and corrective action. | 60–66 |
| Have third-party assessment. | 66–68 |

for Chapter 38 of *The ASQ ISO 9000:2000 Handbook*.[2] Your list of actions and timing will be different, so you need to think it through in the context of your organization. Don't just copy our list; make your own! Once you have the list, we recommend development of a Gantt chart to track progress.

But it is the actual progress tracking system itself that is far more important. A process should be developed and agreed upon by top managers to:

- Track progress
- Review initial results during system development and implementation
- Make decisions on changes needed to the plans

One of the best ways to do this is to hold periodic system implementation review meetings with top managers in which key functional managers provide overviews of progress made and give recommendations to improve the system development and implementation process. Such a process puts top managers right in the middle of the decision making. If the work to identify and map or flowchart processes indicates problems, these meetings provide a ready-made forum to discuss the issues and develop action plans to fix the situation.

## IDENTIFY THE IMPORTANT PROCESSES AND ASSOCIATED CONTROLS

One of the most important items in our list of implementation actions has to be identification of the processes of the quality management system. The "Implementation Tips and Typical Questions to Ask for Conformity" in Chapter 2 provides a brief but useful guide on how to do this. Do not make the mistake of trying to identify every process interaction in your system; in many cases that is impractical. Rather focus on the important ones. And the most important ones may not be the most obvious. For example, if you are in an organization that has a rapidly changing product line, the interactions between the process for planning of product realization and the capital allocation process is the most critical of all. In such a case, poor performance at this interaction may mean you do not have all the resources needed to launch the next product model, resulting in a collapse in market share! Above all, **think** about the processes needed to satisfy customers, to improve products, and to make the organization more efficient at meeting requirements.

## DEVELOP A FOCUS ON CONTINUAL IMPROVEMENT

Continual improvement is a requirement of ISO 9001:2008, so processes are needed to comply. But real continual improvement requires a lot more than written corrective action and preventive action procedures. It requires there be a systematic loop of improvement that operates in the organization all the time. That improvement look is illustrated in Figure 13.2. It includes:

- Planning for continual improvement as described in ISO 9001:2008, clauses 5.4.2 and 8.1.
- A quality policy that includes a commitment to continual improvement of the quality management system as required in clause 5.3.
- Quality objectives in accordance with clause 5.4.1 that are set with the policy in mind. Objectives need to include appropriate improvements.
- Measures required by clause 8.2, including measures of product and process, audit results, and information on customer satisfaction.
- Collection and analysis of data as required in clause 8.4.
- Identification of opportunities as required in clauses 5.6 and 8.4.
- Appropriate corrective action (solving known problems) and preventive action (preventing possible problems) required in clauses 8.5.2 and 8.5.3.
- Active and serious management review of the entire loop as required in clause 5.6.

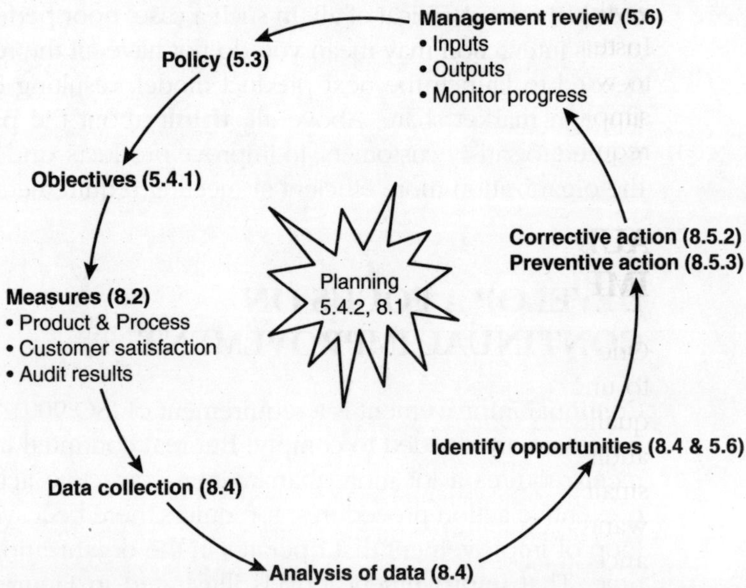


**Figure 13.2** Loop of continual improvement and associated ISO 9001:2008 clauses.

This loop of improvement needs to involve nearly everyone in the organization. Think of it this way: Big problems are worked on by top leaders, smaller problems are the purview of middle managers, while the issues with minor process problems are addressed by the workers. In most organizations there are enough problems, nonconformities, and issues to keep all these people pretty busy. Having a formal process with robust management review can keep everyone on track and working on the right issues.

## KEEP THE PROCESSES, DOCUMENTATION, AND OVERALL QUALITY MANAGEMENT SYSTEM AS SIMPLE AND EASY TO UNDERSTAND AS POSSIBLE

This is a challenge. There is so much to be done that the temptation is to start writing procedures and not stop until everything is written down in great detail. Resist this temptation. Instead, focus on getting the processes and their interactions to work effectively and efficiently. Simple procedures and a simple quality manual are not difficult to develop, but they require thought and discipline.

## AUDIT DURING AND AFTER IMPLEMENTATION

One of the early steps in implementation is a preassessment to understand the gaps you need to close in developing the quality management system. It is always useful to start your audit program during the early stages of implementation. Take small steps, then audit the results and correct the items found wanting. As you start your audit program consider the guidance in Chapter 14.

## MAKE MANAGEMENT REVIEWS MEANINGFUL FOR BOTH THE ORGANIZATION AND TO EACH TOP MANAGER

Successful implementation of the quality management system normally requires an organization to do a lot of work. There is no work more important than that done by top managers—particularly in management review. Management reviews are not the same things as operational reviews or success celebrations. They need to be tough, honest reviews of the system's effectiveness. They need to be rigorous reviews of progress toward achieving quality objectives, including objectives related to improvement. This is necessary to focus the organization on system and product improvements. But there is another important aspect. Management reviews must meet the needs of your top managers themselves. The reviews need to become regular elements of your top managers work routine. This means you will need to spend a great deal of time, commitment, preparation, and study to make the reviews the best they can be. Done poorly, management reviews are frustrating, argumentative, and wasteful. Done well, management reviews result in positive changes and improvements to the system. Done poorly, management reviews cause top managers to feel hopelessly out of control or to take a bored ho-hum attitude toward the quality management system. Done well, they cause top managers to believe the quality management system is *the* key to success. Get it right and take the time to plan effective management reviews.

## SUMMARY

There are many ways to implement a system. If you plan and implement a system that addresses the processes identified in ISO 9001:2008, even if it is not perfect initially, with great management reviews and corrective and preventive action, it will quickly become more effective. If ISO 9004 and any of the excellence models are engaged for improvement guidance to go beyond the minimum requirements of ISO 9001:2008, then the organization will be on its way to achieving exceptional performance.

## ENDNOTES

1. Houser, William F., and Bloom, Russ. Why Use the ISO 9000 Family? *The ASQ 9000: 2000 Handbook,* Cianfrani, Charles; Tsiakals, Joseph J., and West, John E. Jack, Eds.; Quality Press, ASQ; Milwaukee, 2002, Chapter 1, pp. 3–10.
2. Schnoll, Leslie S., Using ISO 9000 to Achieve Customer Requirements, *The ASQ ISO 9000:2000 Handbook,* Chapter 38, pp. 512.

# CHAPTER 14

# Auditing the Process-Based Quality Management System

## QUALITY MANAGEMENT SYSTEMS STRUCTURE AND THE IMPLICATIONS FOR INTERNAL AUDITING

There has been a significant change in the focus of quality management over the past 20 years. The ISO Technical Committee responsible for Quality Management (TC 176) addressed this change in focus in the release of ISO 9001:2000. That standard incorporated thinking and requirements that, if embraced by an organization, can ensure that the quality management system of that organization is consistent with the minimum requirements and expectations of customers. The change in focus that was incorporated into ISO 9001:2000 and retained in ISO 9001:2008 has had an impact on how organizations approach and conduct internal audits of quality management system effectiveness.

Examples of the evolving concepts that are incorporated in ISO 9001:2008 include:

- A change to a focus on customers instead of an internal focus
- A recognition that output that meets customer requirements and expectations really does matter, and must be a prime focus of the quality management system
- A change to an emphasis on managing a system of processes from a system focused on documentation
- A change to an emphasis on quality management and improvement from just controlling or assuring quality
- A change in attitude from quality as the sole purview of specialists to an attitude that all in the organization have something to contribute to quality
- A change to leadership by top management from leadership of quality activities by staff people

ISO 9001:2008 also continues to be based on eight quality management principles that were used as input to the development of ISO 9001:2000. These principles were developed over several years and were based on information collected from around the world. The eight quality management principles in clause 0.2 of ISO 9000:2005 were presented earlier in this book in chapters 1 and 13.

A brochure that discusses these principles may be downloaded from the ISO Web site at http://www.iso.ch. Remember that the principles provide ideas or concepts related to quality management systems. They were developed to provide input to the revision process that resulted in ISO 9001:2000, but they are not a part of the quality management system requirements of that standard. While not formally a part of the standard, each of these principles is embodied in ISO 9001:2008.

From the viewpoint of internal auditing, none of the principles are more important than those related to the "system approach to management" and the "process approach." The use of these two principles together is referred to as the "process approach." Before discussing the auditing of a quality management system based on the process approach, we should review and understand the process approach concept in order to be able to effectively audit the systems. The process approach concept was explained in detail in our book titled *How to Audit the Process-Based QMS,*[1] published by Quality Press, and the figures in this chapter are the same as we used in that book.

Let's start by reviewing the two underlying quality management principles related to the processes of the quality management system in greater detail:

- First, the Process Approach Principle—*"a desired result is achieved more efficiently when activities and related resources are managed as a process."* This principle is best understood when it is applied to an individual process. A process is nothing more than a collection of interrelated activities (see Figure 14.1). These activities are related because they act together to transform inputs into outputs. Effective and efficient operation of the transformation requires coordination among the activities and management of the resources necessary to conduct them. A process approach also requires application of control to ensure that requirements will be met.

Full understanding of the process approach also requires an understanding of the linkage between suppliers and cus-

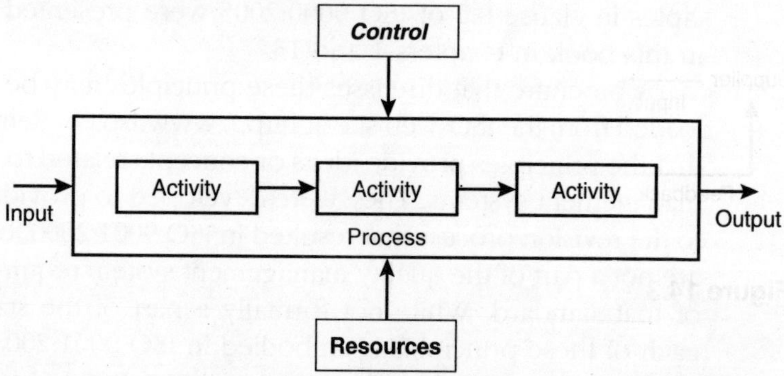


**Figure 14.1** A process is a group of interrelated activities and related resources that transforms inputs to outputs.

tomers. Customers and suppliers can be either internal or external to the organization. Customers provide requirements to the process and feedback how well those requirements have been met. Likewise, the process provides requirements to its suppliers and feedback as to how well those requirements are met. This linkage is often referred to as SIPOC (suppliers, inputs, process, outputs, customers) and can be seen in Figure 14.2.

- The System Approach to Management Principle—*"identifying, understanding, and managing interrelated processes as a system contributes to the organization's effectiveness and efficiency in achieving its objectives."* This principle applies to the whole quality management system. Thus, a system is a collection of interrelated processes with a common set of objectives and outputs. In essence, the quality management system should be a group of interrelated

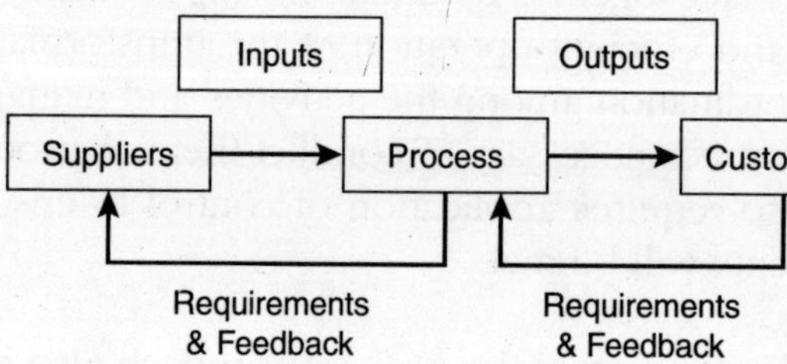


**Figure 14.2** Suppliers provide inputs that the process transforms into outputs for customers.

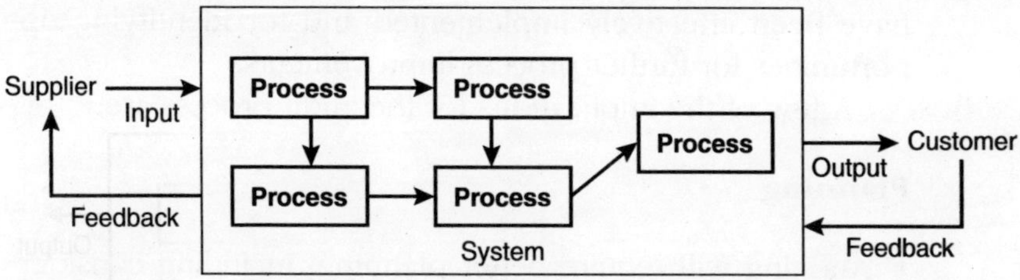


**Figure 14.3** A system is a group of interrelated processes that work together to achieve outputs that meet objectives.

processes focused on effectively and efficiently achieving the organization's quality objectives. An organization may be able to achieve those objectives without the system approach, but the quality objectives can be best achieved if the processes and their interactions are managed together as a system. Figure 14.3 shows a basic system and its relationship to suppliers and customers.

These are the principles that provide a foundation for ISO 9001:2008. To fully implement the process approach to quality management as it is described in ISO 9001:2008, it is also necessary to address the requirements found in the following clauses:

- 4.1, *Quality management system general requirements*
- 5.4, *Planning*
- 7.1, *Planning of product realization*
- 7.5.1, *Control of production and service provision*
- 8.1, *Measurement, analysis, and improvements, general*

It is not sufficient to just read these clauses. When implementing quality management, organizations should consider the requirements contained in these clauses *not only on an individual basis but also as a set of linked and interrelated requirements.*

Because achieving quality objectives and meeting customer requirements depends on the processes of the quality management system, it follows that the audit program of an organization should focus on those processes as well. Auditing is a key means for determining whether these processes have been effectively implemented and for identifying opportunities for further process improvements.

A few of the implications for the audit process are:

**Planning**

- Auditing will require better planning, including consideration of process output information such as customer complaints and process performance data.
- Audits need to be more focused on outcomes and effectiveness of processes.

**Competence**

- Auditors need a working knowledge of the processes they are auditing to be able to assess activities from inputs to outputs.
- Auditors need to understand the entire system, its processes and interactions.
- Ensuring auditor competence may be a challenge. Auditors need to understand both the system and its processes as well as process management concepts and how to apply these concepts to auditing.

**Conducting the audit**

- Individual activities should no longer be considered standalone entities; rather, they will have to be considered in the context of the activities to which they are connected.
- Audit reports should add more value because the reports will have more content related to process outputs and effectiveness.

## AUDITING THE PROCESS-BASED QUALITY MANAGEMENT SYSTEM

There are certainly several ways an organization can structure a quality audit program to meet the internal audit requirement of ISO 9001:2008. One way would be to simply divide the standard into its basic process-related parts and audit each of these without regard to the organization's own processes, organization, and workflows. This is certainly possible, but experience has shown it is not efficient. Since it tends to ignore the organization's processes, it is also not likely to prove very effective in stimulating performance improvements. Or the organization could decide to audit all aspects of the quality management system with a team in one intense effort over a very short period of time. This approach may be disruptive to the normal operating environment. Or, the organization could choose to audit each of its product lines, either in their entirety or by breaking down a high level process into many subprocesses.

Let's look at some of the alternatives.

- *Audit the processes*—Structure the audits around the major management, support, and product realization processes of the quality management system. The interactions between these processes are required to be identified in the quality manual. While it is probably impossible to design a system that audits all of the processes, each major process can be covered to sufficient levels of detail to ensure compliance with ISO 9001:2008. This approach is often called a *horizontal audit*. Because processes tend to flow through the functions of the organization, this approach would cover the major functions as well as the interfaces between the functions and the processes. It may, however, have the disadvantage of missing many of the interactions among the key processes of the system, but this disadvantage can be overcome with careful audit designs.
- *Audit the functions*—Structure the audits around the major organizational functions. Include in each of these audits all the processes for which the function being audited has any responsibility. This approach is often called a *vertical audit*. It is likely to be a somewhat better approach overall than the horizontal approach. It has the advantage of covering all of the key processes and their interfaces within the function being audited. If process "hand-offs" to and from the function are considered, it also provides a window to problems at functional boundaries. It is fairly efficient because each function need be visited once per audit cycle.

In actual practice, audit programs may use a combination of these approaches. This provides **flexibility.** Vertical audits can be used for functional areas that have major parts of the overall system, as may be true for design engineering, purchasing, or the production department. For these major functions, it may be more efficient and effective to conduct a single audit that encompasses all processes for which they have responsibilities. Other processes may have responsibilities so spread out that a horizontal, cross-functional audit is best. As the organizational structure changes over time and the quality management system matures, this approach provides the flexibility to change to meet emerging needs. For example, if several functions seem to have difficulties with a particular cross-functional process that has been audited during prior functional audits, perhaps the next audit cycle should include a cross-functional audit of that process.

No matter what approach is used to conduct internal audits, every process audited should be viewed as consisting of inputs, activities that convert inputs to outputs, and outputs as shown in Figure 1.1. Also, the process has feedback loops to communicate to suppliers to the process and customers of the process, recognizing that the suppliers and customers may be internal or external.

In conducting audits of processes it can be helpful to consider the following questions to ensure that the audit is focused on understanding if the process is capable of meeting requirements in the short term and will be able to sustain performance over time and changing conditions.

Questions to consider asking to audit process based systems performance include the following.

**Typical questions related process inputs:**

- What are the inputs?
- Do inputs meet specified requirements? How do we know?
- Who are the suppliers of the inputs?
- How are the input requirements defined?
- How is internal supplier performance measured?

**Typical questions related to the activities occurring in a process:**

- Who is the customer of the process?
- What does the customer want?
- Is there an understanding of what is necessary to meet (or exceed) customer requirements?
- Are individuals performing work correctly?
- Do they know what to do and have the means to do it, including documentation, time, and tools?
- Are responsibilities clear?
- Are procedures, or work instructions, if applicable, available? Understood? Controlled?
- What are the specific requirements for successful completion?
- How are interactions with other processes monitored or measured?
- How is interaction with other processes controlled?
- How do individuals know that they have performed work to meet requirements?
- What is done with the data that are collected? Who analyzes it? Is there evidence of data analysis?
- How is continual improvement addressed?
- What is the evidence to support each of these?

**Typical questions related to process outputs:**

- Is the process effective in achieving required results?
- How is conformance to customer or specification requirements determined?
- Is the process continually improved?
- How is customer feedback (external or internal) solicited and used?

**Typical questions related to process interfaces:**

- Are interfaces with other processes identified?

- Are requirements to supplier processes clearly communicated?
- Is supplier performance tracked and communicated?
- Are requirements of the customers of the process clearly defined and understood?
- Is "customer" performance and satisfaction tracked as appropriate?

**Typical questions related to process failures:**

- What happens when deviations from requirements are found?
- What are the processes for correction?
- What are the processes for control of nonconforming product?
- What are the processes for disposition of nonconforming product?
- What are the processes for analysis for possible corrective action?
- What are the processes for corrective action?
- What are the processes for use of data for preventive action, when applicable?

**Typical questions related to process improvement:**

- Can this process or some of its activities be combined with other processes for increased effectiveness or efficiency?
- Is there evidence of transferable best practices?
- Are there redundant or unnecessary activities?
- Are there significant risks of future process problems?
- Is the process continually improved?

**Typical general questions that can be asked:**

- Are the processes identified and appropriately described?
- Are responsibilities assigned?

- Are process controls in place?
- Are personnel performing the work competent? How do we know?
- Are procedures (documented or not) implemented and maintained?
- Are the requirements clearly specified and understood?
- Is the process monitored (and, if required, measured) as appropriate?
- Is the process effective in achieving the required results?
- Is the process meeting all of its performance objectives?
- Does the process pose significant risks of future problems or nonconformities?
- Can this process or some of its activities be combined with other processes for increased effectiveness or efficiency?
- Are there redundant or unnecessary activities?

## ADDITIONAL CONSIDERATIONS

While we are auditing we are certainly focused on understanding that all aspects of the process or activity we are auditing have been planned and are operating under controlled conditions and that the entire system is functioning effectively. But we cannot forget that a great audit has many other important activities that need to be addressed. A few examples of considerations beyond the audit itself include:

- Ensuring that we have properly planned our audit
- Reviewing all available procedural and process results materials in advance
- Allowing adequate time to write a great report and archive audit papers and reference materials

Each of these activities deserves attention. Expanded discussion of these activities and others can be found in the book titled *How to Audit the Process-Based QMS*.

## OTHER STANDARDS PROVIDING AUDITING GUIDANCE

Additional requirements for internal auditing are included in sector-specific standards such as AS9100, ISO/TS 16949, and ISO 14001. If your organization is required to comply with any of these standards, refinement of your audit procedures and processes may be required.

Also, guidance to consider for your internal audit program can be found in ISO 9004 and in ISO 19011.

## SUMMARY

The processes of the quality management system are critical to achieving the quality objectives of an organization and meeting customer requirements. It follows that the audit program should focus on those processes as well. Auditing is a key means for determining whether these processes have been effectively implemented and for identifying opportunities for further process improvements.

By asking the questions indicated above and obtaining objective evidence to substantiate the answers received from auditees, an auditor will be able to adequately assess the degree to which the audited processes will be able to conform to requirements and consistently yield outputs that will meet requirements.

## ENDNOTE

1. Cianfrani, Charles A. and West, John E. and Arter, Dennis R., *How to Audit the Process-Based QMS,* Ed., Quality Press, ASQ Milwaukee 2003.

# CHAPTER

# 15

# Use of ISO 9001 and Sector Applications

## INTRODUCTION

The concept and use of quality management systems as expressed through the ISO 9001 quality management standard has been accepted beyond all expectations of the founders of the ISO quality management committee in 1980. No other standard or family of standards has achieved the success of the ISO 9000 family of standards. This phenomenal success has resulted in tremendous visibility for the International Organization for Standardization and has had its intended consequence of reducing trade barriers. For many organizations it also has resulted in improved products, services, and business performance.

There are close to one million documented ISO 9001:2000 certifications worldwide as of the publishing of this book in late 2008. ISO 9001 certification is frequently used in both private and public sectors to increase confidence in the products and services provided by certified organizations. It is also used to improve control and business performance, in the selection of suppliers, and in determining which potential suppliers are asked to bid for procurement contracts.

It is because of the tremendous value created by this standard that significant attention has been paid to keep it pure and to prevent dilution through uncontrolled development of derivative standards. This, in standards language, is referred to as "preventing proliferation." Two main documents are used for this purpose: (1) The ISO/IEC Directive on Sector Policy and (2) ISO Guide 72.

ISO TC 176 is the ISO technical committee for "Quality Management and Quality Assurance," which developed and maintains ISO 9001 and associated generic quality management system standards. ISO TC 176 standards are called "generic" because they are intended to apply generically across all types of organizations. This chapter discusses the use of ISO 9001 and associated standards by specific business sector.

## PREVENTING PROLIFERATION

ISO/IEC Sector Policy was issued to control the development of sector-specific standards on quality management systems. The key objectives of the ISO/IEC Sector Policy are to: (1) maximize the use of generic QMS International Standards; (2) Support international trade and remove trade barriers; and (3) support developing countries.

The sector policy states:

- "In case a sector-specific development of ISO 9001/9004 is necessary, the rules of the ISO/IEC Directives Part 2, paragraph 6.8.2 'Sector Policy' must be applied."
- "All questions concerning the sector policy or interpretations of ISO 9000/9001/9004 standards should be addressed to the ISO/TC 176."
- Instructions and criteria have been issued by ISO/TC 176 Subcommittee 2 for determining the necessity for any sector-specific document as well as for the development of such documents.

Rules to be respected for the development of sector-specific documents include:

- Terms and definitions specified in ISO 9000:2005 must be referred to in a normative manner (Note: "normative" means that the ISO 9000:2005 definition for a term is to be treated as the operative definition in the sector-specific standard).
- Normative reference must be made to ISO 9001:2008 in its entirety or, subject to the 'applicability' provisions detailed in the scope of ISO 9001:2008, to its clauses or sub-clauses.
- If text from ISO 9001:2008 is reproduced, it must be clearly distinguishable from the sector-specific wording.
- Text from ISO 9001:2008 must be reproduced verbatim (any add-on, amendment, deletion, or interpretation of the requirements laid down in ISO 9001 is not permitted)
- Sector-specific requirements may be added.

ISO/TC 176 developed a guidance document on the application of the sector policy. This guidance suggests steps to be followed in the development of a sector specific standard based on ISO 9001. This guidance is applicable to ISO/IEC committees and outside organizations. The steps are:

- Establish the need for a sector document
- Develop the document
- Liaise with ISO/TC 176
- Comply with ISO Guide 72

Within ISO, oversight of the standards writing technical committees is provided by the ISO's Technical Management Board (TMB). The ISO TMB developed *ISO Guide 72, Guidelines for the Justification and Development of Management System Standards* to help prevent the proliferation of standards. Guide 72 applies to all management system standards (MSS) including sector applications of the generic ISO 9001.

New ISO work requires justification including an independent study. Some of the perceived reasons to justify a sector-specific quality management system standard are:

- The existence of sector-specific terminology
- The need for more prescriptive requirements and controls
- The need for an explanation of generic requirements in the language of the sector
- The need to use sector-specific regulatory requirements and/or codes of good practice

There are fairly tight rules for the development of a new MSS standard related to ISO 9001. Guide 72 requires a sector standards writing committee to establish liaison arrangements with ISO TC 176 for the development of a derivative of ISO 9001. It is important that the new sector document not detract from or dilute the generic 9001.

## CLASSIFICATIONS OF MANAGEMENT SYSTEMS STANDARDS

Guide 72 makes a distinction between three different types of management system standards. These MSS types are defined with examples in Guide 72 as presented in Table 15.1.

**Table 15.1** Classification of management systems standards.

| |
|---|
| **Type A — Management Systems Requirements Standard**<br>Standard that is intended to provide the marketplace with relevant specifications for the management system of an organization to demonstrate its capability to meet internal and external requirements (e.g. by assessment of that capability by internal or external parties)<br><br>Examples<br>— Management system requirements standards (specifications).<br>— Management system sector-specific requirements standards. |
| **Type B — Management Systems Guidelines Standards**<br>Standard that is intended to assist an organization to implement and/or to enhance its management system by providing additional guidance to the elements of a management system requirements standard, or stand-alone guidance with no equivalence to a management system requirements standard.<br><br>Examples<br>— Guidance on the use of management system requirements standards.<br>— Guidance on the establishment of a management system.<br>— Guidance on the improvement/enhancement of a management system.<br>— Management system sector-specific guidelines standards. |
| **Type C — Management Systems Related Standards**<br>Standard that is intended to provide further information on specific parts of the management system or guidance on related supporting techniques, in addition to management system standards.<br><br>Examples<br>— Management system terminology documents.<br>— Standards on auditing, documentation, training, monitoring, measurement, and performance evaluation.<br>— Standards on labelling and life–cycle assessment. |

*Source:* ISO Guide 72

## SECTOR APPLICATIONS OF ISO 9001

In spite of the efforts to prevent proliferation, there have been widespread efforts for the development of standards based on ISO 9001. Table 15.2 indicates the use of these derivative standards in 33 sectors for application with products and services. There are 16 standards that are of Type A: management systems requirements standards that can be used for conformity assessment audits by either internal or external parties.

## USE OF ISO 9001

ISO estimates there are close to 1 million third-party certifications for the generic ISO 9001:2000. This is by organization and does not include all of the sites of each organization. These organizations contract with a certification body (sometimes called a registrar) for third-party certification services including audits and other activities related to certification. The total number of organizations that use ISO 9001 with or without certification is well over 1 million.

ISO 9001 is implemented by both private and public organizations in 170 countries. About 20 percent of the certifications are held by organizations in China. Approximately 50 percent of the certifications are held by organizations in Italy, Japan, Spain, the United Kingdom, the United States, Germany, India, France, and Australia. The remaining certificates are held by organizations in other countries.

There are a variety of reasons for incurring the cost associated with obtaining an ISO 9001 certification:

**Internal Use:** Many organizations select ISO 9001 as the basis for their quality management system in a desire to use a widely recognized model that has proved to be effective. Some do this based on actual customer requirements. Others do this based on a perception of market advantage and use the certificates in advertisements promoting their goods and services.

**Supplier Qualification:** The historical use for a quality management system standard is as a basis for qualifying the quality management system of suppliers. Development of quality management system standards dates to the 1950s. One of the early standards of this type was Mil Q 9858A, used by the Department of Defense for use in qualifying some of its suppliers. Today, ISO 9001:2000 is widely used as a qualification requirement for suppliers in many product and service sectors. It can be expected that this will continue with ISO 9001:2008. The automotive, aerospace, telecommunications, and other industries have sector-specific versions of ISO 9001 that are used with suppliers.

A 2006 ISO survey conducted by ACNielsen indicates the total number of certifications for ISO/TS 16949:2002 for the automotive sector. Taking those numbers and projecting the growth rate from 2005 to 2006, projected certifications for ISO/TS 16949:2002 in 2008 was over 40,000 in 90 countries. Certifications are required for Type A standards in telecommunications, aerospace, and certain other sectors without regulatory requirements for ISO 9001 as noted in Table 15.2.

**Regulatory Requirement:** The European Union, FDA, Japan, Australia, Canada, and many other countries use ISO 9001 as the quality management system for meeting certain regulatory requirements.

- **For CE Marking** The European Union has a goal of achieving a single internal market to promote economic competitiveness and to become a powerful economic trading block by removing barriers to trade. Each country had controlled the flow of products and services considered critical from a health and safety perspective by the use of regulations. Harmonizing these national regulations into EU regulations (called "directives") has been a major initiative for easing hindrances to the flow of trade. It is of great value to anyone with products targeted for the European market to only have to meet a single regulation instead of a different regulation for each country.

**Table 15.2** List of ISO 9001 Sector Applications.
This table is an extract from ISO/TC 176 N881R3 dated June 2008. It lists the sector specific documents based on ISO 9001:2000. It is not necessarily a complete list.

| Sector | Document Designation | Doc. Type | Document Title | Date Published | | Website | Language |
|---|---|---|---|---|---|---|---|
| | | | | First | Latest | | |
| *Aerospace* | AS/JISQ/EN 9100 | A | Quality management systems—Aerospace—Requirements | 1999 | 2004 | www.sae.org<br>www.jsa.or.jp<br>www.cenorm.be | English<br>Japanese<br>French<br>German |
| | AS/SJAC/EN 9101 | C | Quality System Assessment | 2000 | 2006 | www.sae.org<br>www.jsa.or.jp<br>www.cenorm.be | English<br>Japanese<br>French<br>German |
| | AS/EN 9110 | A | Quality management systems—Aerospace—Requirements maintenance organizations | 2003 | 2003 | www.sae.org<br>www.cenorm.be | English<br>French<br>German |
| | AS/EN 9111 | C | Quality management systems assessment for maintenance organizations | 2005 | 2005 | www.sae.org<br>www.cenorm.be | English<br>French<br>German |
| | AS/EN 9120 | A | Quality management systems—Aerospace—Requirements for stockist distributors | 2002 | 2002 | www.sae.org<br>www.cenorm.be | English<br>French<br>German |
| | AS/EN 9121 | C | Quality management systems—Aerospace—Requirements for stockist distributors—Revision A | 2003 | 2007 | www.sae.org<br>www.cenorm.be | English<br>French<br>German |

*Source:* ISO / TC 176 N881 R3 June 2008

**Table 15.2** Continued.

| Sector | Document Designation | Doc. Type | Document Title | Date Published | | Website | Language |
|---|---|---|---|---|---|---|---|
| | | | | First | Latest | | |
| *Agriculture* | ISO/DIS 22006 | A | Guidelines on the application of ISO 9001:2000 in crop production | tbd | tbd | www.iso.org | English |
| | UNI 11219 | B | Quality management systems—Guidelines for the application of UNI EN ISO 9001:2000 standard in farms | 2006 | 2006 | www.uni.com | Italian |
| *Architecture* | | B | Quality management system for architects. Guidelines on the application of UNE-EN ISO 9001:2000 | 2005 | 2005 | www.aenor.es | English |
| *Automotive* | ISO/TS 16949 | A | Quality management systems—Particular requirements for the application of ISO 9001:2000 for automotive production and relevant service part organizations | 1999 | 2002 | www.iso.org | English |
| *Chemical* | ÖNORM S 2095-3 | A | Integrated management—Quality assurance, environment, health and safety—Part 3: Requirements in chemical industry | | 2004 | www.on-norm.at | German |

*Continued*

**Table 15.2** Continued.

| Sector | Document Designation | Doc. Type | Document Title | Date Published | | Website | Language |
|---|---|---|---|---|---|---|---|
| | | | | First | Latest | | |
| *Cleaning Services* | EN 13549 | C | Cleaning services. Basic requirements and recommendations for quality measuring systems | 2001 | 2001 | www.cenorm.be | English |
| *Computer Software* | ISO-IEC 90003 | | Software engineering—Guidelines for the application of ISO 9001:2000 to computer software | 1997 | 2004 | www.iso.org www.iec.ch | English |
| *Construction* | ASQ E2014 | B, C | Interpretive Guide for the Design and Construction Project Team | 2002 | 2002 | www .qualitypress .asq.org | English |
| | IRAM 30100 | B | Guidance for the interpretation of ISO 9001:2000 in construction | 2002 | 2002 | www.iram.org.ar | Spanish |
| | HB 90.3 | | The Construction Industry—Guide to ISO 9001:2000 | 2000 | 2000 | www.standards .com.au | English |
| *Consulting Engineering* | 13 | B | Guide to interpretation and application of the ISO 9001: 2000 standard for the Consulting Engineering Industry | 2001 | 2001 | www.fidic.org | English |

**Table 15.2** Continued.

| Sector | Document Designation | Doc. Type | Document Title | Date Published | | Website | Language |
|---|---|---|---|---|---|---|---|
| | | | | First | Latest | | |
| *Education* | ISO IWA 2 | B | Quality management systems—Guidelines for the application of ISO 9001:2000 in education | 2003 | 2007 | www.iso.org | English |
| | IRAM 30000 | B | Guidance for the interpretation of ISO 9001:2000 in education | | 2001 | www.iram.org.ar | Spanish |
| | NTC 541/03 | B | Guia para la educación | 2005 | 2005 | www.icontec.com | Spanish |
| | HB 90.7 | | Education and Training Guide to ISO 9001:2000 | 2000 | 2000 | www.standards.com.au | English |
| | | | | | | | |
| *Electrical* | JEAG 4111 | B | Quality assurance code for safety in nuclear power plants JEA (Japan Electric Association) | 2005 | 2005 | www.denki.or.jp | Japanese |
| | JEAG 4121 | B | Application guide to quality assurance code for safety in nuclear power plants—Operation phase of nuclear power plants JEA (Japan Electric Association) | 2005 | 2005 | www.denki.or.jp | Japanese |

*Continued*

**Table 15.2** Continued.

| Sector | Document Designation | Doc. Type | Document Title | Date Published | | Website | Language |
|---|---|---|---|---|---|---|---|
| | | | | First | Latest | | |
| *Electronics* | IEC 60300-1 | C | Dependability management—Part 1: Dependability management systems | 1993 | 2003 | www.iec.ch | English |
| | IEC 60300-2 | C | Dependability management—Part 2: Guidelines for dependability management | 1995 | 2004 | www.iec.ch | English |
| | CEI 0-12:2002 | | "Process approach and quality indicators for the electrotechnical and electronic sector. Guidelines for the application of ISO 9000:2000 series of standards". | 2002 | 2002 | www.ceiweb.it. | Italian |
| *Environmental Health and Safety* | ÖNORM S 2095-1 | A | Integrated management—Quality-assurance, environment, health and safety—Part 1: Determination of basic requirements | 2003 | 2003 | www.on-norm.at | German |
| *First Aid Stations* | Guide 41 | C | Implementing ISO 9001:2000 in hospital's first aid stations and reception | 2002 | 2002 | www.uni.com | Italian |
| *Food* | ISO 22000 | A | Food safety management systems—Requirements for any organization in the food chain | 2005 | 2005 | www.iso.org | English |
| | HB 90.4 | | ISO 9000 in the Food Processing Industry | 2000 | 2000 | www.standards .com.au | English |

**Table 15.2** Continued.

| Sector | Document Designation | Doc. Type | Document Title | Date Published: First | Date Published: Latest | Website | Language |
|---|---|---|---|---|---|---|---|
| *Food & Drink* | ISO 15161 | B | Guidelines on the application of ISO 9001:2000 for the food and drink industry | 2001 | 2001 | www.iso.org | English |
| *Government* | IWA 4 | B | Quality management systems—Guidelines for the application of ISO 9001:2000 in local government | 2005 | 2005 | www.iso.org | English |
| | IRAM 30300 | B | Guidance for the interpretation of ISO 9001:2000 in government local bodies (municipalities) | 2003 | 2003 | www.iram.org.ar | Spanish |
| | IRAM 30600 | B | Guide for the Interpretation of ISO 9001:2000 in management of judicial operations | 2005 | 2005 | www.iram.org.ar | Spanish |
| | Guide 33 | B | Implementing ISO 9001:2000 in local administrations | 2002 | 2002 | www.uni.com | Italian |
| | Guide 38 | B | Implementing ISO 9001:2000 in local public services | 2002 | 2002 | www.uni.com | Italian |

*Continued*

**Table 15.2** Continued.

| Sector | Document Designation | Doc. Type | Document Title | Date Published | | Website | Language |
|---|---|---|---|---|---|---|---|
| | | | | First | Latest | | |
| *Health and Health Services* | ISO 15378 | A | Primary packaging materials for medicinal products—Particular requirements for the application of ISO 9001:2000, with reference to Good Manufacturing Practice (GMP) | 2006 | 2006 | www.iso.org | English |
| | ISO IWA 1 | B | Quality management systems—Guidelines for process improvements in health service organizations | 2001 | 2005 | www.iso.org | English |
| | CEN/TS 15224 | B | Health services—Quality management systems—Guide for the use of EN ISO 9001:2000 | 2005 | 2005 | www.cenorm.be | English |
| | Guide 26 | B | Implementing ISO 9001:2000 in hospitals | 2002 | 2002 | www.uni.com | Italian |
| | Guide 43 | B | Implementing ISO 9001:2000 in hospitals' management services | 2000 | 2000 | www.uni.com | Italian |
| | HB 90.8 | B | ISO 9000 in Healthcare services | 2000 | 2000 | www.standards.com.au | English |
| | IRAM 30200 | B | Guidance for the interpretation of ISO 9001:2000 in health organizations | 2004 | 2004 | www.iram.org.ar | Spanish |

**Table 15.2** Continued.

| Sector | Document Designation | Doc. Type | Document Title | Date Published | | Website | Language |
|---|---|---|---|---|---|---|---|
| | | | | First | Latest | | |
| *Health and Health Services* Continued | UNE 66928 | B | Quality management systems. Guide for the application of the UNE-EN ISO 9001:2000 standard to pharmacies | 2004 | 2004 | www.aenor.es | Spanish |
| | UNI 10881 | B | Services—Nursing homes—Guidelines for the application of the UNI EN ISO 9000 standards | 2000 | 2000 | www.uni.com | Italian |
| | | | | | | | |
| *Hotels* | Guide 22 | B | Implementing ISO 9001:2000 in hotels | 2002 | 2002 | www.uni.com | Italian |
| | | | | | | | |
| *Insurance* | UNE 66927 | A | Quality management systems. Guide for the application of the UNE-EN ISO 9001:2000 standard to insurance brokers | 2003 | 2003 | www.aenor.es | Spanish |
| | | | | | | | |
| *Legal* | HB 90.6 | B | The Legal Profession—Guide to ISO 9000:2000 | 2000 | 2000 | www.standards.com.au | English |
| | Guide 37 | B | Implementing ISO 9001:2000 in lawyers' offices | 2001 | 2001 | www.uni.com | Italian |

*Continued*

**Table 15.2** Continued.

| Sector | Document Designation | Doc. Type | Document Title | Date Published | | Website | Language |
|---|---|---|---|---|---|---|---|
| | | | | First | Latest | | |
| *Libraries* | IRAM 30500 | B | Guidance for the interpretation of ISO 9001:2000 in libraries | 2005 | 2005 | www.iram.org.ar | Spanish |
| | Guide 39 | B | Implementing ISO 9001:2000 in libraries | 2002 | 2002 | www.uni.com | Italian |
| *Medical Devices* | ISO 13485 | A | Medical devices—Quality management systems—Requirements for regulatory purposes | 1996 | 2003 | www.iso.org | English |
| | ISO/TR 14969 | C | Medical devices—Quality management systems—Guidance on the application of ISO 13485: 2003 | 1997 | 2004 | www.iso.org | English |
| *Medical Laboratory* | DIN 58936-1 | C | Quality management and quality assurance in laboratory medicine—Basic terminology | 2000 | 2000 | www.din.de | German |
| | DIN 58936-1 | C | Quality management and quality assurance in laboratory medicine—Basic terminology | 2000 | 2000 | www.din.de | German |
| | DIN 58936-2 | C | Quality management in laboratory medicine—Part 2: Terminology for quality and application of test procedures | 2001 | 2001 | www.din.de | German |

**Table 15.2** Continued.

| Sector | Document Designation | Doc. Type | Document Title | Date Published | | Website | Language |
|---|---|---|---|---|---|---|---|
| | | | | First | Latest | | |
| *Medical Laboratory* Continued | DIN 58959-1 | C | Medical microbiology—Quality management in medical microbiology—Part 1: Requirements for the QM system | 1997 | 2006 | www.din.de | German |
| | Guide 42 | B | Implementing ISO 9001:2000 in medicine laboratory services | 2002 | 2002 | www.uni.com | Italian |
| *Packaging* | ISO 16106 | B | Packaging—Transport packages for dangerous goods—Dangerous goods packagings, intermediate bulk containers (IBCs) and large packagings—Guidelines for the application of ISO 9001 | 2006 | 2006 | www.iso.org | English |
| *Petro-Chemical* | ISO/TS 29001 | A | Petroleum, petrochemical and natural gas industries—Sectorspecific quality management systems—Requirements for product and service supply organizations | 2003 | 2007 | www.iso.org | English |
| *Public* | NTCGP 1000 | A | Sistema de Gestión de la calidad para la Rama Ejecutiva del Poder Publico y Otras Entidades prestadoras de servicios requisitos | 2004 | 2004 | www .mincultura .gov.co | Spanish |

*Continued*

**Table 15.2** Continued.

| Sector | Document Designation | Doc. Type | Document Title | Date Published | | Website | Language |
|---|---|---|---|---|---|---|---|
| | | | | First | Latest | | |
| *Schools* | Guide 44 | B | Implementing ISO 9001:2000 in schools | 2003 | 2003 | www.uni.com | Italian |
| *Services* | UNE 66929 | A | Quality management systems. Guide for the application of the UNE-EN ISO 9001:2000 standard to legal, economical and/or fiscal professional offices | 2003 | 2003 | www.aenor.es | Spanish |
| | HB 90.2 | C | ISO 9000 in the Service Industry | 2000 | 2000 | www.standards.com.au | English |
| *Small Business* | HB 90.1 | B | ISO 9000 for Small Business | 1994 | 2000 | www.standards.com.au | English |
| *Space* | EN 14736 | A | Space product assurance—Quality assurance for test centres | 2004 | 2004 | www.cenorm.be | English |
| *Telecommunications* | TL 9000 | A | TL 9000 Quality Management System Requirements Handbook version 4.0 | | 2006 | www.tl9000.org | English |

**Table 15.2** Continued.

| Sector | Document Designation | Doc. Type | Document Title | Date Published | | Website | Language |
|---|---|---|---|---|---|---|---|
| | | | | First | Latest | | |
| *Transport* | EN 12507 | B | Transportation services—Guidance notes on the application of EN ISO 9001:2000 to the road transportation, storage, distribution and railway goods industries | | 2005 | www.cenorm.be | English |

NOTE 1–Document Types: A—requirements standard, B—guidance to support a requirements standard, C—supporting tools and techniques guidance
NOTE 2–Shaded items denote international standards

Evidence of conformance to the relevant EU directive is demonstrated by placing a CE Mark on the product. Relevant directives cover 18 product types including pressure vessels, explosives, electromagnetic equipment, flammability of children's sleepwear, toy safety, in vitro diagnostic devices, and medical devices. A number of approaches are available for ensuring product quality including extensive testing for items of great complexity produced individually or in small unit quantities. From a practical standpoint for mass-produced products, however, the only way to meet a directive's product quality requirements incorporates use of ISO 9001 certification. This has resulted in a tremendous surge in the use of this standard. Just imagine, every item that you purchase that has a CE Mark embossed on it or on its label has been produced by a process certified as being in conformance to ISO 9001.

• **For Medical Devices** A notable regulated sector for this standard is the medical device sector. From the ACNielson survey conducted for ISO in 2006, a reasonable projection for 2008 certifications to ISO 13485:2003 is 12,000 in 90 countries.

This sector has a variety of relevant quality system standards that are intended to satisfy manufacturer, customer, and regulatory agency requirements. These standards are embodied by the regulations of the United States (the Quality System Regulation), Japan (the Japanese Good Manufacturing Practices Regulation), and countries that have adopted ISO 13485:2003. Other countries have adopted versions of one or the other of these standards. ISO 13485:2003 is derived from ISO 9001 with particular requirements for medical devices added.

Two requirements of ISO 9001:2000 are not included in ISO 13485:2003, continual improvement and customer satisfaction. ISO 13485:2003 does not require the organization to demonstrate continual improvement but only that the quality system is implemented and maintained. Government regulators have taken the position that an organization must meet regulatory requirements prior to regulatory approval; therefore, continual improvement is not required, just maintenance once the system is implemented. From a practical standpoint, if you desire to continue to meet regulatory requirements, you are well advised to implement the continual improvement requirements of ISO 9001. The ISO 9001:2008 requirement that the organization monitors information relating to customer perception as to whether the organization has met customer requirements is not in ISO 13485:2003. The focus of the medical device sector has been on meeting customer requirements. Customer satisfaction is not considered to be appropriate to use as a basis for regulation. Even so, ISO 13485:2003 includes processes for complaint handling, order handling, and contract review. Even though regulators appear not to be concerned with customer satisfaction, every organization must address this for market place success. Medical device manufacturers would do well to meet not only the requirements of ISO 13485:2003 but also the complete set of requirements in ISO 9001:2008.

## CONCLUSION

The widespread acceptance of quality management systems is evidenced by the total number of third-party certifications and by the large number of sector applications which can be seen from a review of Table 15.2. This table illustrates the breadth of depth of the sector applications related to ISO 9001:2000. It is noteworthy that even though there are 68 listed sector standards relating to ISO 9001: 2000, only sixteen are management system requirement standards (Type A). Of these sixteen Type A standards, only seven are international standards as indicated by shading in Table 15.2. In many industries, meeting or exceeding the requirements of ISO 9001 is recognized as essential to success in an ever more competitive marketplace. While sector-developed quality management system standards are important, their total use is a small fraction of the total number of certifications for the generic ISO 9001. The work at preventing proliferation and maintaining a common approach for organizations' quality management systems has been successful.

# ANNEX A of ISO 9001:2008

**Table A.1** Correspondence between ISO 9001:2008 and ISO 14001:2004

| ISO 9001:2008 | | ISO 14001:2004 | |
|---|---|---|---|
| Introduction (title only)<br>General<br>Process approach<br>Relationship with ISO 9004<br>Compatibility with other management systems | <br>0.1<br>0.2<br>0.3<br>0.4 | | Introduction |
| Scope (title only)<br>General<br>Application | 1<br>1.1<br>1.2 | 1 | Scope |
| Normative references | 2 | 2 | Normative references |
| Terms and definitions | 3 | 3 | Terms and definitions |
| Quality management system (title only) | 4 | 4 | Environmental management system requirements (title only) |
| General requirements | 4.1 | 4.1 | General requirements |
| Documentation requirements (title only) | 4.2 | | |
| General | 4.2.1 | 4.4.4 | Documentation |
| Quality manual | 4.2.2 | | |
| Control of documents | 4.2.3 | 4.4.5 | Control of documents |
| Control of records | 4.2.4 | 4.5.4 | Control of records |

**Table A.1** Continued.

| ISO 9001:2008 | | ISO 14001:2004 | |
|---|---|---|---|
| Management responsibility (title only) | 5 | | |
| Management commitment | 5.1 | 4.2<br>4.4.1 | Environmental policy<br>Resources, roles, responsibility and authority |
| Customer focus | 5.2 | 4.3.1<br>4.3.2<br>4.6 | Environmental aspects<br>Legal and other requirements<br>Management review |
| Quality policy | 5.3 | 4.2 | Environmental policy |
| Planning (title only) | 5.4 | 4.3 | Planning (title only) |
| Quality objectives | 5.4.1 | 4.3.3 | Objectives, targets and programme(s) |
| Quality management system planning | 5.4.2 | 4.3.3 | Objectives, targets and programme(s) |
| Responsibility, authority and communication (title only) | 5.5 | | |
| Responsibility and authority | 5.5.1 | 4.1<br>4.4.1 | General requirements<br>Resources, roles, responsibility and authority |
| Management representative | 5.5.2 | 4.4.1 | Resources, roles, responsibility and authority |
| Internal communication | 5.5.3 | 4.4.3 | Communication |
| Management review (title only) | 5.6 | 4.6 | Management review |

**Table A.1** Continued.

| ISO 9001:2008 | | ISO 14001:2004 | |
|---|---|---|---|
| General | 5.6.1 | 4.6 | Management review |
| Review input | 5.6.2 | 4.6 | Management review |
| Review output | 5.6.3 | 4.6 | Management review |
| Resource management (title only) | 6 | | |
| Provision of resources | 6.1 | 4.4.1 | Resources, roles, responsibility and authority |
| Human resources (title only) | 6.2 | | |
| General | 6.2.1 | 4.4.2 | Competence, training and awareness |
| Competence, training and awareness | 6.2.2 | 4.4.2 | Competence, training and awareness |
| Infrastructure | 6.3 | 4.4.1 | Resources, roles, responsibility and authority |
| Work environment | 6.4 | | |
| Product realization (title only) | 7 | 4.4 | Implementation and operation (title only) |
| Planning of product realization | 7.1 | 4.4.6 | Operational control |
| Customer-related processes (title only) | 7.2 | | |

**Table A.1** Continued.

| ISO 9001:2008 | | ISO 14001:2004 | |
|---|---|---|---|
| Determination of requirements related to the product | 7.2.1 | 4.3.1<br>4.3.2<br>4.4.6 | Environmental aspects<br>Legal and other requirements<br>Operational control |
| Review of requirements related to the product | 7.2.2 | 4.3.1<br>4.4.6 | Environmental aspects<br>Operational control |
| Customer communication | 7.2.3 | 4.4.3 | Communication |
| Design and development (title only) | 7.3 | | |
| Design and development planning | 7.3.1 | 4.4.6 | Operational control |
| Design and development inputs | 7.3.2 | 4.4.6 | Operational control |
| Design and development outputs | 7.3.3 | 4.4.6 | Operational control |
| Design and development review | 7.3.4 | 4.4.6 | Operational control |
| Design and development verification | 7.3.5 | 4.4.6 | Operational control |
| Design and development validation | 7.3.6 | 4.4.6 | Operational control |
| Control of design and development changes | 7.3.7 | 4.4.6 | Operational control |
| Purchasing (title only) | 7.4 | | |

**Table A.1** Continued.

| ISO 9001:2008 | | ISO 14001:2004 | |
|---|---|---|---|
| Purchasing process | 7.4.1 | 4.4.6 | Operational control |
| Purchasing information | 7.4.2 | 4.4.6 | Operational control |
| Verification of purchased product | 7.4.3 | 4.4.6 | Operational control |
| Production and service provision (title only) | 7.5 | | |
| Control of production and service provision | 7.5.1 | 4.4.6 | Operational control |
| Validation of processes for production and service provision | 7.5.2 | 4.4.6 | Operational control |
| Identification and traceability | 7.5.3 | | |
| Customer property | 7.5.4 | | |
| Preservation of product | 7.5.5 | 4.4.6 | Operational control |
| Control of monitoring and measuring equipment | 7.6 | 4.5.1 | Monitoring and measurement |
| Measurement, analysis and improvement (title only) | 8 | 4.5 | Checking (title only) |
| General | 8.1 | 4.5.1 | Monitoring and measurement |
| Monitoring and measurement (title only) | 8.2 | | |
| Customer satisfaction | 8.2.1 | | |

**Table A.1** Continued.

| ISO 9001:2008 | | ISO 14001:2004 | |
|---|---|---|---|
| Internal audit | 8.2.2 | 4.5.5 | Internal audit |
| Monitoring and measurement of processes | 8.2.3 | 4.5.1<br>4.5.2 | Monitoring and measurement<br>Evaluation of compliance |
| Monitoring and measurement of product | 8.2.4 | 4.5.1<br>4.5.2 | Monitoring and measurement<br>Evaluation of compliance |
| Control of nonconforming product | 8.3 | 4.4.7<br>4.5.3 | Emergency preparedness and response<br>Nonconformity, corrective action and preventive action |
| Analysis of data | 8.4 | 4.5.1 | Monitoring and measurement |
| Improvement (title only) | 8.5 | | |
| Continual improvement | 8.5.1 | 4.2<br>4.3.3<br>4.6 | Environmental policy<br>Objectives, targets and programme(s)<br>Management review |
| Corrective action | 8.5.2 | 4.5.3 | Nonconformity, corrective action and preventive action |
| Preventive action | 8.5.3 | 4.5.3 | Nonconformity, corrective action and preventive action |

**Table A.2** Correspondence between ISO 14001:2004 and ISO 9001:2008

| ISO 14001:2004 | | ISO 9001:2008 | |
|---|---|---|---|
| Introduction | | <br>0.1<br>0.2<br>0.3<br>0.4 | Introduction (title only)<br>General<br>Process approach<br>Relationship with ISO 9004<br>Compatibility with other management systems |
| Scope | 1 | 1<br>1.1<br>1.2 | Scope (title only)<br>General<br>Application |
| Normative references | 2 | 2 | Normative references |
| Terms and definitions | 3 | 3 | Terms and definitions |
| Environmental management system requirements (title only) | 4 | 4 | Quality management system (title only) |
| General requirements | 4.1 | 4.1<br>5.5<br>5.5.1 | General requirements<br>Responsibility, authority and communication (title only)<br>Responsibility and authority |
| Environmental policy | 4.2 | 5.1<br>5.3<br>8.5.1 | Management commitment<br>Quality policy<br>Continual improvement |
| Planning (title only) | 4.3 | 5.4 | Planning (title only) |

**Table A.2** Continued.

| ISO 14001:2004 | | ISO 9001:2008 | |
|---|---|---|---|
| Environmental aspects | 4.3.1 | 5.2<br>7.2.1<br>7.2.2 | Customer focus<br>Determination of requirements related to the product<br>Review of requirements related to the product |
| Legal and other requirements | 4.3.2 | 5.2<br>7.2.1 | Customer focus<br>Determination of requirements related to the product |
| Objectives, targets and programme(s) | 4.3.3 | 5.4.1<br>5.4.2<br>8.5.1 | Quality objectives<br>Quality management system planning<br>Continual improvement |
| Implementation and operation (title only) | 4.4 | 7 | Product realization (title only) |
| Resources, roles, responsibility and authority | 4.4.1 | 5.1<br>5.5.1<br>5.5.2<br>6.1<br>6.3 | Management commitment<br>Responsibility and authority<br>Management representative<br>Provision of resources<br>Infrastructure |
| Competence, training and awareness | 4.4.2 | 6.2.1<br>6.2.2 | (Human resources) General<br>Competence, training and awareness |
| Communication | 4.4.3 | 5.5.3<br>7.2.3 | Internal communication<br>Customer communication |
| Documentation | 4.4.4 | 4.2.1 | (Documentation requirements) General |

**Table A.2** Continued.

| ISO 14001:2004 | | ISO 9001:2008 | |
|---|---|---|---|
| Control of documents | 4.4.5 | 4.2.3 | Control of documents |
| Operational control | 4.4.6 | 7.1 | Planning of product realization |
| | | 7.2 | Customer-related processes (title only) |
| | | 7.2.1 | Determination of requirements related to the product |
| | | 7.2.2 | Review of requirements related to the product |
| | | 7.3.1 | Design and development planning |
| | | 7.3.2 | Design and development inputs |
| | | 7.3.3 | Design and development outputs |
| | | 7.3.4 | Design and development review |
| | | 7.3.5 | Design and development verification |
| | | 7.3.6 | Design and development validation |
| | | 7.3.7 | Control of design and development changes |
| | | 7.4.1 | Purchasing process |
| | | 7.4.2 | Purchasing information |
| | | 7.4.3 | Verification of purchased product |
| | | 7.5 | Production and service provision (title only) |
| | | 7.5.1 | Control of production and service provision |
| | | 7.5.2 | Validation of processes for production and service provision |
| | | 7.5.5 | Preservation of product |
| Emergency preparedness and response | 4.4.7 | 8.3 | Control of nonconforming product |
| Checking (title only) | 4.5 | 8 | Measurement, analysis and improvement (title only) |

**Table A.2** Continued.

| ISO 14001:2004 | | ISO 9001:2008 | |
|---|---|---|---|
| Monitoring and measurement | 4.5.1 | 7.6<br>8.1<br>8.2.3<br>8.2.4<br>8.4 | Control of monitoring and measuring equipment<br>(Measurement, analysis and improvement) General<br>Monitoring and measurement of processes<br>Monitoring and measurement of product<br>Analysis of data |
| Evaluation of compliance | 4.5.2 | 8.2.3<br>8.2.4 | Monitoring and measurement of processes<br>Monitoring and measurement of product |
| Nonconformity, corrective action and preventive action | 4.5.3 | 8.3<br>8.4<br>8.5.2<br>8.5.3 | Control of nonconforming product<br>Analysis of data<br>Corrective action<br>Preventive action |
| Control of records | 4.5.4 | 4.2.4 | Control of records |
| Internal audit | 4.5.5 | 8.2.2 | Internal audit |
| Management review | 4.6 | 5.1<br>5.6<br>5.6.1<br>5.6.2<br>5.6.3<br>8.5.1 | Management commitment<br>Management review (title only)<br>General<br>Review input<br>Review output<br>Continual improvement |

# ANNEX B of ISO 9001:2008

**Table B.1** Changes between ISO 9001:2000 and ISO 9001:2008

| ISO 9001:2000 Clause No. | Paragraph/ Figure/ Table/ Note | Addition (A) or ~~Deletion~~ (D) | Amended text |
|---|---|---|---|
| Foreword | Para 2 | D + A | International Standards are drafted in accordance with the rules given in the ISO/IEC Directives, ~~Part 3~~ Part 2. |
| Foreword | Para 3, Sentence 1 | A | The main task of technical committees is to prepare International Standards. |
| Foreword | Para 4, Sentence 1 | D + A | Attention is drawn to the possibility that some of the elements of this ~~International Standard~~ document may be the subject of patent rights. |
| Foreword | Para 5 | D | ~~International Standard~~ ISO 9001 was prepared by Technical Committee ISO/TC 176, *Quality management and quality assurance,* Subcommittee SC 2, *Quality systems.* |
| Foreword | Para 6 | D | ~~This third edition of ISO 9001 cancels and replaces the second edition (ISO 9001:1994) together with ISO 9002:1994 and ISO 9003:1994. It constitutes a technical revision of these documents. Those organizations which have used ISO 9002:1994 and ISO 9003:1994 in the past may use this International Standard by excluding certain requirements in accordance with 1.2.~~ |
| | | A | This fourth edition cancels and replaces the third edition (ISO 9001:2000), which has been amended to clarify points in the text and to enhance compatibility with ISO 14001:2004. |
| Foreword | Para 7 | D | ~~The title of ISO 9001 has been revised in this edition and no longer includes the term "Quality assurance". This reflects the fact that the quality management system requirements specified in this edition of ISO 9001, in addition to quality assurance of product, also aim to enhance customer satisfaction.~~ |

**Table B.1** Continued.

| ISO 9001:2000 Clause No. | Paragraph/ Figure/ Table/ Note | <u>Addition</u> (A) or ~~Deletion~~ (D) | Amended text |
|---|---|---|---|
| Foreword | Para 8 | D | Annexes A ~~and B of this International Standard are for information only.~~ |
| Foreword | New para 7 | A | <u>Details of the changes between the third edition and this fourth edition are given in Annex B.</u> |
| 0.1 | Para 1, Sentence 2 | D | ~~The design and implementation of an organization's quality management system is influenced by varying needs, particular objectives, the products provided, the processes employed and the size and structure of the organization.~~ |
| | | A | <u>The design and implementation of an organization's quality management system is influenced by</u><br>a) <u>its organizational environment, change in that environment, and the risks associated with that environment;</u><br>b) <u>its varying needs;</u><br>c) <u>its particular objectives;</u><br>d) <u>the products it provides;</u><br>e) <u>the processes it employs;</u><br>f) <u>its size and organizational structure.</u> |
| | Sentence 3 | Now a new para | It is not the intent of this International Standard to imiply uniformity in the structure of quality managment systems or uniformity of documentation. |
| 0.1 | Para 4 | A | This International Standard can be used by internal and external parties, including certification bodies, to assess the organization's ability to meet customer, <u>statutory and</u> regulatory requirements <u>applicable to the product</u>, and the organization's own requirements. |

**Table B.1** Continued.

| ISO 9001:2000 Clause No. | Paragraph/ Figure/ Table/ Note | <u>Addition</u> (A) or ~~Deletion~~ (D) | Amended text |
|---|---|---|---|
| 0.2 | Para 2 | D + A | For an organization to function effectively, it has to ~~identify~~ <u>determine</u> and manage numerous linked activities. An activity <u>or set of activities</u> using resources, and managed in order to enable the transformation of inputs into outputs, can be considered as a process. |
| 0.2 | Para 3 | A | The application of a system of processes within an organization, together with the identification and interactions of these processes, and their management <u>to produce the desired outcome</u>, can be referred to as the "process approach". |
| 0.3 | Para 1 | D + A | ~~The present editions of~~ ISO 9001 and ISO 9004 ~~have been developed as a consistent pair of~~ are quality management system standards which have been designed to complement each other, but can also be used independently. ~~Although the two International Standards have different scopes, they have similar structures in order to assist their application as a consistent pair.~~ |
| 0.3 | Para 3 | D + A | ~~ISO 9004 gives a guidance on a wider range of objectives of a quality management system than does ISO 9001, particularly for the continual improvement of an organization's overall performance and efficiency, as well as its effectiveness. ISO 9004 is recommended as a guide for organizations whose top management wishes to move beyond the requirements of ISO 9001, in pursuit of continual improvement of performance. However, it is not intended for certification or for contractual purposes.~~ |

**Table B.1** Continued.

| ISO 9001:2000 Clause No. | Paragraph/ Figure/ Table/ Note | Addition (A) or ~~Deletion~~ (D) | Amended text |
|---|---|---|---|
| 0.3 | Para 3 *(continued)* | | At the time of publication of this International Standard, ISO 9004 is under revision. The revised edition of ISO 9004 will provide guidance to management for achieving sustained success for any organization in a complex, demanding, and ever changing, environment. ISO 9004 provides a wider focus on quality management than ISO 9001; it addresses the needs and expectations of all interested parties and their satisfaction, by the systematic and continual improvement of the organization's performance. However, it is not intended for certification, regulatory or contractual use. |
| 0.4 | Para 1 | D + A | ~~This International Standard has been aligned with ISO 14001:1996 in order to enhance the compatibility of the two standards for the benefit of the user community.~~<br><br>During the development of this International Standard, due consideration was given to the provisions of ISO 14001:2004 to enhance the compatibility of the two standards for the benefit of the user community. Annex A shows the correspondence between ISO 9001:2008 and ISO 14001:2004. |
| 1.1 | Bullet a) | A | a) needs to demonstrate its ability to consistently provide product that meets customer and applicable statutory and regulatory requirements, and |
| | Bullet b) | A | b) aims to enhance customer satisfaction through the effective application of the system, including processes for continual improvement of the system and the assurance of conformity to customer and applicable statutory and regulatory requirements. |

**Table B.1** Continued.

| ISO 9001:2000 Clause No. | Paragraph/ Figure/ Table/ Note | Addition (A) or ~~Deletion~~ (D) | Amended text |
|---|---|---|---|
| | Note | D | ~~NOTE In this International Standard, the term "product" applies only to the product intended for, or required by, a customer.~~ |
| | | A | NOTE 1 In this International Standard, the term "product" only applies to<br>a) a product intended for, or required by, a customer,<br>b) any intended output resulting from the product realization processes. |
| | New Note 2 | A | NOTE 2 Statutory and regulatory requirements can be expressed as legal requirements. |
| 1.2 | Para 3 | A | Where exclusions are made, claims of conformity to this International Standard are not acceptable unless these exclusions are limited to requirements within Clause 7, and such exclusions do not affect the organization's ability, or responsibility, to provide product that meets customer and applicable statutory and regulatory requirements. |
| 2 | Para 1 | D + A | ~~The following normative document contains provisions which, through reference in this text, constitute provisions of this International Standard. For dated references, subsequent amendments to, or revisions of, any of these publications do not apply. However, parties to agreements based on this International Standard are encouraged to investigate the possibility of applying the most recent edition of the normative document indicated below. For undated references, the latest edition of the normative document referred to applies. Members of ISO and IEC maintain registers of currently valid International Standards.~~ |

**Table B.1** Continued.

| ISO 9001:2000 Clause No. | Paragraph/ Figure/ Table/ Note | Addition (A) or ~~Deletion~~ (D) | Amended text |
|---|---|---|---|
| | | A | The following referenced documents are indispensable for the application of this document. For dated references, only the edition cited applies. For undated references, the latest edition of the referenced document (including any amendments) applies. |
| | | D + A | ISO 9000:~~2000~~2005, *Quality management systems—Fundamentals and vocabulary* |
| 3 | Para 1 | D + A | For the purposes of this document ~~International Standard~~, the terms and definitions given in ISO 9000 apply. |
| 3 | Paras 2, 3 | D | ~~The following terms, used in this edition of ISO 9001 to describe the supply chain, have been changed to reflect the vocabulary currently used:~~<br>~~**supplier → organization → customer**~~<br>~~The term “organization” replaces the term “supplier” used in ISO 9001:1994, and refers to the unit to which this International Standard applies. Also, the term “supplier” now replaces the term “subcontractor”.~~ |
| 4.1 | Bullet a) | D + A | a) ~~identify~~ determine the processes needed for the quality management system and their application throughout the organization (see 1.2), |
| 4.1 | Bullet e) | A | e) monitor, measure where applicable, and analyse these processes, and |
| 4.1 | Para 4 | D + A | Where an organization chooses to outsource any process that affects product conformity ~~with~~ to requirements, the organization shall ensure control over such processes. The type and extent of control to be applied to these outsourced processes shall be defined within the quality management system. |

**Table B.1** Continued.

| ISO 9001:2000 Clause No. | Paragraph/ Figure/ Table/ Note | <u>Addition</u> (A) or ~~Deletion~~ (D) | Amended text |
|---|---|---|---|
| 4.1 | Note 1 | D + A | NOTE 1 Processes needed for the quality management system referred to above ~~should~~ include processes for management activities, provision of resources, product realization, ~~and~~ measurement, <u>analysis and improvement.</u> |
| 4.1 | New Notes 2 & 3 | A | <u>NOTE 2 An "outsourced process" is a process that the organization needs for its quality management system and which the organization chooses to have performed by an external party.</u> |
| | | | <u>NOTE 3 Ensuring control over outsourced processes does not absolve the organization of the responsibility of conformity to all customer, statutory and regulatory requirements. The type and extent of control to be applied to the outsourced process can be influenced by factors such as</u><br><u>a) the potential impact of the outsourced process on the organization's capability to provide product that conforms to requirements,</u><br><u>b) the degree to which the control for the process is shared,</u><br><u>c) the capability of achieving the necessary control through the application of Clause 7.4.</u> |
| 4.2.1 | Bullet c) | A | c) documented procedures <u>and records</u> required by this International Standard, <u>and</u> |
| 4.2.1 | Bullet d) | A + D | d) documents<u>, including records</u>, ~~needed~~ <u>determined</u> by the organization <u>to be necessary</u> to ensure the effective planning, operation and control of its processes. ~~and~~ |
| 4.2.1 | Bullet e) | D | ~~e) records required by this International Standard (see 4.2.4)~~. |

**Table B.1** Continued.

| ISO 9001:2000 Clause No. | Paragraph/ Figure/ Table/ Note | Addition (A) or ~~Deletion~~ (D) | Amended text |
|---|---|---|---|
| 4.2.1 | Note 1 | A | NOTE 1 Where the term "documented procedure" appears within this International Standard, this means that the procedure is established, documented, implemented and maintained. A single document may address the requirements for one or more procedures. A requirement for a documented procedure may be covered by more than one document. |
| 4.2.3 | Bullet f) | A | f) to ensure that documents of external origin determined by the organization to be necessary for the planning and operation of the quality management system are identified and their distribution controlled, and |
| 4.2.4 | Para 1 | D + A | Records ~~shall be~~ established ~~and maintained~~ to provide evidence of conformity to requirements and of the effective operation of the quality management system shall be controlled. ~~Records shall remain legible, readily identifiable and retrievable.~~<br>The organization shall establish a documented procedure ~~shall be established~~ to define the controls needed for the identification, storage, protection, retrieval, retention ~~time~~ and disposition of records.<br>Records shall remain legible, readily identifiable and retrievable. |
| 5.5.2 | Para 1 | A | Top management shall appoint a member of the organization's management who, irrespective of other responsibilities, shall have responsibility and authority that includes |
| 6.2.1 | Para 1 | A + D | Personnel performing work affecting conformity to product ~~quality~~ requirements shall be competent on the basis of appropriate education, training, skills and experience. |

**Table B.1** Continued.

| ISO 9001:2000 Clause No. | Paragraph/ Figure/ Table/ Note | Addition (A) or ~~Deletion~~ (D) | Amended text |
|---|---|---|---|
| | New Note | A | NOTE Conformity to product requirements can be affected directly or indirectly by personnel performing any task within the quality management system. |
| 6.2.2 | Clause title | A + D | Competence, training and awareness ~~and training~~ |
| 6.2.2 | Bullets a) & b) | A + D | a) determine the necessary competence for personnel performing work affecting conformity to product ~~quality~~ requirements,<br>b) where applicable, provide training or take other actions to ~~satisfy these needs~~ achieve the necessary competence, |
| 6.3 | Bullet c) | A | c) supporting services (such as transport, communication or information systems). |
| 6.4 | New Note | A | NOTE The term "work environment" relates to those conditions under which work is performed including physical, environmental and other factors (such as noise, temperature, humidity, lighting, or weather). |
| 7.1 | Bullet b) | A + D | b) the need to establish processes and documents, and to provide resources specific to the product; |
| 7.1 | Bullet c) | A | c) required verification, validation, monitoring, measurement, inspection and test activities specific to the product and the criteria for product acceptance; |
| 7.2.1 | Bullet c)<br>Bullet d), | D + A<br>D + A | c) statutory and regulatory requirements ~~related~~ applicable to the product, and<br>d) any additional requirements ~~determined~~ considered necessary by the organization. |

**Table B.1** Continued.

| ISO 9001:2000 Clause No. | Paragraph/ Figure/ Table/ Note | Addition (A) or ~~Deletion~~ (D) | Amended text |
|---|---|---|---|
| | New Note | A | NOTE Post-delivery activities include, for example, actions under warranty provisions, contractual obligations such as maintenance services, and supplementary services such as recycling or final disposal. |
| 7.3.1 | New Note | A | NOTE Design and development review, verification and validation have distinct purposes. They can be conducted and recorded separately or in any combination, as suitable for the product and the organization. |
| 7.3.2 | Para 2 | D + A | ~~These~~ The inputs shall be reviewed for adequacy. Requirements shall be complete, unambiguous and not in conflict with each other. |
| 7.3.3 | Para 1 | D + A | The outputs of design and development shall be ~~provided in a form that enables~~ in a form suitable for verification against the design and development input and shall be approved prior to release. |
| 7.3.3 | Bullet b) | D | b) provide appropriate information for purchasing, production and ~~for~~ service provision, |
| 7.3.3 | New Note | A | NOTE Information for production and service provision can include details for the preservation of product. |
| 7.3.7 | Paras 1 & 2 | No text change. Paras now merged | Design and development changes shall be identified and records maintained. The changes shall be reviewed, verified and validated, as appropriate, and approved before implementation. The review of design and development changes shall include evaluation of the effect of the changes on constituent parts and product already delivered. Records of the results of the review of changes and any necessary actions shall be maintained (see 4.2.4). |

**Table B.1** Continued.

| ISO 9001:2000 Clause No. | Paragraph/ Figure/ Table/ Note | Addition (A) or ~~Deletion~~ (D) | Amended text |
|---|---|---|---|
| 7.5.1 | Bullet d) | D + A | d) the availability and use of monitoring and measuring ~~devices~~ equipment, |
| 7.5.1 | Bullet f) | A | f) the implementation of product release, delivery and post-delivery activities. |
| 7.5.2 | Para 1 | D + A | The organization shall validate any processes for production and service provision where the resulting output cannot be verified by subsequent monitoring or measurement. ~~This includes any processes where~~ and, as a consequence, deficiencies become apparent only after the product is in use or the service has been delivered. |
| 7.5.3 | Para 2 | A | The organization shall identify the product status with respect to monitoring and measurement requirements throughout product realization. |
| 7.5.3 | Para 3 | D + A | Where traceability is a requirement, the organization shall control ~~and record~~ the unique identification of the product and maintain records (see 4.2.4). |
| 7.5.4 | Para 1, Sentence 3 | D + A | If any customer property is lost, damaged or otherwise found to be unsuitable for use, ~~this shall be reported to the customer and records maintained~~ the organization shall report this to the customer and maintain records (see 4.2.4). |
| | Note | A | NOTE Customer property can include intellectual property and personal data. |
| 7.5.5 | Para 1 | D + A | The organization shall preserve the ~~conformity of~~ product during internal processing and delivery to the intended destination in order to maintain conformity to requirements. ~~This~~ As applicable, preservation shall include identification, handling, packaging, storage and protection. Preservation shall also apply to the constituent parts of a product. |

**Table B.1** Continued.

| ISO 9001:2000 Clause No. | Paragraph/ Figure/ Table/ Note | Addition (A) or ~~Deletion~~ (D) | Amended text |
|---|---|---|---|
| 7.6 | Title | D + A | Control of monitoring and measuring ~~devices~~ equipment |
| 7.6 | Para 1 | D + A | The organization shall determine the monitoring and measurement to be undertaken and the monitoring and measuring ~~devices~~ equipment needed to provide evidence of conformity of product to determined requirements ~~(see 7.2.1)~~. |
| 7.6 | Bullet a) | A | a) be calibrated or verified, or both, at specified intervals, or prior to use, against measurement standards traceable to international or national measurement standards; where no such standards exist, the basis used for calibration or verification shall be recorded (see 4.2.4); |
| 7.6 | Bullet c) | D + A | ~~c) be identified to enable the calibration status to be determined;~~<br>c) have identification in order to determine its calibration status; |
| 7.6 | Para 4, Sentence 3 | Now new para 5, without change. | Records of the results of calibration and verification shall be maintained (see 4.2.4). |
| 7.6 | Note | D + A | ~~Note See ISO 10012-1 and ISO 10012-2 for guidance~~<br>NOTE Confirmation of the ability of computer software to satisfy the intended application would typically include its verification and configuration management to maintain its suitability for use. |
| 8.1 | Bullet a) | D + A | a) to demonstrate conformity ~~of the product~~ to product requirements, |

**Table B.1** Continued.

| ISO 9001:2000 Clause No. | Paragraph/ Figure/ Table/ Note | Addition (A) or ~~Deletion~~ (D) | Amended text |
|---|---|---|---|
| 8.2.1 | New Note | A | NOTE Monitoring customer perception can include obtaining input from sources such as customer satisfaction surveys, customer data on delivered product quality, user opinion surveys, lost business analysis, compliments, warranty claims, and dealer reports. |
| 8.2.2 | Para 2 Sentence 3 | A | The selection of auditors and conduct of audits shall ensure objectivity and impartiality of the audit process. |
| 8.2.2 | New Para 3 | A | A documented procedure shall be established to define the responsibilities and requirements for planning and conducting audits, establishing records and reporting results. |
| 8.2.2 | Para 3 | Now para 4 D + A | ~~The responsibilities and requirements for planning and conducting audits, and for reporting results and maintaining records (see 4.2.4) shall be defined in a documented procedure.~~ Records of the audits and their results shall be maintained (see 4.2.4). |
| 8.2.2 | Para 4 Sentence 1 | Now para 5 A | The management responsible for the area being audited shall ensure that any necessary corrections and corrective actions are taken without undue delay to eliminate detected nonconformities and their causes. |
| 8.2.2 | Note | D + A | NOTE ~~See ISO 10011-1, ISO 10011-1 and ISO 10011-3.~~ See ISO 19011 for guidance. |
| 8.2.3 | Para 1 Sentence 3 | D | When planned results are not achieved, correction and corrective action shall be taken, as appropriate~~, to ensure conformity of the product~~. |

**Table B.1** Continued.

| ISO 9001:2000 Clause No. | Paragraph/ Figure/ Table/ Note | Addition (A) or ~~Deletion~~ (D) | Amended text |
|---|---|---|---|
| 8.2.3 | New Note | A | NOTE When determining suitable methods, it is advisable that the organization consider the type and extent of monitoring or measurement appropriate to each of its processes in relation to their impact on the conformity to product requirements and on the effectiveness of the quality management system. |
| 8.2.4 | Para 1 | A | The organization shall monitor and measure the characteristics of the product to verify that product requirements have been met. This shall be carried out at appropriate stages of the product realization process in accordance with the planned arrangements (see 7.1). Evidence of conformity with the acceptance criteria shall be maintained. |
| | Para 2 | D + A | ~~Evidence of conformity with the acceptance criteria shall be maintained.~~ Records shall indicate the person(s) authorizing release of product for delivery to the customer (see 4.2.4). |
| | Para 3 | D + A | ~~Product release and service delivery~~ The release of product and delivery of service to the customer shall not proceed until the planned arrangements (see 7.1) have been satisfactorily completed, unless otherwise approved by a relevant authority and, where applicable, by the customer. |
| 8.3 | Para 1, Sentence 2 | D + A | ~~The controls and related responsibilities and authorities for dealing with nonconforming product shall be defined in a documented procedure.~~<br><br>~~A documented procedure shall be established to define the controls and related responsibilities and authorities for dealing with nonconforming product.~~ |

**Table B.1** Continued.

| ISO 9001:2000 Clause No. | Paragraph/ Figure/ Table/ Note | Addition (A) or ~~Deletion~~ (D) | Amended text |
|---|---|---|---|
| 8.3 | Para 2 | A | <u>Where applicable,</u> the organization shall deal with nonconforming product by one or more of the following ways: |
| 8.3 | New bullet d) | A | <u>d) by taking action appropriate to the effects, or potential effects, of the nonconformity when nonconforming product is detected after delivery or use has started.</u> |
| | Para 3 | Moved to be Para 4 | ~~Records of the nature of nonconformities and any subsequent actions taken, including concessions obtained, shall be maintained (see 4.2.4)~~ |
| | Para 4 | Moved to be Para 3 | When nonconforming product is corrected it shall be subject to re-verification to demonstrate conformity to the requirements.<br>Records of the nature of nonconformities and any subsequent actions taken, including concessions obtained, shall be maintained (see 4.2.4). |
| | Para 5 | Now new bullet d) | ~~When nonconforming product is detected after delivery or use has started, the organization shall take action appropriate to the effects, or potential effects, of the nonconformity.~~ |
| 8.4 | Bullet b) | D + A | b) conformity to product requirements ~~(see 7.2.1)~~ <u>(see 8.2.4),</u> |
| | Bullet c) | A | c) characteristics and trends of processes and products, including opportunities for preventive action <u>(see 8.2.3 and 8.2.4)</u>, and |
| | Bullet d) | A | d) suppliers <u>(see 7.4).</u> |
| 8.5.2 | Para 1 | D + A | The organization shall take action to eliminate the ~~cause~~ <u>causes</u> of nonconformities in order to prevent recurrence. |

**Table B.1** Continued.

| ISO 9001:2000 Clause No. | Paragraph/ Figure/ Table/ Note | Addition (A) or ~~Deletion~~ (D) | Amended text |
|---|---|---|---|
| 8.5.2 | Bullet f) | A | f) reviewing the effectiveness of the corrective action taken. |
| 8.5.3 | Bullet e) | A | e) reviewing the effectiveness of the preventive action taken. |
| Annex A | All | D + A | *Updated to reflect ISO 9001:2008 versus ISO 14001:2004* |
| Annex B | All | D + A | *Updated to reflect ISO 9001:2008 versus ISO 9001:2000* |
| Bibliography | New and amended references | D + A | *Updated to reflect new standards (including ISO 9004, currently under revision), new editions of standards, or withdrawn standards.* |

# Index

**Also Available from ASQ Quality Press Exclusively Published by New Age International Pvt.Ltd.**

*Analysis of Customer Satisfaction Data*
Derek R. Allen, Tanniru R. Rao
ISBN: 978-81-224-2800-1, Original Edition Price: $ 66.00, Indian Edition Price: Rs. 395.00

*An Introduction to Design of Experiments: A Simplified Approach*
Larry B. Barrentine
ISBN: 978-81-224-3112-4, Original Edition Price: $ 40.00, Indian Edition Price: Rs. 150.00

*Computer-Based Robust Engineering Essentials for DFSS*
Genichi Taguchi, Rajesh Jugulum, Shin Taguchi
ISBN:978-81-224-2791-2, Original Edition Price: $ 57.75, Indian Edition Price: Rs. 395.00

*Common Sense Project Management*
Wayne Turk
ISBN:978-81-224-3102-5, Original Edition Price: $ 46.00, Indian Edition Price: Rs. 250.00

*Customer Satisfaction Research Management*
Derek R. Allen
ISBN: 978-81-224-2797-4, Original Edition Price: $ 66.00, Indian Edition Price: Rs. 395.00

Design of Experiments with Minitab
Paul Mathews
ISBN: 978-81-224-3111-7, Original Edition Price: $ 116.00, Indian Edition Price: Rs. 595.00

*Effective Implementation of ISO 14001*
Marilyn R. Block
ISBN: 978-81-224-3114-8, Original Edition Price: $ 110.00, Indian Edition Price: Rs. 495.00

*Environmental Management Quick and Easy: Creating an Effective ISO 14001 EMS in Half the Time*
Joe Kausek
ISBN: 978-81-224-3113-1, Original Edition Price: $ 87.00, Indian Edition Price: Rs. 395.00

*Enabling Excellence: The Seven Elements Essential to Achieving Competitive Advantage*
Timothy A. Pine
ISBN: 978-81-224-3105-6, Original Edition Price: $ 41.00, Indian Edition Price: Rs. 150.00

*Fundamental Concepts for the Software Quality Engineer, Volume-2*
Sue Carroll and Taz Daughtrey, *Editors*
ISBN: 978-81-224-3107-0, Original Edition Price: $ 72.00, Indian Edition Price: Rs. 399.00

*Integrating Reengineering with Total Quality*
Joseph N. Kelada
ISBN: 978-81-224-3110-0, Original Edition Price: $ 88.00, Indian Edition Price: Rs. 495.00

*Improving Performance Through Statistical Thinking*
Galen C. Britz, Donald W. Emerling, Lynne B. Hare, Roger W. Hoerl
Sturat J. Janis, Janice E. Shade
ISBN: 978-81-224-2796-7, Original Edition Price: $ 39.00, Indian Edition Price: Rs. 200.00

*ISO 9001:2008 Explained Third Edition*
John E. "Jack" West, Charles A. Cianfrani, Joseph J. Tsiakals
ISBN:978-81-224-3101-8, Original Edition Price: $ 105.00, Indian Edition Price: Rs. 395.00

*Integrating ISO 14001 into a Quality Management System, Second Edition*
Marilyn R. Block and I. Robert Marash
ISBN: 978-81-224-3115-5, Original Edition Price: $ 39.00, Indian Edition Price: Rs. 395.00

*Measuring Customer Satisfaction and Loyalty*
(Survey Design, Use, and Statistical Analysis Methods)
Bob E. Hayes
ISBN: 978-81-224-2799-8, Original Edition Price: $ 53.00, Indian Edition Price: Rs. 395.00

*Principles and Practices of Organizational Performance Excellence*
Thomas J. Cartin
ISBN: 978-81-224-2793-6, Original Edition Price: $ 44.00, Indian Edition Price: Rs. 495.00

*Quality Engineering Statistics*
Robert A. Dovich
ISBN: 978-81-224-3108-7, Original Edition Price: $ 43.00, Indian Edition Price: Rs. 150.00

*SPC Essentials and Productivity Improvements: A Manufacturing Approach*
*William A. Levinson, Frank Tumbelty*
ISBN: 978-81-224-3116-2, Original Edition Price: $ 40.00, Indian Edition Price: Rs. 399.00

*Statistical Engineering An Algorithm for Reducing Variation in Manufacturing Processes*
*Stefan H. Steiner and R. Jock Mackay*
ISBN: 978-81-224-3109-4, Original Edition Price: $ 99.00, Indian Edition Price: Rs. 395.00

*Six Sigma Project Management (A Pocket Guide)*
Jeffrey N. Lowenthal
ISBN: 978-81-224-2802-5, Original Edition Price: $ 24.00, Indian Edition Price: Rs. 50.00

*Six Sigma for the New Millennium: A CSSBB Guidebook, Second Edition*
Kim H. Pries
ISBN: 978-81-224-3103-2, Original Edition Price: $ 97.00, Indian Edition Price: Rs. 399.00

*The ASQ Auditing Handbook, Third Edition*
J.P. Russell, Editor
ISBN: 978-81-224-3104-9, Original Edition Price: $ 139.00, Indian Edition Price: Rs. 495.00

*The Certified Software Quality Engineer Handbook*
Linda Westfall
ISBN: 978-81-224-3117-9, Original Edition Price: $ 133.00, Indian Edition Price: Rs. 699.00

*The Certified Reliability Engineer Handbook*
Donald W. Benbow and Hugh W. Broome
ISBN: 978-81-224-2792-9, Original Edition Price: $ 121.00, Indian Edition Price: Rs. 495.00

*The Certified Quality Engineer Handbook*
Connie M. Borror, Editor
ISBN: 978-81-224-2794-3, Original Edition Price: $ 139.00, Indian Edition Price: Rs. 795.00

*The Certified Quality Process Analyst Handbook*
Eldon H. Christensen, Kathleen M. Coombes-Betz, Marilyn S. Stein
ISBN: 978-81-224-3106-3, Original Edition Price: $ 76.00, Indian Edition Price: Rs. 495.00

*The Certified Quality Technician Handbook*
Donald W. Benbow, Ahmad K. Elshennawy, H. Fred Walker
ISBN: 978-81-224-2790-5, Original Edition Price: $ 121.00, Indian Edition Price: Rs. 495.00

*The Desk Reference of Statistical Quality Methods: Second Edition*
Mark L. Crossley
ISBN: 978-81-224-3118-6, Original Edition Price: $ 104.00, Indian Edition Price: Rs. 499.00

*The Metrology Handbook*
Jay L. Bucher, Editor
ISBN:978-81-224-2789-9, Original Edition Price: $ 121.00, Indian Edition Price: Rs. 695.00

*The Making of a World-Class Organization*
E. David Spong and Debbie J. Collard
ISBN: 978-81-224-2798-1, Original Edition Price: $ 42.00, Indian Edition Price: Rs. 150.00

*The Supplier Management Handbook*
James L. Bossert, Editor
ISBN: 978-81-224-2801-8, Original Edition Price: $ 81.00, Indian Edition Price: Rs. 395.00